The Master Musicians Series

HAYDN

SERIES EDITED BY

SIR JACK WESTRUP

M.A., Hon. D. Mus.(Oxon.), F.R.C.O.

Joseph Haydn

THE MASTER MUSICIANS SERIES

HAYDN

by

ROSEMARY HUGHES

*With eight pages of plates
and music examples in the text*

LONDON
J. M. DENT AND SONS LTD

FARRAR, STRAUS AND GIROUX, INC.
NEW YORK

FOREWORD

IT is strange that the personality and work of the friendliest and most approachable of composers should be so imperfectly known. Yet it was with good reason that the late Sir Donald Tovey called Haydn 'the inaccessible.' Our approach to Haydn is in fact hedged by a double paradox. On the musical side, thanks to the popularity of his work during his lifetime, Haydn, the most orderly of men, left behind him a jungle of conflicting editions and opus numbers and works of doubtful attribution, largely unexplored as the result of that breakdown in the Collected Edition of his works which is in part responsible for the neglect of all but a small proportion of his total output. On the human side, in this country at least, is the queer fact that he, on whom England made, and who made on England, a sharper impression than any of the great composers save Handel, should have aroused so little interest among English biographers.

Recently Karl Geiringer's book *Haydn: a Creative Life in Music* (written in America, the country of his adoption, but also published in England) has given the English-speaking world a vivid and scholarly picture of Haydn's life and work. My own indebtedness to Dr. Geiringer is apparent throughout this book, and in addition I owe him my thanks for much personal kindness. The immensely detailed German biography by Carl Ferdinand Pohl (completed some forty years after his death by Hugo Botstiber) and his monograph *Mozart und Haydn in London* are still, however, indispensable as works of reference. I have also made use of such valuable studies as E. F. Schmid's *Joseph Haydn: ein Buch von Vorfahren und Heimat des Meisters,* and of all available contemporary sources—Haydn's own published letters and notebooks, memoirs of him written by those who knew him and, as far as possible, diaries and newspapers. Translations from these sources are my own except where otherwise stated.

On the musical side, Dr. Larsen's great work *Die Haydn-Überlieferung,* the brilliant specialized studies of Miss Marion M. Scott and Sir Donald Tovey's analytical essays are the essential foundations for any discussion of Haydn's work. The opinions of these great scholars and musicians have inevitably influenced mine; but the views I have expressed are as much my own as direct and loving attention to Haydn's music can make them.

A word must be said about the Catalogue of Works which replaces that contained in the earlier volume in this series. Although more complete than the previous list, it is no more than an interim report, setting forth the results of recent research for the convenience of students, and will doubtless be superseded within measurable time by a more exhaustive catalogue. The list deals only with Haydn's works in their original form, and makes no attempt to classify the innumerable arrangements of them—many dating from his lifetime, and still current—for instrumental com- binations other than those for which they were written.

I am deeply grateful to Dr. Alfred Einstein for the light he has thrown on Haydn for me, directly in conversation and in- directly in his work on Mozart, and for his great kindness in reading and criticizing this book in proof; to Mr. Oliver Strunk, of Princeton University, New Jersey, for generously allowing me to make use of his unpublished material on Haydn, and for his constant readiness to help me with advice and information; to Dr. Egon Wellesz for a conversation and two or three letters which taught me more about eighteenth-century Austria than I could have learned in years of reading; to Mr. Paul Hirsch for offering me the hospitality of his home and library while that great collec- tion was still at Cambridge; to Mr. C. B. Oldman and Mr. A. Hyatt King, of the British Museum, Mr. Richard Hill, of the Library of Congress, Washington, and to the staffs of the West- minster City Library, the historical section of Somerset House and the Enoch Pratt Free Library, Baltimore, Maryland, for their patient and unfailing help; to Dr. and Mrs. Walter Breitenfeld and Dr. and Mrs. Wendell Muncie for much helpful advice; and to Miss Phyllis Holt-Needham, who not only read the proofs but also made a number of valuable criticisms. If despite so much generous help there are still errors and inaccuracies, I need hardly say that the responsibility is entirely mine.

I should also like to thank Mrs. W. Murray Crane, of New York, the owner of the portrait attributed to Fuseli, for her kindness in allowing me to reproduce it, and to the Royal College of Music for permission to reproduce the portrait of Haydn by Thomas Hardy.

This book first appeared in 1950; in the same year a new phase in Haydn research began with the launching of the projected new Complete Edition of Haydn's works by the Haydn Society Incorporated. The present reprint has provided the opportunity of revising the book in the light of the most recent explorations and discoveries, and of correcting such errors as had crept into the first edition. I am most grateful to reviewers and personal friends for pointing out mistakes and for their constructive suggestions, which I have followed wherever possible.

The Catalogue of Works, pending the completion of the Haydn Society Complete Edition, is still an interim report, and lists only those works which are known to be authentic, or which for any reason call for clarification. It has, however, been brought up to date with the help of Mr. H. C. Robbins Landon, founder of the Haydn Society, who, with the most generous kindness, not only examined and corrected the revised draft but also added to it a number of works (especially among the divertimenti, smaller church works and occasional arias) discovered or authenticated by him in the course of his researches. I am deeply indebted to him for placing at my disposal his vast knowledge of everything connected with Haydn, on this and every other occasion.

R. H.

1956.

The six years since the first reprint of this book have seen far-reaching changes in the field of Haydn research. The Haydn

Society Incorporated, Boston, has ceased to function, but the work of preparing a Complete Edition of Haydn's works has now been undertaken by the Joseph Haydn Institute, Cologne. H. C. Robbins Landon's great book, *The Symphonies of Joseph Haydn*, has become a major, and permanent, feature of the landscape, and his continuing researches are steadily recovering for us lost or hitherto unknown works. He has also been in part responsible for the reappearance of a number of Haydn's operas in modern editions; and this, with the publication by two Hungarian scholars of an important study of Haydn's work as an operatic director (*Haydn als Opernkapellmeister. Die Haydn-Dokumente der Esterházy-Opernsammlung*, by Dénes Bartha and László Somfai), has led to a revival of interest in that aspect of Haydn's music and a reassessment of its importance. Finally, the appearance of Vol. I of Anthony Van Hoboken's *Thematisch-bibliographisches Werk-verzeichnis* has at last given us, at least for the instrumental works with which that volume deals, a permanent and standard frame-work of numerical reference, which will eventually extend to the vocal works also.

The results of these changes on the present reprint are, firstly, the inclusion of a new section on Haydn's work as a director and composer of opera, and secondly, a complete revision of the Catalogue of Works. In this the main grouping and classifica-tion of works follow Van Hoboken's Catalogue throughout, and his numbering has been adopted for the instrumental works. In the groups devoted to the vocal works, numbers, where given, are those of the Complete Edition now being issued by the Joseph Haydn Institute, Cologne. In Group I (Symphonies) the numbering adopted (with additions) by Van Hoboken is that of the original Breitkopf & Härtel Collected Edition; this was taken over in the volumes brought out by the Boston Haydn Society, which also included a thematic list with revised dates. These dates have been used in this book except where more recent research has enabled a corrected date to be assigned.

Once more I wish to thank Mr. H. C. Robbins Landon for his endless generosity with his time, knowledge and findings, and Dr. Egon Wellesz for the help and advice which led to the inclusion of the section on Haydn's operatic work. I am also most grateful to Mr. Harry Newstone and Mr. Andrew Porter for their kindness in calling my attention to new publications and in lending me books and scores.

In quoting Van Hoboken's Catalogue numbers, roman numerals indicate the Group (e.g. I, Symphonies; III, String Quartets), arabic numerals the individual work.

R. H.

1962.

CONTENTS

ILLUSTRATIONS

CHAPTER I

EARLY YEARS

IF Joseph Haydn had been given to self-analysis, he could, at any time before his fifty-ninth year, have said with the Viennese poet Grillparzer that whoever had looked out from the Kahlenberg would understand both him and his work. For the low wooded hills girdling Vienna to the west and south—the famous *Wiener-wald,* of which the Kahlenberg is the foremost spur—bear a double aspect. To Vienna they are, in a sense, what the heights of Hampstead and Highgate are to London: a view-point, a place of recreation and a home of poets and artists; but to Europe these, the last foothills of the Alps as they die away into the plains of Hungary, stand as a frontier and breakwater against the invading east—a breakwater against which, in 1683, the Turkish armies dashed themselves in vain.

It was from the Kahlenberg that King John Sobieski and his relieving armies looked down on the beleaguered city. And for Haydn, if he ever visited the little Baroque chapel which enshrines that heroic memory, the prospect before him would not only have virtually contained his world—which, until he set out for England in 1790, lay within a sixty-mile radius of Vienna—but would have worn the same double aspect.

Immediately below, within the converging arms of the Danube and the *Wienerwald,* lies Vienna itself, the Gothic spire of St. Stephen's, massive yet delicate, drawing the eye to the city's centre as the pole draws a compass-needle. Here, in this city where the architecture and music of north and south also converge, within the walls of the Cathedral, in the Baroque palaces and churches of the surrounding streets, and in those streets themselves, he learned and taught himself his art. But beyond its eastward limits, where the watcher's eyes follow the shining ribbon of the Danube till it loses itself in haze, lies the border country where he and his ancestors were born and bred, and where he himself spent the greater part of his working life.

Boundaries were not very sharply drawn among the rivers, lakes and low hills where Hungary marches with Austria, and countless little towns and villages have still an Austrian and a Hungarian form to their name. Migrations of Swabian peasant farmers seeking better territory, or of Lutherans taking refuge from persecution, had filled Hungary with German-speaking enclaves, while similar waves of migration had deposited whole Hungarian- and Croatian-speaking villages on the Austrian side of the border. Hungarian and Croat peasants were familiar neighbours to Haydn for most of his life, and their songs were woven into his memories from childhood onwards. It would not have been surprising if their blood had flowed in his veins too, and indeed he has been claimed as a Croat by Dr. Kuhač, supported by Sir Henry Hadow,[1] and by other investigators as being of Hungarian and even of gypsy origin. Recently a German scholar, E. F. Schmid,[2] has not only traced his ancestry, on both his father's and mother's side, to villages peopled largely by Swabian immigrants, but has also shown that the name Haydn (of which the root is the German word *Heide*, meaning both 'heath' and 'heathen') was widely distributed in Germany as far back as the Middle Ages. But if by blood he was German, he was, as Karl Geiringer justly observes, an Austrian by nationality, and thus heir to all the varied racial cultures held together by their allegiance to the Habsburg monarchy. The extent to which he claimed his inheritance is a matter of musical and not of genealogical history.

Border country, as our own ballads remind us, is far from peaceful. Haydn's forbears lived in dread of the Turks and of the Hungarian *Kuruzzen*—the peasant armies who followed Prince

[1] In his book *A Croatian Composer* (London, 1897), in which he brought Dr. Kuhač's theory before the English-speaking world.

[2] His book *Joseph Haydn: ein Buch von Vorfahren und Heimat des Meisters* (Cassel, 1934) not only deals exhaustively with the genealogical and etymological sides of Haydn's name and ancestry, but also gives a detailed, vivid and fascinating picture of the daily life and social conditions of the villages and little towns where Haydn and his forbears lived, and of the stresses and emergencies which shaped their destinies.

Rákoczy and his fellow insurgents in their revolt against the Habsburgs. The Turkish invasion of 1683, which encircled Vienna, engulfed the little Danubian town of Hainburg, which lay in the track of its advance, and Haydn's great-grandfather Caspar, a vineyard labourer, with his wife, fleeing with a crowd of terrified fellow citizens towards the Danube gateway, found it barred by a traitor and were hewn down in the narrow alley where they were trapped. Their son, Thomas, a journeyman wheelwright of twenty-three, escaped the massacre with his sister and established their joint claim to their dead father's property. He married four years afterwards, and in the following year, 1688, was enrolled as a citizen. His early death, thirteen years later, left his wife with six little boys to bring up, and within a year she married a man named Seefranz, also a wheelwright, who apprenticed three of her sons to the family trade. The next ten years, constantly threatened with invasion by the *Kuruzzen* and with epidemics of plague, must have put a breaking strain on all nerves in Hainburg; the little town was crowded beyond its capacity with billeted imperial soldiers and with refugees from the surrounding villages, and every adult male had to take his turn at digging entrenchments and keeping watch on the walls. Young Matthias Haydn, who was twelve when the war ended in 1711, and had been brought up by a hot-tempered stepfather and an overworked mother among nine other children, had probably been none too happy, and at eighteen, after being apprenticed as a wheelwright by his stepfather, he left Hainburg to seek his fortune. After five years, during which he had travelled as far afield as Frankfort-on-Main, he turned up in his home town demanding a birth certificate; then he vanished again, to reappear in 1727, five years later, and settle down as a master wheelwright, not at Hainburg but in the tiny village of Rohrau, some ten miles to the south.

By the following year he was sufficiently established to build himself a house—a long, low cottage at one end of the village street—and take a wife; his bride was a girl of twenty-one, Anna Maria Koller, who worked as under-cook at the castle of the local overlord, Count Harrach. As she parted from her employers

3

neither she nor they can have dreamed that, sixty-five years later, their son would erect on their estate a monument to hers.

Their first child was a girl, Franziska, born in September 1730. Then, after another eighteen months, on 31st March 1732, their eldest son, Franz Joseph, was born, and baptized on the following day, 1st April, in the village church of St. Vitus.[1]

Ten more births and baptisms followed, and it says much for Anna Maria Haydn that in those days of primitive hygiene she managed to rear six of her twelve children. Life in Rohrau was hard and precarious; the lowlying village was constantly threatened by the periodic flooding of the Leitha, and twice during the wars it had been burned to the ground. The little community was entirely dependent on its vineyards and—in a different sense—on its overlords, the Harrach family. Joseph's father, besides doing all Count Harrach's coach repairs, was elected *Marktrichter*,[2] and as such had twofold responsibilities, towards his overlord and towards the community. Joseph must often have trotted beside him as he went from house to house arranging the rota for fire-guard duty and for the *Robotdienst* (labour dues) on the Harrach estates, though his short legs would have given out long before his father had finished touring the acres of vineyard, settling boundary disputes and seeing that paths and fences were in repair. Year in year out, Rohrau had to struggle for a livelihood, and Haydn in his old age used to proclaim his thankfulness to his parents for bringing him up in the fear of God and for training him, 'of necessity, because they were poor,' in thrift and hard work. Of his mother in particular he used to say that she was 'accustomed to cleanliness, hard work and tidiness' and that she 'kept her children strictly to the same standards from their earliest years.' She seems, indeed, to have been of that fine type of working

[1] There is some uncertainty whether Haydn was born on 31st March or 1st April; the latter date was given wide currency during his lifetime, but he himself insisted that it was 31st March, and the custom of the time makes it probable that he was, like Mozart, baptized on the day following his birth.

[2] Literally 'Market Judge.' His wife's father had held the same position.

woman whose very strictness, when coupled with real love, inspires deep devotion in her children.

Life was not all made up of the sterner virtues, however, and in the evenings there was singing in the big living-room of the Haydn cottage. Both husband and wife could sing, accompanied by Matthias on the harp he had picked up at Frankfort and learned to play by ear, and as soon as the two children had voices at all he made them join in and learn the songs. One of them, at any rate, needed no encouragement, and the neighbours who passed by the open door began to remark on the way in which the little boy was picking up the tunes, and smile at him as he carolled them all over the village the next day. Besides his small, sweet voice and his good memory, Joseph—Sepperl to his family, for Austrians always give a name a diminutive form when they can— had a more than ordinary sense of rhythm. One day, when he was five years old, the hard-worked schoolmaster and choir-master from Hainburg, Johann Matthias Franck, visited Matthias Haydn, whose half-sister Rosina he had married. Sepperl—with that insatiable interest in the workings of things which he kept to the end of his life—had been intently watching the village school-master playing the fiddle, and of late had taken to accompanying the family music-making by tucking a bit of wood under his chin and sawing away with a stick across its imaginary strings with such vigour and precision that his 'Cousin Franck' had an idea. If, he said, Sepperl's parents would let him take the child to Hainburg, his wife would look after him with her own children and he could learn his lessons and the rudiments of music, sing in the parish choir, and so find out if his musical capacities were sufficient to earn him a living.

Maria Haydn objected. Like so many Catholic mothers, she dreamed of having 'a son a priest,' and Sepperl's intelligence had raised her hopes. But Franck assured her that such a start as he proposed giving Sepperl would increase his chances of acceptance, later on, as a student for the priesthood. The village priest and schoolmaster were called in to advise, and supported the plan, and at last the parents agreed to it.

So, at an age when the child Mozart was beginning his triumphal round of the courts of Europe, Sepperl Haydn jolted his slow way along the ten miles or so of rough road across the plain, past the great ruined Roman arch, gateway to vanished Carnuntum, and up the hilly approach to Hainburg. The little walled town which was his journey's end was about ten times the size of Rohrau and, on its wooded crest above the great sweep of the Danube, must have seemed vast compared with his home on the sluggish Leitha. Near the Vienna Gate lived his grandmother, scanning his face sharply for likenesses to his father and chilling his blood with stories of the Turks. And near by, in a small house adjoining the courtyard of the town hall, was the slovenly and casual home into which 'Cousin Franck' and his wife received him.

His aunt may have looked after him 'like one of her own children,' but if so, that only proved that her standards were very different from his mother's. Small boys are not usually much worried by dirt, but this small boy, whose mother had included a wig 'for cleanliness' sake' in the scanty wardrobe she had scraped together for his venture into the world, soon 'noticed with distress that dirt was in the ascendant, and, although I thought a lot of my small person, I could not prevent traces of dirt appearing on my clothing now and then, which caused me agonies of shame.' The discipline to which he was subjected was also very different from that of his home, and he said afterwards of his stormy music-lessons with 'Cousin Franck': 'I am eternally indebted to the man for having taught me so much, even though I got more beatings than I got to eat.'

There was some excuse for this state of things. Johann Michael Franck, as schoolmaster and choirmaster, had to run the school for about seventy children, pay two assistant teachers out of his own meagre salary, conduct the choir and be responsible for all the church music, act as sacristan, keep the parish register, see to the upkeep of the church clock and bells and ring the bells as a warning of thunderstorms. Small wonder that meals were scanty and tempers short in that household. But there were compensations for Sepperl. The big Baroque church of St. Philip and St. James had a fine organ, recently rebuilt, and every Sunday

6

there was sung mass, accompanied by the organ and two violins, supplemented on feast days by a cello, a double bass, horns, trumpets, and drums. Moreover, in his second year at Hainburg, 1738, the whole musical strength of the town was deployed during the processions and ceremonies of the fourteen-day *Jubilaeum Universale* proclaimed by the Church to beg for victory over the Turks. At Corpus Christi came more processions, and also his father, to attend the celebrations held by the Wheelwrights' Guild in honour of the great feast held by all guilds in special veneration. Secular ceremonies in the town hall accompanied the state visit of the Imperial Electoral Commissioner in the following year, and during the lengthy formalities a choirboy of seven may have sought distraction in neck-cricking glances at the gay frescoes on the ceiling, painted to celebrate the peace of 1711; they depicted the Four Seasons.

But it was the Rogation Week ceremonies of 1738 that brought him the first chance to distinguish himself. Processions of the Blessed Sacrament, to pray for God's blessing on the harvest, took place daily, to a different shrine or church each day, and on Ascension Day itself round the actual fields; as usual, the choir and the town band were to provide the music. At the last moment the drummer fell sick and died. Faced with this emergency, *Schulrektor* Franck recalled the rhythmic sawing of a stick on non-existent fiddlestrings which had caught his eye months ago in Rohrau, and, clutching at a straw, told Sepperl to be prepared to beat the drums in the procession. Sepperl did not need telling twice. He flew to the back of the house, seized a flour-bin as being the nearest object of about the right size, tied a cloth tightly across its mouth, armed himself with a couple of sticks and set to work with concentrated delight, oblivious of the clouds of flour that rose from the bin and enveloped him and the surrounding furniture. Wrath broke about his head; the mess was too much even for the Franck household. But the harassed *Schulrektor* was quickly mollified when he found that the child had acquired skill enough on his improvised drum to enable him to fill the gap. So the procession set out—the priest bearing the Sacred Host under its canopy, followed by choir and verger, mayor and town

7

council, schoolchildren, representatives of the guilds and pious confraternities, and, of course, the town band. The gravity of the watching citizens may have been disturbed despite the solemnity of the occasion, for the drums were slung on the shoulders of a hunchback, the only man in the town short enough to match the stature of the drummer, who, small and comically bewigged, played away blissfully regardless of nudges and titters.

Haydn said afterwards that it was largely this episode that made his kinsman look upon him as a potential musician. But others, in particular the parish priest, Father Palmb, had remarked on the intense seriousness with which the child flung himself into his musical training—to such effect that he could say, looking back, 'Almighty God (to Whom alone my thanks are due for this immeasurable grace) gave me such facility in music that in my sixth year I could already sing several masses in the choir without hesitation, and play the clavier [1] and violin a little.' And so it came about that when, the following summer, that important personage Georg Reutter, Imperial Court Composer and newly appointed Cathedral choirmaster, came to Hainburg from Vienna in search of new talent and began inquiring about the treble soloist at the Sunday High Mass, Father Palmb sent for *Schul-rektor* Franck to bring Sepperl Haydn round to the presbytery.

Reutter was expansive and encouraging to the shabby little boy. He flung him a handful of cherries from a bowl on the table that had very obviously caught his eye, and put him through a variety of voice and sight-singing tests, which he sailed through with ease. At last he asked: 'Now, my lad, can you sing a trill?' In a shocked voice Sepperl replied: 'But Cousin Franck can't do *that!*' With perhaps a glance of malicious amusement at his

[1] The German term 'clavier' is a general one meaning any keyboard instrument (it bears this sense in the title of Bach's 'Forty-eight'—*Das Wohltemperierte Clavier*). Haydn uses it equally for the harpsichord (*cembalo*) and for the pianoforte (*forte piano*) which by the second half of the eighteenth century was coming rapidly to the fore, and for which, indeed, both his and Mozart's mature keyboard works were written. The word 'clavier' is retained, here and elsewhere, if used in a general sense, in order to avoid clumsiness or pedantry.

discomfited colleague, Reutter replied: 'Now look, I am going to sing you a trill. Pay great attention to the way I do it.' Sepperl watched him absorbed, as he had watched the Rohrau schoolmaster with his fiddle; all his self-consciousness was gone. The moment Reutter had finished he jumped up to try it. Two attempts broke down, but at the third he produced such an accomplished trill that Reutter cried: 'Bravo! You shall come along with me!' and thrust a coin and another handful of Father Palmb's cherries into his hands. Haydn used to say in later life that he never sang a trill without being reminded of the taste of cherries.

His father's consent had to be obtained, and Matthias Haydn came to Hainburg to talk it over. Reutter made lavish promises, and the delighted father must have felt that Franck's optimism had been more than justified. Joseph was summoned once more to the conclave and informed of his wonderful good fortune; he was to be admitted to St. Stephen's choir when he was turned eight, and Reutter solemnly bade him profit by the nine months' interval to practise scales.

Joseph took him at his word. There was no one to teach him *solfège*—Franck was far too busy—so he worked out a method all by himself, singing and naming the notes by their letters. When Reutter returned after the promised nine months he was amazed and delighted at his progress. For the second time preparations were made and good-byes were said, and at the age of eight the boy stood at last in the heart of Vienna, looking up at the soaring spire of St. Stephen's Cathedral and the modest building near by, the choir school, which was to be his home for the next nine years.

CHAPTER II

VIENNA—THE CHOIR SCHOOL

THE sheltering walls of the cathedral and choir school lay between the country-bred child and the immediate impact of the imperial city. Nerve-centre of Catholic south-eastern Europe and its junction-point with the northward-streaming commerce, art, architecture and music of Italy, Vienna embodied that unique blend of Latin and German elements which characterizes Austria's civilization. The younger Canaletto has captured its classic beauty, the noble Gothic of St. Stephen's contrasting sharply with the great Baroque churches and palaces of the seventeenth and eighteenth centuries. As the seat of court and government, it carried its full complement of greater and lesser nobility, civil servants, well-off professional classes and purveyors of luxury goods, as well as the merchants, shopkeepers, craftsmen and workpeople that form the backbone of any great city.

The house of Habsburg had indeed lost that pre-eminent position in Europe which it had held in the sixteenth and seventeenth centuries: in 1740, the year in which Joseph Haydn first saw Vienna, the youthful Maria Theresa ascended her precarious throne under the menace of invasion by Frederick the Great of Prussia. But what the dynasty had lost in international power, she herself was to regain in the intimate affection of her own people. As a lovely and threatened queen she gained their loyalty, as wife and mother she earned their interest and respect, and at length, by a lifetime of devotion to their welfare, she won their hearts and the venerable epithet of *Landesmutter*. How real this relationship was is shown by the incident when, on the birth of a baby to the wife of her son Leopold, she ran in her dressing-gown down the corridors of the palace and into the imperial box of the adjoining Burg Theatre, leaned over to the cheering people and called out, in broad Viennese dialect: 'Le'pold's got a boy—just in time to give me a present on my wedding-day!'

The Catholic faith was the state religion and that of the whole country. Its feasts punctuated the year with their varied yet unchanging rhythm; and its teachings, though they sat lightly on an easy-going people in an easy-going and rationalistic age—that in which the Church itself is poorest in saints—were the bedrock and background and surrounding air of their lives. The Church was there, like their beds and their meals, and they would no more have thought of doing without the one than the other. The choirboy Joseph Haydn's yearly routine was woven into this pattern of moving feasts, to which he was accustomed from babyhood as to a coloured picture-book: the solemnity of Advent, the warmth and glow of Christmas, Epiphany and Candlemas; Lent, when instruments were banished from the choir and the austere purity of unaccompanied sixteenth-century polyphony reigned supreme; the long and solemn services of Holy Week; Easter, when organ, orchestra and the newer music reappeared in a blaze of glory; Whitsun, Corpus Christi with its great processions, the summer feasts of SS. Peter and Paul and the Assumption of Our Lady; then those of St. Michael, St. Theresa of Avila (the queen's name-day), All Saints and All Souls and St. Leopold, the country's patron—then Advent once more. But alongside the Church's year, and in addition to the daily High Mass and Vespers, ran the celebration of events in the life of the royal family or the nation: the successive births of Maria Theresa's children and the vicissitudes of the war were marked by special ceremonies, culminating in the thanksgiving services following the state entry into the city of Maria Theresa and her consort, Francis Stephen of Lorraine, after his coronation as emperor in 1745.

Of the political happenings that shook their country the choirboys knew little; but their musical commentary on the great events of Church and State led them through a vast and varied repertory. The polyphonic school of Palestrina's time had not completely died out, but it was regarded as the 'ancient style,' something archaic and venerable, to be used at the penitential seasons of Advent and Lent, and as a model for the training of young composers. In the hands of Fux, the court *Kapellmeister*, whose *Gradus ad Parnassum* was the indispensable textbook of strict counterpoint for generations of students—it was still a living language, and his noble masses shared the honours of performance with those of Palestrina and Lassus. The newer style, rich in the melodic freedom, instrumental colour and contrapuntal craftsmanship of the Baroque period—the great Italianborn style which Handel and the instrumental works of Corelli, Vivaldi and their school have made familiar to us—was represented in Vienna by such lesser lights as Caldara, Tuma and Palotta. Reutter himself composed numerous masses, some good, others showing that fatal decline into mere facility that was to drive thinking musicians into revolt against the Italian school.

Together with this wide range of music, Joseph made the acquaintance of his fellow performers—the five other choirboys and the nine men (three altos, three tenors and three basses) who made up the choir; the organist, the ten members of the string orchestra and the subcantor, Adam Gegenbauer, who also played in the orchestra and taught him the violin. Brass and drums were lent by the court for festal occasions; the only regular wind players were a cornettist[1] and a bassoonist.

In the intervals there were other lessons. Joseph got a smattering of allround elementary instruction, 'Latin, religion, arithmetic and writing,' besides his violin lessons with Gegenbauer and some training in singing from the 'elegant tenor,' Finsterbusch. Of teaching in musical theory he received hardly any. Reutter (ennobled in 1740) had greedily accumulated jobs and emoluments, and, as court composer and assistant court *Kapellmeister*, in addition to his duties at the cathedral, he was, or fancied himself, too busy and important to take any great part in the musical education of the choirboys, though nominally it was his responsibility. He only gave the boy Haydn two lessons, though he would advise him to arrange or write variations on the church music he sang, and at his leisure glance through and correct them. But this casualness did not daunt Joseph, accustomed as he was to erratic tuition. 'When my comrades were at play, I took my clavier under my arm and went up to the attic so that I could practise

[1] The 'cornett' of those days was a woodwind instrument with a cup mouthpiece.

there undisturbed.' Alone and unaided, he pored over such textbooks as Mattheson's *Der vollkommene Capellmeister*, and even got hold of Fux's *Gradus ad Parsassum* and began ploughing his way through the exercises.

Ambition he certainly had, and a youthful itch to attempt the grand manner. 'I thought then that everything was all right if only the paper was chock-full of notes. Reutter laughed at my crude efforts, and at passages that no throat or instrument could ever have compassed.' On one occasion Reutter caught him composing a twelve-part *Salve Regina*. The absurdity of the attempt was all that struck him, and he said, with a laugh: 'You silly lad, aren't two parts enough for you?'

These hole-and-corner struggles to master the art that so irresistibly attracted him were squeezed into what free time remained after services, practices, lessons and frequent excursions into the musical life of the city at large. The Jesuit fathers often enlisted their co-operation in theatrical performances by their pupils; true to their principle of becoming 'all things to all men, that they might save all,' they had sailed with that stream of passion for theatre and opera that swept Europe in the seventeenth century, and their schools and colleges regularly put on grand-scale plays, religious or classical in theme, with operatic solos, choruses, orchestra and all the scenic elaboration which characterized stage productions of the Baroque period. The choirboys were also frequently summoned to join the court choir and orchestra at festival seasons. Such a summons was issued for the Whitsun celebrations in 1745, which the imperial court was to spend at Schönbrunn, just outside the city. The scaffolding was not yet removed from the gracious golden façade of the rebuilt summer palace, and the choirboys, their duties over, found it irresistible. Their shrieks and laughter soon brought angry signals from the palace windows to stop their acrobatics. When these were ignored, Reutter was summoned to the presence of the empress who, pointing out the obvious ringleader, asked who 'that fair-haired idiot' was, and on being informed, retorted: 'Well, give him a good hiding.' The command was faithfully carried out.

It was not only the court that made use of the Cathedral choir.

The nobility, when giving entertainments, would often ask for a party of choirboys to diversify the music and, incidentally, to help with the serving. These assignments were eagerly sought after by the boys, chiefly because, in addition to their fee, they were usually given a meal below stairs; the feeding at the choir-school was inadequate for growing lads—Reutter's expensive tastes made him chronically short of money—and Joseph described it as 'a perpetual fast.' Hence arose his sudden zeal to distinguish himself in singing, so that he might be one of the lucky ones chosen for these outings. On such evenings the little party, laden with music sheets and instruments, threaded its way through the city's streets and alleys to the stately *palais* where the entertainment was being given. Lights would be streaming from open windows into the courtyard and on to the cobbled streets and the clusters of people gazing up at the fine dresses or listening to the orchestra playing while the company dined or danced. As the sounds reached the choirboys, waiting to perform their piece or dashing to and fro with piles of plates and silver, none listened more intently than Joseph, who, though he may have come for the chance to stuff himself in the back premises, had ears alert for the lively, undemanding overtures and suites and *divertimenti*, of which the guests who took music for granted as a background to social intercourse were only half aware.[1] Then home in the lamp-lit darkness, once or twice encountering in the narrow lanes serenading parties playing away for the few groats that sufficed to serenade a lady in a city alive with music and with musicians scraping together a hand-to-mouth livelihood. Joseph had no inkling then of the days when he himself would be thankful to join such a party for the price of a meal.

But with the passing months and years the inevitable doom of all choirboys crept steadily nearer—the dreaded break of voice.

---

[1] A *Servizio di tavola* by Reutter himself, written in 1757 for just such an occasion, is preserved in the *Denkmäler der Tonkunst in Oesterreich*. It is in four movements, the first and last in 'sonata form' as far as key relations go, but consisting mainly of lively passage-work and entirely devoid of development in the true sense. The pensive *Larghetto* is in the minor mode, and the third movement is a minuet and trio.

At first, weeks would go by without that wild, uncontrollable fluctuation breaking in; but when it did, the empress, herself an accomplished singer, was quick to comment, tartly, 'That boy doesn't sing, he crows.' Faced with the loss of a competent and reliable singer, Reutter suggested that Joseph should undergo the operation that would preserve his boy's voice and secure him a permanent livelihood in the ranks of the *castrati* for whose powerful and brilliant sopranos many of the leading operatic parts of the century were written.[1] The barbarous ethics of this proceeding did yet, however, require parental agreement. No sooner had word of the proposal reached Matthias Haydn than he set off for Vienna, frantic with anxiety lest his consent had been already presumed. But his stammered-out questions to his son received a reassuring answer, and in the ensuing heated interview with Reutter he received unexpected support from a *castrato* who chanced to be at the choir-school that day. Between them they saved Joseph for normal manhood and, though they did not know it, for a glory far greater than that of a second Farinelli.

The immediate outlook was gloomy, however, and the rising brilliance of his brother Michael, whom his father had sent to join him two years earlier, did not help matters. Though five years his junior, Michael took to school life quickly and easily, and not only did better at his lessons than the slower and less bookish Joseph,[2] but proved a dangerous rival as a singer. Maria Theresa was as quick to spot him as she had been to remark on Joseph's decline; after the celebration of St. Leopold's feast at the Benedictine Abbey of Klosterneuburg in November 1748, she and the emperor summoned Michael before them to praise his exquisite singing, inquired about his family and origin, and gave him

[1] The truth of this story has been disputed, but the sources are reliable: Le Breton and Framéry, who heard it from Haydn's pupil Pleyel, and Griesinger, who, besides being himself a friend of Haydn's, had heard the tale vouched for by others to whom Haydn had related it.

[2] He acquired a sound knowledge of Latin and Italian, read widely, began composing early and—with a touch of youthful priggishness—formed a club among his schoolfellows for the detection of plagiarism in each other's compositions.

twenty-four ducats. When asked by Reutter what he was going to do with the money, he replied: 'I shall send half to my father, who lost one of his animals a little while ago. Will you please keep the other half for me till *my* voice breaks?'

It was plain to others beside the canny Michael that Joseph could not last much longer. He did, in fact, hang on another year. Although he was by now a tolerably good violinist, it does not seem to have occurred to any one to transfer him to the orchestra; Reutter had lost interest by this time, and was merely anxious to be rid of him. Joseph himself provided Reutter with his opportunity. Many must have known in their youth an uncontrollable itch to cut off a pigtail; Joseph Haydn is one of the few who have actually done it. The projecting queue of the choir-boy sitting in front of him and the possession of a new pair of scissors afforded all the stimulus necessary. Retribution was prompt and drastic: Reutter condemned him to be caned in front of the school. Appalled at the indignity to one of his seventeen years, Joseph cried out that he would rather be dismissed than caned. Reutter snatched the proffered pretext, without mercy. 'Certainly you may go,' he said, 'but you'll get your caning first!' And so it came about that, on a November evening in 1749, Joseph, clutching 'three poor shirts and a worn-out coat' under his arm, heard the door of the choir-school slam behind him. He had nowhere to go and not a penny in his pocket.

HAYDN'S BIRTH-HOUSE AT ROHRAU
From an early engraving

E.N.A

CHAPTER III

THE SCHOOL OF EXPERIENCE

HE spent the first night on a bench in the open. He had been brought up to poverty, but destitution was something new. He could, of course, make his way home; but that would fling him on his parents' support, and proclaim to the entire village his failure and disgrace and the collapse of the high hopes that had been set on him. Besides, there was no future for him at Rohrau; he was not brought up to his father's craft, nor to any other. Worst of all, his return would mean the abandonment of that life of music on which, dumbly but irrevocably, he had set his heart. He knew that, with the training he had received, he could scrape together a living of sorts in Vienna—but how to start, alone and empty-handed?

Suddenly, in the chill of the early morning, a friendly greeting broke in upon the bleak procession of his thoughts. It was one of the tenors of St. Michael's Church, Spangler by name, who knew the Cathedral choir through countless joint performances and must have been surprised at seeing one of the choir-school lads out alone at such an hour. As he heard young Haydn's story his sympathies quickened. He knew what it was to be hard up, for his own earnings as a choir singer, composer and tutor only sufficed for the rent of a tiny attic for himself, his wife and a son of eight months. In such cramped quarters he might well have held himself excused from offering hospitality; but shelter was the homeless boy's immediate and pressing need. Spangler accordingly offered him a corner in his attic—a kindness which Haydn thankfully accepted and never forgot. The impending arrival of a second baby, and Haydn's own sturdy independence, ended the arrangement after a few months; but eighteen years later Haydn was to repay his debt to Spangler in the person of this unborn baby, who through him secured a job—and a husband—in Prince Nicholas Esterházy's opera company.

Meanwhile the outlook was grim. Clavier lessons at two florins a month hardly brought in enough for bare necessities, and the winter was no time for street serenading parties. Plan after plan formed in his mind, only to be discarded as fruitless. Moreover, his parents' anxiety on his account had revived their old desire for him to become a priest, as a practical and providential way of escape from his difficulties; his mother wept, his father urged, and between them they gave him no peace. They could not believe that he would refuse. But refuse he did, with a doggedness that amazed them. It may well have amazed him too, for he could find no reasons with which to justify his stubbornly reiterated 'I don't want to be a priest.' Humble and unselfconscious as he was, it never occurred to him to tell them that he had his vocation already.

What his parents' entreaties failed to accomplish, the pressure of sheer hunger nearly achieved. In a fit of black depression, the result of physical exhaustion and undernourishment, he made up his mind to enter the Servite order, if only to eat his bellyful. But before he had taken the decisive step his natural resilience returned with the spring—the soft, incalculable Austrian spring of Schubert's *Frühlingsglaube*—and the same spring-time longing 'to go on pilgrimage' that had seized Chaucer and his companions long ago turned young Haydn's feet away from the monastery door and set them on the road to Mariazell.

Mariazell, one of the most venerable shrines of Our Lady in Europe, lies in a fold of the Styrian Alps; the little town scrambling up the hillside is dominated by its great church, sheltering the wonder-working statue of Mary and her Child brought by the Benedictine monk who in the tenth century came to preach Christ to the wild shepherd people of the mountains. Athwart the centre of the nave stands the silver-canopied altar where the little carved figure, now stiffly cased in brocade, still draws pilgrims in their thousands who, like Haydn and his fellow travellers, end their journey on their knees around her shrine. But for Haydn prayer was followed by action. He sought out the choirmaster, Father Wrastil, told his story and asked to be taken into the choir. The request was curtly refused; the choirmaster had been plagued

18

too often by ragamuffins from Vienna claiming to be former choirboys but unable to sing a note. Undefeated, Haydn crept up into the gallery and begged the tenor soloist to let him take his part in the next Mass. In vain the singer nervously demurred; when he stood up for his first solo, the music was tweaked from his hand, and Haydn sang the part, with such accomplishment that the choir listened enchanted, the choirmaster made his apolo-gies and the Father Superior sent round to ask who he was. They kept him for a week, with free board and lodging, and put the proceeds of a whip-round collection into his pocket as he went away.

Refreshed in body and spirit, he returned to the grinding struggle of his life in Vienna. He was now in a room of his own—a garret in the Altes Michaelerhaus at the corner of the Kohlmarkt and the Michaelerplatz, adjoining St. Michael's Church, where his friend Spangler sang; Spangler probably helped him to find it. It was small and dark, hot in summer, cold in winter; it lacked a stove and let in the weather. Even so, the rent would have overtaxed his meagre and irregular earnings but for the generous help to which his long-lived gratitude bore witness in his will of 1801, containing a legacy of 100 florins to one Anna Buchholz 'because her grandfather, in my youth and utmost need, lent me 150 florins free of interest, which sum however I repaid fifty years ago.'

Hard living went hand in hand with hard work—teaching by day, playing in the streets by night. The fact that he paid off Buchholz's loan within a year is eloquent of his perseverance and self-denial. There was little enough time for study; but his actual way of life was all the time subjecting him to what was, perhaps, the strongest single influence on his development as a composer.

Vienna's climate, the Italian vein in her culture and the love of her citizens for music and for being amused, had made her for centuries a city of serenades and serenaders. A Viennese journalist, writing towards the end of the century, observed that these serenades, which occurred almost every fine summer evening,

do not consist, as in Italy or Spain, merely in the accompaniment of the voice by a guitar or mandora . . . (for a serenade here is not a declaration of love . . . for which a thousand more suitable opportunities present themselves), but in trios and quartets, mainly from operas, with several voices, wind instruments, often a whole orchestra. . . . On the eve of the more common name-days, especially on St. Anne's Eve, the streets fairly swarm with serenading parties . . . however late it is, even at an hour when most people are hurrying home to bed, heads soon appear at the windows and a crowd gathers round the players, clapping, applauding, demanding encores, and seldom dispersing till the serenade is over, when they will often troop after the players to another district.

Poor musicians without regular employment made up serenading parties to supplement their meagre incomes, as did young Haydn. But to his eager mind and ears it was the doorway to a new world, glimpsed at intervals in his choirboy days through church and *salon* windows: a world where operatic arias and popular songs met on equal terms, and the dances of the suite and the *sinfonia avanti l'opera*, jostling in a gay and sociable welter with marches, hunting-songs and variations on familiar airs, helped to fuse the diverse elements that make up the symphony as we know it. It was moreover a world of musicians out of doors and on the move, who could not carry a harpsichord about with them, and from which, therefore, the *basso continuo*, with its harmonic support and control, was automatically banished. Haydn was no conscious revolutionary, and as a *salon* musician he frequently conducted from the keyboard; but he never forgot the sound of emancipated strings and wind in those Viennese summer nights under the stars, and the keyboard, with him, though it never formally abdicated, was a strictly constitutional monarch.

Besides money and experience, his serenading parties brought him companionship and an outlet for his unquenchable sense of fun. On one occasion he posted his party, some on and some below the bridge that still spans the narrow lane known as the Tiefer Graben, with instructions to strike up at a given signal. The signal was given, and pandemonium broke out, for each man had been given a different tune to play. Furious citizens flung open their windows and called the watch, under whose very noses the trick had been perpetrated, for their 'police station' was in the Tiefer Graben itself. A violinist and a drummer were caught in full flight, but resolutely refused to give the ringleader away, and were released after a couple of days. The police, if they ran true to Viennese type, doubtless relished the joke.

In the end it was a serenade that brought Haydn, at nineteen, his first commission as a composer. One fine evening in the year 1751 his team elected to serenade the pretty wife of Vienna's most popular comedian—Johann Joseph Kurz. He was known to the whole city as Kurz-Bernardon, owing to his triumphant representation of 'Bernardon' (*alias* Kasperl, *alias* Hanswurst), that stock 'Simple Simon' figure of the Viennese variety stage, rich in gags and topical allusions in the local dialect.[1] No sooner was the music at an end than this gentleman appeared and demanded the composer. He was devising a new musical show, half operetta, half pantomime, and wanted music for it. Undeterred by Haydn's youth and shabbiness, Kurz dragged him upstairs, outlined to him the plot of his opera, *Der krumme Teufel* ('The Crooked Devil')[2] and urged him to the keyboard, where he improvised music for one scene after another. At last they came to the entr'acte or so-called 'pantomime,' the story of which (entirely irrelevant to the main plot) dealt with a desert-island shipwreck. Kurz wanted an opening tone-picture depicting the fury of the winds and waves; but Haydn, who was not to see the sea for another forty years, met his graphic descriptions with blank puzzlement. At last, exasperated, Kurz flung himself across an armchair, brandishing arms and legs in the manner of a drowning swimmer, and cried out in a fury: 'But can't you see me swimming?' Something in the actor's frenzied gestures communicated itself to Haydn. He broke into a surging 6–8 movement which brought him a torrent of embraces from the mercurial Kurz, and a definite commission to write the music.

The opera duly appeared and the composer received twenty-five ducats, 'with which he regarded himself as a very rich man.'

[1] We meet this character, transfigured by Mozart's genius, under the guise of Papageno in *The Magic Flute*.

[2] Karl Geiringer (*Joseph Haydn*, Potsdam, 1932) points out that the title *Der neue krumme Teufel*, frequently quoted as the title of Haydn's first opera, properly belongs, not to this original version, but to the revised version of 1758.

Unfortunately an influential Italian nobleman regarded it, rightly or wrongly, as a caricature of himself, and it was withdrawn after a few performances. Six years later Kurz put on a new version, the title-page of which bears the modest footnote:

N.B.—Die Musique, sowohl von der Opera comique, als auch von der Pantomime ist componiret/von/Herrn Joseph Heyden [*sic*].

It was the only time Kurz ever mentioned the composer's name on the title-page of a work of his, and it was all the immortality Haydn's music was to get, for the music of both versions is entirely lost. The only surviving works of this period in his life (unless his biographer Griesinger is right in dating his first quartets in 1750) are a few of his earliest trios and clavier sonatas, and the gay little F major Mass which in his failing years he was so pathetically pleased to rediscover and revise.

Despite this success, the growth of his musical experience made him sharply and depressingly conscious of his own deficiencies as a composer, which he had little time to remedy, for the intermittent serenading did not, of itself, bring in enough to keep him. Looking back, he said of this period of his life:

I had to spend eight whole years trailing wretchedly around giving lessons to children (many a genius earning his bread in this miserable way comes to grief for lack of time for study), this was unfortunately my own experience and I would never have made such little progress as I did if I had not pursued my zeal for composition far into the night.

One cannot but marvel at the picture of courage and tenacity which this flat statement unconsciously draws for us: of days spent trudging from house to house, nerves and patience worn thin by the exacting balance of self-communication and self-restraint which teaching demands, by casual treatment and the carelessness of reluctant pupils; then, at the end of such a day, the climb up five flights of stairs to the bleakness of an attic and a few cold odds and ends of food; and after all that, hours of solitary wrestling with the art which he knew full well he had only imperfectly grasped, haunted by uncertainty whether he was working on the right lines and whether anything would ever come of it, and without a soul to stimulate, correct and advise.

But he was one day to find—if only on paper—a friend and guide on this lonely pilgrimage, far longer and harder than the road to Mariazell. He had worked his way right through the strict counterpoint exercises of Fux's *Gradus ad Parnassum*, and was rummaging in search of some book to help him further, when the bookseller, interested in his quest, thrust into his hands a set of keyboard sonatas by Carl Philipp Emmanuel Bach.[1] He took them home to the old worm-eaten clavier in his attic and 'never left it until he had played the sonatas right through.' 'I played them time and again for my own pleasure, especially when I was discouraged or depressed by worry, and always left the instrument cheered and in good spirits.' He said later that any one who really knew him must recognize how much he owed to C. P. E. Bach, and proudly recalled that Bach had himself described him as 'the only one *fully* to understand his work.' It may have been in part the structure of Bach's sonatas, with their use of 'sonata form' so much discussed by later historians, that caught his interest; but far stronger than this structural capacity— so much inferior to Haydn's own—was the impact of his emotional warmth and melancholy on one young, impressionable, hungry in mind and heart as well as in body, and with a latent romantic streak even stronger than C. P. E. Bach's. The old clavier now became his friend and comforter, and as he played—so he recalled as an old man—he 'envied no king his happiness.'

At last the Providence which had planted him in the Altes Michaelerhaus brought him a master in the flesh. The old house, like others of its kind, sheltered a cross-section of Viennese life. Aristocracy lived on the first floor, middle-class culture occupied the floors above, and servants, tradespeople and poor devils such as music teachers lived under the roof. In this house the pattern of Haydn's life was freakishly crystallized, for the occu-pant of the first floor was the Dowager Princess Esterházy whose two sons he was destined to serve for close on thirty years. Of more immediate importance, however, was the occupant of a

---

[1] Two sets had been published at this date—those dedicated to Frederick the Great of Prussia and to the Duke of Württemberg.

six-room apartment on the third floor—none other than the Abbate Metastasio, court poet and prince of opera librettists, whose exquisitely turned verse-dramas had been set by every composer of note in the past three decades. Burney, who met him twenty years later, described him as

. . . at least seventy-two and for that time of life . . . the handsomest man I ever beheld. There are painted on his countenance all the genius, goodness, propriety, benevolence and rectitude which constantly characterize his writings.[1]

Even at fifty his placid, conservative temperament led him to a semi-retired life, sharing his big apartment with a friend employed at the Papal Nunciature, Niccolò de Martinez, and exercising his benevolence by taking charge of the education of Martinez's two little girls.

It was the eldest of these, Marianne, aged nine—with whom Mozart played duets in the 1780s—who was to be the instrument of fate for Haydn. She was a brilliant little creature, and Meta-stasio had already arranged singing-lessons for her with Niccolo Porpora, the irascible old Neapolitan whose 'method' had launched on their course to fame some of the most renowned *castrati* of their day; as he thought it beneath his dignity to accom-pany his own lessons, the Abbate was now looking out for an accompanist, who could also start the child on the clavier. Finding that there was a young music master under the same roof, he engaged Haydn, who for nearly two years taught and accompanied Marianne in return for free meals at Metastasio's table—an arrangement advantageous to him and economical for the Abbate. But what Haydn valued immeasurably more was the opportunity of contact with Porpora, who, besides his vast repute as a teacher of singing, was a prolific and experienced composer. Humbly and painfully aware that he had 'written perseveringly but without proper grounding,' Haydn would have jibbed at nothing in order to obtain 'the privilege of learning the true fundamentals of composition from the famous Herr Porpora.' As there could be no question of his paying for lessons in cash,

[1] *The Present State of Music in Germany* (1773), vol. i, p. 300.

Porpora took him on as accompanist and unofficial valet; Haydn trailed round with him to his various lessons and in the intervals blacked his boots and cheerfully put up with kicks and abuse from the foul-mouthed old man 'because I learned so much from him in singing, composition and Italian.'

Among Porpora's pupils was the mistress of the Venetian ambassador, who insisted on continuing her lessons during the summer season at Mannersdorf, an elegant watering-place at the foot of the Leitha hills. Porpora and his factotum were accordingly attached to the ambassador's *ménage* for three months; Haydn was boarded with the servants, discreetly made himself useful and received six florins [1] a month. He accompanied the lady when she sang at the ambassador's *soirées* and, as an appendage of Porpora's, received an occasional word of encouragement from the eminent musicians who—like his own friend Dittersdorf some years later—performed at these functions alongside the aristocratic *dilettanti* whose patronage they enjoyed. Gluck counselled him to continue his studies in Italy—well-meant advice which he was never in a position to follow.

While at Mannersdorf he would not have missed the opportunity of visiting his home, less than twenty miles away. Even from Vienna he and his brother Michael—now rising seventeen and capable of deputizing for the cathedral organist—used to make their way over to Rohrau, where their father, recapturing in these re-unions the memory of their early days, used to get out his harp and gather his family round him to sing their childhood's songs once more. But these happy interludes were soon to end. Anna Maria Haydn, 'my good mother . . . who always cared most tenderly for my welfare,' died in 1754, and in the same year Michael left St. Stephen's and went to Hungary. In the following year Matthias Haydn married again. Not long afterwards, while moving into new lodgings in the Seilerstätte, Joseph had all his clothing stolen and received nothing but good advice in response to his appeal to his father for linen for new shirts; doubtless his

[1] The florin, or *gulden*, was the equivalent of about two shillings, but its purchasing power, as in England at that time, was of course far more than it would be to-day.

stepmother felt that her husband's grown-up sons were perfectly well able to fend for themselves.

In fact, she was not far wrong. In the musical world, as elsewhere, it is the securing of the first foothold that matters. The Metastasio-Martinez-Porpora connection, and the fact of having been seen in Porpora's wake in high society at Mannersdorf, were bringing him pupils. He was also lucky enough to arouse the interest of the Countess Thun; the story goes that, admiring a manuscript sonata of Haydn's which she picked up at a dealer's, she caused the composer to be sought out and sent to her. Suspicious at first of the raw appearance of the stocky, bony-featured young man who presented himself, she put him through a searching examination as to the circumstances of his expulsion from the choir school, was convinced by the straightforward simplicity of his manner and his answers, engaged him as her clavier teacher and sent him away with money to buy a more presentable suit of clothes. His growing repute enabled him to put up his charges for clavier lessons from two to five florins a month, and he even acquired two composition pupils. His Sundays were also busy with a succession of jobs: first violin at the eight o'clock Mass at the Brothers of Mercy in the Leopoldstadt suburb (to which order one of his composition pupils belonged)—this brought him sixty gulden a year; organist at Count Haugwitz's chapel at ten, and at eleven, back to the Cathedral choir for seventeen kreutzers (about sixpence) a time; Reutter was still nominally in charge, but, being a chronic absentee, was probably unaware that his old pupil and victim had turned up again. Serenading was still his evening's occupation. With so much regular employment he could afford the larger apartment in the Seilerstätte and treat himself to violin lessons: money well spent, for it brought to his music that insight into the instrument's capacities that only comes with practical performing experience.

So far he had written—besides the early F major Mass and the *Crooked Devil* music—a quantity of light, ephemeral stuff for his serenaders and numerous easy sonatas for his clavier pupils, which in his innocence he gave away and felt himself honoured if they were accepted, unaware that the music dealers were doing a brisk

trade in them. (He was later to become considerably more
hard-headed.) Now, at twenty-five or thereabouts, his slow
but tenacious mind, assimilating Porpora's teaching and putting
it into practice through all this apprentice work, had acquired
a technique and a language of its own, and the Providence which
had led him thus far was prompt in giving him the occasion to
use them.

In a narrow lane called Paternostergasserl, not far from the
Seilerstätte, was the town house of the Baron von Fürnberg, who—
possibly on the recommendation of Countess Thun—engaged
Haydn as music master to his family. The baron also possessed
a country property, Weinzierl, on the Danube near Melk, some
sixty miles upstream from Vienna, and in the summer used to
invite the young music master to join him for months at a time,
carrying on the lessons by day and taking the viola in the nightly
music-making, in which the other players were the parish priest
and the baron's steward, both violinists, and a cellist named
Albrechtsberger. He had already produced a handful of modest
trio sonatas, and now he was urged to try his hand at producing
something fresh for the little band of four. And so, if his own
memory can be trusted, came the historic evening when he
diffidently laid out on the desks the parts of his first string
quartet.[1] A German officer taken prisoner in the Seven Years

[1] The date is uncertain. Griesinger puts his first quartets as early
as 1750, and Karl Geiringer thinks that his earliest trios, for two violins
and cello with figured bass, probably date from then; but if the quartets
written for Count Fürnberg were in fact his first, they can hardly have
been written earlier than 1755. Fritz Dworschak in his article 'Joseph
Haydn und Karl Joseph Weber von Fürnberg' (in *Unsere Heimat*,
1932) suggests that, on the reckoning of the 'eight whole years,' from
1749, which Haydn described himself as having spent giving casual
lessons, it may even have been as late as 1757, and on that assumption
advances the theory that the Albrechtsberger of these musical evenings
was in fact the famous Johann Georg Albrechtsberger who taught
Beethoven counterpoint, for he was organist at Maria Taferl, only twelve
kilometres away, from 1757 to 1759, and is described by Gerber's *Lexicon*
as having been a good cellist in his youth.

War and quartered on Baron Fürnberg recalled years later that Haydn,

modest to the point of nervousness, could not be persuaded, although every one present was delighted with his compositions, that his work was worthy of becoming known in the musical world.

But his companions' pleasure in them was unmistakable, and as there are few things more heartening than an appreciative clamour for more, the first attempt was followed by others. Dies says that 'the quartets and other pieces' written at this period—which probably include nearly all the two sets of six Quartets known as Op. 1 and Op. 2—'won him the increasing favour of amateur musicians, so that he became recognized everywhere as a genius.'

All the same it was Michael who, though five years younger, was the first to secure a regular post; he became *Kapellmeister* to the Bishop of Grosswardein, at the age of twenty, in 1757. Joseph's turn did not come till two years later, when, on Baron Fürnberg's recommendation, he was appointed *Kapellmeister* and *Kammer-compositeur* to Count Morzin at a salary of 200 florins a year. The job took him to Lukaveč, the Count's castle in Bohemia, for the greater part of the year, and involved writing *divertimenti* and *Feldpartien* [1] for the wind band and directing the count's small orchestra (of strings supplemented by players from the wind band on occasion), for which he composed his first symphonies, slight and simple in structure like the *divertimenti* and quartets—or, as he called them, *quadri*—with which, at this period of flux, the term *sinfonia*, as Marion Scott points out, was practically interchangeable.[2] His characteristic comment on the appointment was:

My good mother . . . was no longer alive, but my father lived to have the joy of seeing me a *Kapellmeister*.

---

[1] 'Partie' is the German version of 'partita' or suite, and the 'Feld-musik,' 'Feldharmonie' or simply 'Harmonie,' was the wind band, maintained by most noblemen even when they could not afford a larger orchestra, for performing at hunting parties and other outdoor enter-tainments.

[2] 'Haydn's "83,"' *Music & Letters*, July 1930.

In the autumn and winter of 1760 the count and his suite were in Vienna for the marriage of the future Emperor Joseph II to Isabella of Parma. During these months Haydn met Dittersdorf, then a talented youth of twenty attached to the household of the Prince of Hildburghausen, and the two spent their off-duty hours roaming the streets and whetting their critical faculties on the music they heard and performed.[1]

It was also at this time that Haydn began to pay visits of increasing length to the house of a certain hairdresser in the Ungargasse, Johann Peter Keller, whose daughters had both been pupils of his. He had in fact fallen in love, some years back, with the younger, Therese. She, however, had become a nun, and for her profession ceremony, in 1756, her disappointed lover had written an organ concerto, slight, cheerful and non-committal. He continued to visit the family, who had shown him great kindness, and at length Keller began urging him to marry his elder daughter Maria Anna, who was thirty-one (two years older than Haydn) and looked like being left on his hands an old maid. It was against the terms of Haydn's engagement with Count Morzin to marry; but he admits with disarming candour that the prohibition only strengthened his natural desires. From his upbringing and from his own memory of his blind confusion one day when the beautiful Countess Morzin's fichu fell open as she turned the pages of the song he was accompanying for her, it seems likely that he had so far kept them in check. But he was now nearly twenty-nine and eager for marriage, and this, together with his strong sense of gratitude and his kindness of heart, made it peculiarly hard for him to say 'No' in a matter of such delicacy—the more so as he had no particular objection to his proposed bride. On 26th

[1] One of their joint adventures shows that Haydn's growing recognition was not confined to high circles, and sometimes took odd forms. Hearing a group of fiddlers scraping out a minuet of his in a tavern, they went in and Haydn dryly asked the composer's name. On being told, he ferociously replied that it was 'a perfectly filthy minuet,' whereupon the players nearly broke his head with their instruments; Dittersdorf, who was the taller, shielded him with his arm till he had safely pushed him outside the door.

November 1760 he and Maria Anna Aloysia Apollonia Keller were married in St. Stephen's Cathedral.

The pitiful sequel is summed up in two remarks made by Haydn as an old man:

We grew fond of each other, but I soon found that my wife was very irresponsible.

and

My wife was incapable of childbearing, and I was therefore less indifferent to the charms of other women.

Their initial incompatibility in age and temperament might indeed have been bridged by children; but there were none, and his consequent intermittent infidelities widened the gap between them. His wife, too, must have suffered bitterly, and cannot be made to bear the entire blame for the failure of their loveless marriage. But instead of seeking comfort in a closer understanding of her husband's life as a musician—for which, instead, she cared so little that he said it was 'all one to her whether her husband is an artist or a cobbler'—she turned *dévote* and spent an undue proportion of their modest income on charity and on entertaining at their house a continuous and distracting procession of clergy. He on his side must have given her equal irritation by his constant generosity to his numerous poor relations. Unhappiness and frustration turned her shrewish, and their forty years of married life were an almost unrelieved grind of petty friction and misery, no less tragic than the violent drama to which the name of tragedy is generally given.

The irony of it was that Therese, his real beloved, left her convent.[1] Perhaps, unlike him, she had mistaken her real vocation.

Haydn must have awaited with some anxiety the consequences of his defiance of Count Morzin's ban, which could not have been kept secret indefinitely. The issue was never put to the test, for the count's financial difficulties forced him to disband his orchestra.

[1] No details are known, save that both Haydn and his wife describe her in their wills as 'the ex-nun.'

HAYDN
From a contemporary engraving, after the bust by Grassi, 1799

But before this happened it chanced that the count had invited to one of his evening entertainments Prince Paul Anton Esterházy. The prince had been struck by the competence of the orchestra and its director and—so Griesinger tells us—by the music they were performing, which included the first Symphony, in D major. His own *Kapellmeister*, Gregor Werner, was old and failing and, on hearing some months later that Count Morzin's orchestra had been disbanded, he jumped at the chance of securing a young and capable assistant. On 1st May 1761 Joseph Haydn, then aged twenty-nine, signed the contract which determined the course of his life for as many years again.

CHAPTER IV

LIFE IN A PRINCELY HOUSEHOLD

THE princely house to whose service Haydn was now pledged was the greatest of the Hungarian noble families owing allegiance to the Habsburg dynasty. Successive Esterházys had distinguished themselves in the Imperial service, and the title of Prince of the Holy Roman Empire had been conferred in 1687 on Prince Paul Esterházy and his heirs as a reward for his exertions in securing the promulgation of the law making the Austrian sovereign hereditary king of Hungary. This many-sided man, composer and theologian as well as soldier and statesman, had in 1683 built the family castle at Eisenstadt, on a quadrangular plan of noble proportions, with four corner towers, and laid out the surrounding park with the avenues, lakes, grottoes and classic temples that were the inevitable adornments of a seventeenth-century palace garden. Both he and his sons had maintained a suitable musical establish-ment, and when his second son Prince Joseph died in 1721, leaving Prince Paul Anton to succeed him at the age of ten, the dowager Princess Octavia—whom we have met in her retirement as a fellow inhabitant of Haydn's in the Altes Michaelerhaus—carried on the administration of the estates and the artistic tradition of the family until her son came of age in 1734.

Prince Paul Anton himself had, during the wars of 1740 to 1763, twice raised and equipped a regiment of hussars, served at their head and received the rank of field marshal, besides having held for some years the post of ambassador at the court of Naples. From his mother he inherited the family love of music (he played both violin and cello), a small choir and orchestra and an excellent *Kapellmeister* of the old school, Gregor Joseph Werner; and during his twenty-eight years' rule he enlarged his musical establishment and built up a fine collection of manuscript scores. But by 1760 the ill health of old Werner was preventing him from doing his job properly, and Prince Paul Anton was looking out for a younger man to understudy him and eventually take his place.

He could not have found a better man for this delicate and invidious position than Haydn, who genuinely admired Werner, having schooled himself on the same old strict model,[1] and whose patience, kindness and competence were equal to shouldering the responsibilities of an establishment considerably larger than Count Morzin's, under the critical eye of an ageing and crabbed superior who constantly carped at him for a 'fashion-plate' and a mere 'song-scribbler.' His years with Porpora had taught him a cheerful indifference to humiliating situations, while his limitless capacity for hard work was fully called forth by the duties laid down in the contract which he signed, six months after his marriage, with the prince's secretary.

Under the terms of this contract he is to be subordinate to Werner, who in consideration of his long and faithful service is to be retained as *Oberkapellmeister*, but 'where Music is required, everything appertaining to the music . . . is the responsibility of the Vice-*Kapellmeister*.' He is to rank as a household officer and be maintained as such, in consideration of which His Serene Highness 'is graciously confident that he will conduct himself as befits a loyal and self-respecting officer in a princely household, soberly, without harshness to the musicians under him, but with gentleness, modesty, calm and fairness.' When music is to be performed the Vice-*Kapellmeister* and his subordinates are to appear in uniform, all alike in clean white stockings and linen, and with hair powdered and either in a pigtail or a bag. His behaviour is to be the more exemplary as the other musicians are placed under his authority and should be able to follow his good example; he is therefore to eat and drink apart from them and avoid all undue familiarity with them. He is under obligation to compose at all times whatever works His Highness may require, and may give such works to no one else, nor write for any one else without His Highness's knowledge and permission. He is to present himself in the antechamber daily, morning and afternoon, to receive his orders, and is responsible for the punctuality of the musicians and for reporting late-comers and absentees. All

[1] Years later he arranged six of his fugues for string quartet in homage to his memory. They were published by Artaria in 1804.

small disputes and complaints among the musicians are to be dealt with by him on the spot; only in serious cases, in which he is unable to mediate, is he to report the matter respectfully to His Highness. He is to be responsible for the care and upkeep of all music and musical instruments; coach the singers and not allow them to 'forget, while in the country, all that they have learned, with much trouble and expense, from the best masters in Vienna'; and, as he is a performer on several instruments, he must be prepared to make himself useful on all of them. It is considered unnecessary to enumerate his other duties, as His Highness graciously hopes that he will of his own accord perform the above-mentioned services and all other commands with the utmost exactitude, and set the music on such a footing and maintain it in such good order that he will do himself credit and render himself worthy of His Highness's favour; in consideration of which he is to receive 400 florins a year and either his meals at the officers' table or half a florin a day in lieu.

The contract was to last three years. Haydn was to give six months' notice if he wished to leave at the end of that time. The prince for his part promised him the reversion of the *Kapellmeister's* post if he gave satisfaction, but reserved the right to dismiss him at any time if he failed to do so.

The terms of this contract have been regarded as degrading to any artist, let alone one of genius. But the musican of this period was still primarily a craftsman, and the romantic conception of the composer as priest and prophet had not yet supervened to turn his objective pride in his craft into a subjective and personal pride in his status. The courts of Europe, great and small, provided the livelihood of thousands of musicians—singers, instrumentalists and men of all-round talent capable of taking charge, as *Kapellmeister*, of a musical establishment, directing its performances and composing for it as a matter of routine. Composing 'to order,' and for the demands of set occasions, was the rule, not the exception, and the thought of writing for posterity was as foreign to Bach, Mozart, or Haydn as to their hundreds of forgotten contemporaries.

Nor would it have occurred to the musicians of the seventeenth and eighteenth centuries to seek their living on other terms. The only choice that presented itself lay between the liberty and financial risk of free-lance work and the relative security of a contract with a single employer—whether a court, a municipality, a religious house or a church. Mozart, who experienced court service at its worst under the Archbishop of Salzburg, gave it up in disgust, and the poverty and misery that were the price of his freedom hastened his death. Haydn, having also known the strain of poverty and insecurity in his young manhood, entered, in his thirtieth year, upon a contract favourable by the current standards, and upon a relationship with his masters which exemplified court service at its best. It was one in which there were many incidental restrictions and disadvantages, but in which the respect freely accorded to rank and dignity on the one hand, and to special-ized skill on the other, ripened into a regard bordering on affection.

The practical scope of Haydn's duties was formidable. The palace routine called for two operas and two concert 'academies' a week, and after attending on the prince to receive his orders he had to rehearse his orchestra of twelve (three violinists, a cellist, a double bass, a flautist, two oboes, two bassoons and two horns),[1] coach the six singers severally in their operatic parts and practise the Sunday masses with them as a choir. On opera nights he was not only in charge of the performance, but had also to cope with such minor production details as the provision of a prompter. He was responsible for the upkeep of instruments and music library, and if he did not, as Griesinger affirms he did, actually do the clavier tuning, he certainly did not think it beneath his dignity to copy out parts himself rather than burden the prince's exchequer with copyists' fees.

Eisenstadt itself, climbing the eastern slopes of the Leitha hills and surrounded with woods and vineyards, must have been a pleasant enough place for the Haydn couple, not yet disillusioned with each other, to set up their home. The house lay in a quiet lane in the lower town, still surrounded by its ancient walls and divided from the upper town by the castle and its grounds.

---

[1] This was its composition when Haydn took over. It received many additions during his years of service, and numbered between six-teen and twenty-two players.

Above the castle and upper town rises the domed Bergkirche, where Haydn lies buried; this in turn is dominated by the Kal-varienberg, an artificially constructed hill set with fourteen little shrines representing the Stations of the Cross—a common sight in Austria—and crowned by a chapel which drew many pilgrims.

On 1st March 1762 Prince Paul Anton died childless, less than eleven months after he had engaged Haydn, but not before his commands had evoked from him three lively and picturesque symphonies depicting the different times of day and accordingly named *Le Matin, Le Midi* and *Le Soir* (numbers 6 to 8 of the Col-lected Edition).[1] His successor was his brother Nicholas, the 'most gracious prince' to whom Haydn gave his longest and most devoted service. Like Paul Anton, he was a loyal adherent of the Empress Maria Theresa, placed his Hungarian regiments at her disposal and received the field marshal's baton from her in 1770. He punctiliously attended court functions, whether in Vienna or abroad, and it was at Frankfort, at the election and coronation of the Archduke Joseph as King of the Romans in 1764, that Goethe saw him and described him as '. . . not tall, but well-built, animated but at the same time refined, without pride or coldness.' His love of pomp, which earned him the nickname of 'the Magnificent,' displayed itself in the richness of his attire (his jewel-encrusted hussar's uniform was particularly resplendent) and in the lavishness with which he surrounded himself with every cultural adornment appertaining to a prince. He was an ardent and dis-criminating music-lover and himself an aspiring performer, like most noblemen of that time. The instrument of his choice was one now obsolete, the baryton, a curious hybrid between a *viola da gamba* and a guitar: its difficulty and its oddness appealed alike to his vanity.[2]

[1] The numbering of the symphonies is that of the original Breitkopf & Härtel Collected Edition, also adopted in that of the Haydn Society of Boston and in Van Hoboken's Catalogue.

[2] Geiringer quotes from Burney's *General History of Music* his account of the performance of Andreas Lidl, a former member of Prince Esterházy's orchestra, on 'this ungrateful instrument, which has the additional embarrassment of base [*sic*] strings at the back of the neck, and

Prince Paul Anton's death, closely followed by that of the Dowager Princess Octavia, and the formal entry of Prince Nicholas into Eisenstadt on 17th May 1762, provided heavy work for the choir, orchestra and Vice-*Kapellmeister*—two successive Requiem masses, followed by a brisk change of mood calling for Italian operettas [1] and orchestral music of all descriptions. Haydn came through the ordeal to his new master's satisfaction, and his salary was raised to 600 florins—half as much again as his contract stipulated, and considerably more than Werner's; a fact which can hardly have sweetened the old man's temper. Early in the following year came yet another celebration—the wedding of the prince's eldest son, Prince Anton, to Countess Maria Theresa Erdödy. For this occasion Haydn wrote his *Acide e Galatea* (described as a *festa teatrale*) which was performed in the course of the three days' brilliant festivities.

Back at Rohrau, Matthias Haydn had good reason to be satisfied with the way his two sons had made good. True, Michael's new post as *Konzertmeister* to Archbishop Sigismund von Schrattenbach at Salzburg put many miles between them, but the salary was some improvement on his first post at Gross-wardein. As for Joseph, he had not only fallen on his feet at last, but was within easy reach, so that Matthias was able to see him in his comfortable home and elegant blue-and-gold uniform [2] and actually hear him praised by Prince Nicholas, who graciously bade Haydn present his father to him. Only a few months later he was dead—crushed, while at work, by a falling wood-pile. His death brought his son not only personal grief but also those

---

he accompanied himself with these; an admirable expedient in a desert, or even in a house, where there is but one musician, but to have the bother of accompanying yourself in a great concert, surrounded by idle performers who could take the trouble off your hands, and leave them more at liberty to execute, express and embellish the principal melody, seemed at best a work of supererogation.'

[1] Of these only four titles and a handful of arias have survived. See footnote to entry in Catalogue of Works.

[2] Later, in the well-known painting of an operatic performance at Esterház (probably about 1775) Haydn is in grey, the orchestra in red.

family responsibilities which all his life he shouldered so readily and discharged so faithfully. True, his sisters were all married, or about to be; but his youngest brother Hansl (Johann Evangelist), aged twenty, though trained as a wheelwright, was delicate and quite incapable of carrying on his father's extensive business. He hung on at home for a year, but when, in 1764, his stepmother married again, the position became untenable. In 1765 Joseph— who had already made over to him his share of their father's property —took him into his own home and persuaded the prince to take him on as an unpaid member of the choir. Hansl Haydn was not a very good singer,[1] and it was six years before he began to draw pay; even after that his brother continued to supplement his insufficient salary out of his own pocket. What Frau Haydn thought of this arrangement is not recorded, but it must be owned that she had some cause for an occasional grumble.

If she did complain, she was not alone in doing so. A draft memorandum in the Esterházy archives, dated 1765, speaks of slackness and bad feeling among the musicians and neglect in the upkeep of the instruments, and instructs ' *Capel-Meister Heyden* ' to list the instruments and music in triplicate, supervise the distribution and storage of sheet-music with greater care, check absenteeism on the part of his staff and finally 'to devote himself more zealously to composition than hitherto, and especially to compose such pieces as can be played on the gamba, of which we have seen very few as yet. . . .'

Overwork and personal worry had, for the first and only time in his life, defeated Haydn. With so heavy a burden of practical, administrative and sheer manual work on his shoulders, it is a wonder that it did not happen earlier, and indeed that he ever found time and energy to compose at all. Most of what he wrote must have been—as he scribbled at the end of his 1762 horn concerto —'written in my sleep,' and one can only marvel, not at the lack of inspiration in his *pièces de circonstance*, but at the amount of experimental vigour in the thirty odd symphonies written in his first five years at Eisenstadt.

[1] Salieri is reputed to have said of one of his pupils, many years later, that she 'sang through her nose like Hansl Haydn.'

E.N.A.

NICOLAS ESTERHÁZY
From a portrait by J. L. Tocque, 1758

As so many overstrained people do, he had, however, added to his own burdens. In order to gratify his prince's passion for the baryton and show him that it could be played in a wider range of keys than His Highness had mastered or thought possible, Haydn had decided to learn the instrument himself. He started practising on it late at night, 'although disturbed by the scolding and abuse of his wife'—for which, this time at least, the poor woman had ample excuse. But when, at the end of six months, he demonstrated his skill and the new modulations, the prince calmly observed: 'Ah well, Haydn, it's your job to know that.' Characteristically, Haydn swallowed his pride, 'reproached my-self with having neglected composition for half a year, and re-turned to it with renewed zeal': to such effect that early in 1766 we find a note from the prince ordering his chief steward to pay Haydn a *douceur* of twelve ducats for three pieces, 'with which I am very pleased.'

This note is significantly dated from 'Süttör,' that modest hunting-box to the south of Neusiedler Lake which was at that very moment in process of transformation into a rival Versailles. Two years earlier, on the occasion of his journey to Frankfort for the Archduke Joseph's coronation, Prince Nicholas Esterházy had visited the French capital, and the glories of Versailles had spurred him to emulation. Now, in 1766, the metamorphosis of hunting-box into palace was almost complete and the name of Esterház had, appropriately, been bestowed by the prince on his creation. For Haydn, who on Werner's death in March 1766 had become *Kapellmeister* in name as well as in fact, this meant, hence-forth, a yearly uprooting and transplanting, for months on end, to the place which he used to call 'my desert,' but which, as is the way with deserts, provided the setting and the means for his strong and victorious development.

CHAPTER V

GROWTH IN ISOLATION

PRINCE NICHOLAS ESTERHÁZY's choice of the unhealthiest locality in the whole of his domain for the erection of his new residence was dictated largely by his passion for duck-shooting, but also, perhaps, by the urge to impose his will and personality on the most intractable material. In winter icy north winds swept across the surrounding marshes, which in the warmer months teemed with insects as well as wildfowl and subjected the local inhabitants—Haydn included—to recurring fevers. The prince's extensive and costly drainage operations effected only a partial improvement.

The palace itself was a triumph. A whole volume would be required—and was actually produced in 1784, probably by Prince Nicholas himself—to do justice to its spacious Italianate façade, its frescoed hall, its picture gallery and library, its countless rooms lit by crystal chandeliers, panelled in Japanese lacquer and furnished with gold-upholstered chairs and precious marquetry cabinets. The opera house, with its elaborately equipped stage, seated four hundred, while the marionette theatre was built in the form of a grotto and lined with sparkling stones and shells. The grounds far outshone those of Eisenstadt in the richness and variety of their terraces, avenues and vistas, cascades and temples, and their wealth of game.

It is however, characteristic of such princely residences, which (as Osbert Lancaster aptly observes) 'fulfilled just about as many of the ordinary requirements of a home as do the pyramids,' that the musicians' living-accommodation was too cramped to allow of married quarters being allotted to any one but the *Kapellmeister,* the first violinist and the leading male singers.

Here, every summer, and for increasingly long periods each year, as the prince's love for his 'stately pleasure-dome' grew upon him, the regular round of attendance and rehearsal, of opera, concert and Sunday Mass went on. Certain events stood out in high relief—weddings and anniversaries in the Esterházy family, and state visits such as that in 1772 of the French ambassador, the Prince de Rohan, who declared, with a mixture of diplomacy and genuine admiration, that in Esterház he had 'rediscovered Versailles.' In the following year the widowed Empress Maria Theresa herself visited Esterház and vastly enjoyed the symphony and the two operas composed and produced by Haydn in her honour.[1] There was indeed an instinctive sympathy between the elderly *Landesmutter* and Haydn, of all her country's sons most racy of his native soil. The year before her visit to Esterház she had attended a concert given by an orchestra of aristocratic *dilettanti* during a festivity arranged at Pressburg by Prince Nicholas's son-in-law, Count Grassalkovicz, in honour of her favourite daughter, the Archduchess Christine, and her husband. Noticing Haydn and his first violinist Tomasini discreetly providing the 'professional stiffening' among the strings, she signalled to them to remove themselves, which they did, under the pretext of broken strings and nose-bleeding, and shared with their empress the joke of watching the collapse of the amateur team. Thus when Haydn was formally presented to her at Esterház and ventured to remind her of the punishment earned by his early indiscretions on the scaffolding at Schönbrunn, she was delighted, wagged a playful forefinger at him and replied: 'But my dear Haydn, look what good fruit that thrashing bore!' So vivid were her memories of the occasion that she used to say afterwards: 'If I want to hear a good opera I go to Esterház'; and in fact she asked Prince Nicholas, five years later, to lend his orchestra, opera and marionettes to the imperial court for her beloved Christine's entertainment.

But before and after these great occasions, with their preliminary weeks of intensive planning and rehearsing, stretched the feature-less months of routine work and administration, of limited recreation and limited society. Haydn, being a countryman, could amuse himself in his scanty leisure hours by fishing and shooting,

[1] The symphony was No. 48 of the Collected Edition, nicknamed the 'Maria Theresa'; the operas were *L'infedeltà delusa* and the marionette opera *Philemon und Baucis*.

41

while the friendship of the nearby village children, readily given
in return for pocketsful of sweets, comforted him for his own childless home. We know too that he had his own little puppet
theatre, with which he and the other musicians used to entertain
themselves, for Prince Nicholas once arranged to borrow it to give
his wife a surprise on her birthday.

As for his choir and orchestra, he won their individual con-
fidence and loyalty, and secured the highest standards of performance from them as a body, by working far harder than he asked
any of them to do, by knowing exactly what he wanted [1] and by the
firm yet gentle ways by which he set about getting it. Individually
they loved him for his unfailing personal kindness and the fear-
lessness with which he championed their interests with the prince,
supporting their petitions and requests and averting his anger,
if they were in trouble, by a tactful word, backed up on occasion
by a new piece for the baryton. In their filial affection and trust
they took to calling him 'Papa,' which to them meant 'Father,'
no more and no less, and had none of the half-jocular Victorian
overtones which it has for our ears.

Doubtless they were a quarrelsome and undisciplined lot, but
there was much talent among them, which Haydn had often been
the first to recognize. Luigi Tomasini, the leading violinist, had
originally come from Italy as Prince Paul Anton's valet. He may
have played in the orchestra as well, as the servants of many noble
houses were expected to do in addition to their regular duties; [2]
but his outstanding gifts appear to have been discovered by Haydn,

[1] How fastidious he was over details of performance is shown in the
lengthy instructions which he sent with the score of a cantata, the *Applausus*,
written in 1768 for the birthday of a Benedictine abbot. He points
out that 'there is a very great difference between *piano* and *pianissimo*,
forte and *fortissimo*, *crescendo* and *sforzando* and the like,' and even asks the
copyist so to arrange the parts that the players do not all have to turn their
pages at once, 'as this weakens a lightly scored passage.'

[2] Geiringer's *Haydn* quotes this advertisement from the *Wiener
Zeitung* (1789): 'Wanted by nobleman a servant who plays the violin
well and is able to accompany difficult piano sonatas.' This also
reflects the current view of the violin as the accompanying instrument
in works for violin and keyboard.

who had him transferred to the orchestra as a full-time member, wrote several violin concertos for him and declared that 'no one played his quartets so gratefully' as he. Haydn was also responsible for the engagement of that fine cellist Joseph Weigl, of the horn player Franz, who later, as a baryton virtuoso, repaid him by carrying his works all over Europe, and of the young Magdalene Spangler, daughter of his old friend and rescuer. Marriages (also, doubtless, more irregular liaisons) were frequent within the little community: Magdalene Spangler became the wife of the leading tenor Karl Friberth, Haydn's lifelong friend, and Weigl married the first soprano Anna Maria Scheffstos. Haydn and his wife were consequently in steady demand as godparents at the parish church at Eisenstadt, and one of his godsons, the Weigls' eldest boy Joseph, delighted his fatherly heart by winning fame as a composer before the century was out.

One other name must be mentioned, though not a performer— that of the copyist Joseph Elssler, whose son Johann (another godchild of Haydn's, as were all his brothers and sisters) has a double claim to remembrance, as the faithful servant and copyist of Haydn's later years and as the father of the celebrated dancer Fanny Elssler.

These virtuosi were a shifting population, and Haydn in his thirty years of service often had the pain of parting with old friends and valuable musicians. They however carried their former *Kapellmeister's* music with them on their travels and were in part responsible for the astonishing growth of its popularity in the 1770s and 1780s.[1] It is indeed one of the most remarkable aspects of

[1] Besides Franz, there was Costanza Baldesturla, who sang Haydn's 'Lament for the Death of Frederick the Great,' accompanied by Franz on the baryton, at Leipzig in 1788, and subsequently married J. G. Schicht, the cantor of the Thomasschule, who in 1802 conducted the first Leipzig performance of Haydn's oratorio *Il ritorno di Tobia*; the violinist Antonio Rosetti, whose new master Prince Kraft Ernst von Oettingen-Wallerstein became an avid collector of Haydn scores; and Andreas Lidl, the baryton virtuoso referred to by Burney, who, as 'the celebrated Mr. Lydel,' won fame for himself as a performer, and for Haydn as a composer, in London and Oxford in the 1770s.

Haydn's career that he, who—unlike Mozart and Beethoven—was, by his own admission, 'no wizard' as a performer, and who, anchored by his duties to one spot, was unable to promote the spread of his works by his personal presence and drive as Handel did, should have won fame throughout Europe, as a composer alone, years before his English visits brought him before a wider public.

But it was not merely restlessness that made Prince Nicholas's musicians leave, despite salaries and treatment that were on the whole generous. The enforced separation from their families at Eisenstadt during the prince's increasingly protracted periods at Esterház turned the palace into the proverbial gilded cage. They did for a time attempt to squeeze their wives and children into their already overcrowded quarters, but the resulting chaos was such that in 1772 the prince expressly forbade them to bring their families to Esterház at all. The extra maintenance grant they demanded and received did nothing to relieve the tension among the young married men condemned to celibacy for the greater part of the year —and this very year the prince chose to prolong his sojourn at Esterház far beyond the normal term. In desperation the musicians turned to their *Kapellmeister* for help.

Haydn doubtless knew that complaints had been reaching the prince's ears, and that it might be undiplomatic to make a frontal attack; on the other hand, the flanking manœuvre which his ingenuity devised and his genius perfected could hardly have attained its object if Prince Nicholas had had no inkling at all of what was in the wind. There must have been some nervousness in the orchestra when, a few weeks later, they plunged into the restless and stormy opening of the 'Farewell' Symphony, and as the finale drew to its close and one musician after another, as the score directed, snuffed his candle and tiptoed out, the temptation to steal a backward glance at their master's face must have been overwhelming. But when the last muted notes of first and second violin had died away, the prince, touched, amused and doubtless delighted by one of the most original and exciting works Haydn had yet written, exclaimed: 'I see what you 're after—the musicians want to go home! Very well, we 'll pack up to-morrow.'

Jubilation reigned among the musicians. Only Haydn himself, returning that night to his married quarters and his unloving and unloved wife, got nothing out of the evening's work beyond the satisfaction of having made his 'children' happy.[1]

It is impossible to tell the whole of Haydn's story. Unlike Mozart, whose letters to his family reveal his personality in all its iridescent complexity, he left few intimate documents to disclose its inner springs. And the outward events of his first ten years in the service of the Esterházy family throw no light on the sudden swift ripening of his art between 1767 and 1770. The process can be measured by the advance in technical and emotional maturity from the Op. 3 quartets (probably written between 1765 and 1767) to the Op. 9 quartets of 1768–9, and by the gulf separating the delightfully effortless little B flat Symphony of 1767, No. 35, from its more pedestrian forerunners on the one hand and, on the other, from the abrupt and brooding passion of its two successors in F minor and G minor, Nos. 49[2] and 39. But it cannot be explained. Still less (apart from a severe attack of fever in 1770, which may have precipitated the crisis) can we account for the volcanic eruption of his genius in the early 1770s, when in the space of three years he composed six outstanding symphonies (Nos. 44, 45—the 'Farewell'—46, 48, 51 and 52), the wonderful single piano Sonata in C minor, No. 20, and the warm-hearted and romantic set Nos. 21–6, the Op. 17 quartets, and above all the Op. 20 quartets, which for the first time reveal his personality in its full stature and power.

Some writers—notably Teodor de Wyzewa and Karl Geiringer —regard the impact of that early romantic tendency in German letters known as the *Sturm und Drang* (the 'storm and stress') movement as being in part the cause of this 'romantic crisis' in Haydn's art. But this movement, essentially intellectual, literary

[1] There are several other versions of this story, but this, related by both Dies and Griesinger as having been told them by Haydn himself, is the one generally accepted as true.

[2] Since the publication of the thematic list in the Breitkopf & Härtel Collected Edition the autograph of No. 49 has been found, and bears the date 1768, four years earlier than the date originally assigned to it.

and city-bred, originated outside Austria and outside the Catholic world. It eventually touched Austria, and indeed filtered through to Eisenstadt and Esterház, chiefly by way of the drama: the travelling companies engaged to entertain the prince included in their repertory such works as Lessing's *Emilia Galotti* and Schiller's *Die Räuber* and *Kabale und Liebe*. But Haydn's 'romantic crisis' of the early 1770s antedates most, if not all, of such performances. As for reading, he was, besides being intensely busy, the most unliterary of men. Carpani, who knew him in his later years, called him 'an illustrious idiot' in relation to all knowledge outside his art, and his library consisted very largely of technical treatises on music. If he was affected by the *Sturm und Drang* movement, it can only have been by an entirely unconscious attunement to the spirit of the time.

In any case, there is no need to seek for external stimuli. The events and experiences of an artist's life and the production of his works are not necessarily linked in a sequence of chronological or emotional cause and effect. His outward experiences influence his art indeed, in so far as they shape his personality, which is the well-spring both of his art and of his actions; but the two streams of his creative and his active life rarely converge outwardly, but, flowing back into their common source, which is the artist's inmost being, there replenish, in a timeless and wholly unaccountable way, themselves, each other and the source itself. It is even true to say, as a recent writer suggests,[1] that, as artistic receptivity increases, 'the relation between impact and response becomes less obvious and less congruous,' so that 'almost any sense impression may effect the creative explosion.'

As far as his actual conditions of life and work were concerned, Haydn was on the whole content, though the isolation of his 'desert' became increasingly irksome as the years went by, and Prince Nicholas was too much attached to him ever to allow him that longed-for trip to Italy which, he always felt, would have made a first-rate opera composer of him. But the prince's real appreciation, and the co-operation of a skilled and devoted orchestra, were a precious stimulus, which he rightly valued.

[1] Rosalind Murray, *The Forsaken Fountain* (Hollis & Carter, 1948).

My prince was satisfied with all my works, I was praised, as head of an orchestra I could experiment, observe what heightened the effect and what weakened it, and so could improve, expand, cut, take risks, I was cut off from the world, there was no one near me to torment me or make me doubt myself, and so I had to become original.

This much-quoted statement of Haydn's presents his situation in an ideal light; but if it was ideal, it was only because he had it in him to make it so. The monotony and isolation, heavy work and petty personal frictions would have broken the nerves and staying-power of a more mercurial temperament. But Haydn's patience and toughness of fibre, and the very slowness of his develop-ment, gave him the strength not only to endure but actually to thrive on the uniformity and solitude of his life.

He worked to a daily plan, rising early and getting through a considerable amount of composition before it was time to wait on the prince and embark on practical duties. He would launch himself off by improvising at the keyboard. Indeed, when a visitor once asked him 'how he ever *began*' to write so many admirable works, he took the question perfectly literally, and replied:

Well, you see, I get up early, and as soon as I have dressed I go down on my knees and pray God and the Blessed Virgin that I may have another successful day. Then when I 've had some breakfast I sit down at the clavier and begin my search. If I hit on an idea quickly, it goes ahead easily and without much trouble. But if I can't get on, I know that I must have forfeited God's grace by some fault of mine, and then I pray once more for grace till I feel I 'm forgiven.

And at the end of his life he told his friend Griesinger that when he was stuck he would walk up and down, rosary in hand, and after a few 'Hail Mary's' the ideas would begin to flow again.

So, in revealing his modest device for setting the machinery of composition in motion, he also disclosed the motive power behind that machinery and behind his whole life. It was the practical immediacy of his faith, the matter-of-factness with which he took his relationship with God for granted, that integrated and gave purpose to his genius and his natural gifts of temperament, and was the secret of his capacity to make his wilderness flower and trans-mute the deadening routine of his days into a living rhythm.

CHAPTER VI

WIDENING HORIZONS

THE fame that, unknown to Haydn himself, had been steadily growing for the past fifteen years had, by 1775, reached considerable proportions. In Austria itself he had, as early as 1766, been compared by a musical essayist to the much-admired poet Gellert (to us the comparison with that edifying but insipid writer seems hardly flattering), and in 1770 the production of his gay little opera *Lo speziale* in Vienna, at the residence of a certain Baron von Sumerau, had brought his operatic achievements before the aristocratic connoisseurs of the capital. The empress's praises following her Esterház visit, and the successful first performance in 1775 of his oratorio *Il ritorno di Tobia* by the Tonkünstlersocietät[1] in aid of their members' widows and orphans, led to his being commissioned by the court, in 1776, to compose an opera, and to his being invited, that same year, to contribute autobiographical notes to *Das gelehrte Oesterreich*, a sort of 'Who's Who' of Austria's literary and artistic world.

Success bred opposition and jealousy. When the opera for the court, *La vera costanza*, went into rehearsal Haydn found his requirements and projected casting overruled on every point— possibly at the instigation of the Italian composer Anfossi, who was at work on the same libretto. Haydn appealed to the Emperor Joseph II, now co-ruler with his ageing mother Maria Theresa; but despite his intervention the difficulties remained insurmountable, and Haydn withdrew the score. Perhaps the emperor's appeals were somewhat half-hearted, for it was characteristic of the temperamental difference between Maria Theresa and her high-minded, doctrinaire son that to him Haydn's music seemed purely frivolous and that—as Mozart later found to his cost—his allegiance was

[1] A contributory benefit society for musicians and their dependants.

48

entirely given to the traditional Italian school represented by Gassmann and Salieri.

In 1778 he was involved in another dispute, this time with the Tonkünstlersocietät, to whom he had applied for membership as a form of insurance for himself and his wife in illness or old age. He had deposited the usual 300 florins, but requested the remission of the further 368 florins required from country members, offering instead to compose, on request, further works for the society's concerts. The society approved his application in 1779, but demanded that he should make his offer binding by a written contract. This Haydn indignantly and very properly refused to do, as being inconsistent with his obligations to his prince and with his own artistic freedom, and withdrew his application. To its discredit, the society accepted his withdrawal. Two years later, during the Grand Duke Paul of Russia's state visit to the imperial court, the society asked Haydn to make certain alterations in the score of *Tobia* for a new performance. Haydn offered to do so and conduct both rehearsals and performance himself, in return for a supply of complimentary tickets. This offer was refused, as the request for complimentary tickets might create a precedent, and Hasse's oratorio *Santa Elena al Calvario* was performed instead.

Abroad, his growing reputation, though—and doubtless because—it brought him less material profit, went forward unchecked by jealousies and, as we have seen, actively promoted by his former colleagues. Even in the 1760s his work had been published in France, Holland and England,[1] and by the 1770s his symphonies and quartets appear with increasing frequency in Paris and London concert programmes. His name was familiar to Dr. Burney when he set out on his musical journey through Germany, Austria and the Netherlands in 1772, though unfortunately he was at Esterház when Burney tried to trace him in Vienna.

[1] Larsen (*Die Haydn-Überlieferung*, p. 103) points out that Haydn probably knew nothing of these early editions, and that there are as yet no grounds for challenging Pohl's statement that until the end of the 1770s there is no indication that Haydn drew any profit from the publication of his works in Leipzig, Berlin, Speyer, Amsterdam, Paris and London.

In 1779 the violinist Fonteski introduced a fresh batch of his symphonies to Paris—with such success that the Concert de la Loge
Olympique, five years later, commissioned from him the set of
six now known as the 'Paris' Symphonies—while in Madrid the
poet Yriarte devoted a considerable section of his lengthy poem
La Música to Haydn, praising his inexhaustible novelty, the nobility
of his modulations and the strangeness of his 'learned and har-
monious sallies'; and also, significantly, acclaiming him as the
sole champion of 'the German regions' in the musical field.
In the light of the musical pre-eminence accorded to Germany and
Austria in the nineteenth century, we are apt to forget that in the
eighteenth century Italy held the foremost place, virtually un-
challenged.[1] It was Haydn who, in this respect as in so many
others, unconsciously gave the impetus to far-reaching changes
in opinion and practice.

From Spain, too, Boccherini sent him messages of enthusiastic
admiration through their common publisher in Vienna, Artaria,
and the Cadiz cathedral chapter commissioned from him, for
the Three Hours' Devotion on Good Friday 1785, the set of
instrumental meditations known as *The Seven Words of the Saviour
on the Cross*.[2] An Italian tribute came from the Philharmonic
Society of Modena, which elected him to honorary membership
in 1780.

Growing fame extended Haydn's business contacts considerably.
It was probably true at the outset that, as Griesinger said, he did
not know how famous he was. But by the 1780s he was in no
doubt whatever but that his work was known and appreciated,
both in Austria and abroad, and that he could command his price.

---

[1] Handel did something to break down the prejudice in England—
Swift, on his being announced as a caller, cried 'O pray let me see a
German genius before I die!'—but his music was purely Italian in style.

[2] In its original form the work was orchestral. Haydn himself
arranged it for string quartet, in which latter version, somewhat illogically, its seven movements (though *not*, illogically again, the self-contained Introduction) are reckoned among his string quartets as seven
separate numbers. Haydn later rearranged it as an oratorio, and it was
first performed in this version in 1799.

In 1780 his long-standing connection with the firm of Artaria was opened by their publication of the six pianoforte sonatas dedicated to the talented Auenbrugger sisters—Nos. 35–39 of the Collected Edition, with the magnificent earlier Sonata in C minor, No. 20, to make up the set; No. 37 is the charming but overplayed little work in D major. Artaria obviously realized Haydn's artistic and commercial value, for in the following year, besides publishing his first set of songs, he had his portrait engraved by J. E. Mansfeld for inclusion in the series of portraits of eminent Austrians brought out by his firm. Prince Nicholas Esterházy was almost as pleased and flattered as Haydn was himself at the publicity accorded to his *Kapellmeister*. In the same year, 1781, Haydn entered into relations with the London firm of Forster, and also undertook the task of announcing the issue of his new set of quartets (the 'Russian' quartets, Op. 33) in manuscript to private subscribers prior to their publication by Artaria. His much-quoted statement that these quartets are written 'in an entirely new and special manner' ('auf eine ganz neue besondere Art') occurs in his letter to Prince von Oettingen-Wallerstein, and whatever its value as musical criticism, certainly gives evidence of good salesmanship. In all his business dealings Haydn shows himself shrewdly aware of the merits and saleability of his works, quick to stand upon his rights and not above an occasional piece of double-dealing; his sale of the Op. 33 quartets, and of *The Seven Words*,[1] to both Artaria and Forster got him into trouble with both firms, and eventually cost him the Forster connection; not-withstanding which he sold to another English publisher, Bland, while in London, a trio which he had previously sold to Artaria with a written undertaking not to dispose of it elsewhere.

In assessing these transactions it has to be remembered that in the eighteenth century the relationship between composer and publisher was such that the cheating of publishers—like smuggling by travellers to-day—ranked as one of the 'permissible'

[1] The trouble over *The Seven Words* arose through the fact that Artaria sent the string quartet arrangement to a rival London firm, Longman & Broderip, which to Forster was an infringement of his right, as sole possessor (so he thought) of the original version, to issue arrangements.

dishonesties.[1]   There was no law of copyright, and if a publisher could acquire a manuscript—usually through that common source of leakage, a dishonest copyist [2]—or, as was more usual with a work published abroad, a printed copy, there was nothing to stop his publishing a pirated edition, from which neither the composer nor, for that matter, the original publisher, earned a penny.   Such a procedure could only be forestalled by either composer or publisher selling the rights of the work themselves to a foreign publisher, who could then label his edition as the sole authentic one; and it is clear that Haydn, who often freely discussed with Artaria his foreign negotiations regarding works that Artaria was bringing out, did this with his publisher's knowledge and consent.   His relationship with Artaria survived the strain put on it by his occasional duplicities on the one hand and Artaria's dilatory methods and careless engraving on the other and, though other firms also handled his work later, remained unbroken for twenty-six years.

Less justifiable is the fact that in 1789 he met Prince von Oettingen-Wallerstein's request—and payment—for three new symphonies which were to be his exclusive property with the three symphonies Nos. 90–2, which, though musically more than value for money, did not fulfil the terms of the bargain, for Haydn had written them the year before, for a certain Comte d'Ogny [3] and also

[1] Mozart tried it also, for he boasts to his father in his letter of 3rd October 1778 of having sold 'two overtures and the *sinfonia concertante*' to Le Gros, who 'thinks he alone has them, but it is not true, for they are still fresh in my head, and as soon as I get home I shall write them down again.'   His phenomenal musical memory would have been a formidable weapon if his business capacity had matched it.

[2] Haydn accuses Artaria's copyist of having offered his copyist eight ducats for a copy of *The Seven Words* (letter of 7th October 1787).

[3] According to the autograph of No. 90 and photostats of parts of No. 91 in the Library of Congress, Washington.   Larsen, in *Die Haydn-Überlieferung* (pp. 85–93) proves that the three symphonies commissioned by Prince von Oettingen-Wallenstein, which were previously thought to have been lost, can be no other than Nos. 90–2.   It is in this connection that he makes the suggestion that Haydn's multiple disposal of various compositions was due to the pressure of work and the difficulty

disposed of them to his Viennese patron von Kees, and editions quickly appeared in Vienna, Paris and London. This is perhaps explained—though not excused—by his natural reluctance to turn down a lucrative commission, even though the constant pressure of his regular duties and his self-confessed slowness ('I was never a quick writer'), aggravated by eye strain, made it increasingly hard for him to keep abreast of the growing demand for his music. Neither his wife's extravagances nor his habit of supporting his own poor relations made saving easy for him; yet he was always anxious to save. This anxiety sprang partly from his peasant instincts of thrift, partly from the scar left by his early experiences and partly from a latent streak of 'nearness' about money, which became a mild obsession in his failing years; though (as Carpani finely observes) 'Haydn, when he was at the height of his powers, that is, when he was truly *Haydn*, was never rich, because he was never miserly,' and his very anxieties were as much on his family's behalf as on his own.

There was by now another reason why he may have been anxious to make a little extra money. In 1779 an Italian couple named Polzelli had joined Prince Nicholas's musical establishment, the husband, Antonio, as violinist, his wife Luigia as a mezzo-soprano. The prince appears to have found them unsatisfactory; Antonio was consumptive and often unfit for duty, while Luigia, aged nineteen, was only capable of undertaking minor operatic parts, and in 1780 they were dismissed, though with full pay, before their contract had expired. In spite of this they were kept on—obviously at Haydn's instance, for a passionate and open attachment had blazed up between him and the Italian girl with her bright dark eyes and shapely figure[1] whom he had to coach in her unimportant parts.

---

of filling the growing demands upon him; though it is surely a little uncharitable of him to hint that Haydn's plea of eyestrain in his correspondence with the prince's agent is a mere pretext, for he is known to have suffered from it while in England.

[1] There is no portrait of her; this—all that we know of her appearance—is taken from her passport description.

Haydn never pretended to be above the average in sexual morality, and his late and slow development and unsatisfactory marriage had left him with unspent reserves of passion and protective tenderness. At forty-eight he was years younger in vitality and ardour than his fifty-year-old wife, and, with the charm which, to his own ironical surprise, he found he could exert over women, fully capable of capturing the love of a girl unhappy herself in her marriage with an elderly and ailing husband. Both of them looked forward to an eventual marriage, and when, in 1791, Luigia's husband died, Haydn wrote, with dry realism (and a characteristic touch of sympathy for the dead man—'poor fellow, he has suffered enough') that 'perhaps the time will come when two pairs of eyes will close. One pair has shut already, but the other—well, God's will be done.'

That Luigia's love for Haydn cooled off before his for her is, considering her youth, not surprising, though it is hurtful to read his still ardent letters of the 1790s with the realization that by this time all she cared for was what she could get out of him financially. But she probably loved him, at the outset, as much and as truly as her nature allowed. On his side (as Geiringer acutely remarks) an additional attraction may well have been her two little boys, whose guardian he became on their father's death. The younger, Antonio (born in 1783), was reputed to be his, but this has never been conclusively proved, and in fact he seems to have preferred the elder, Pietro, who was two years old when the Polzellis arrived at Esterház, and to whom he was devotedly attached.

Amid all the happenings of a singularly active year, 1781—the year of the Op. 33 quartets and of lively contact with the outside world—the event which was to mark Haydn's life most deeply was one of which, at the time, he knew nothing: a brief wrangle between the Archbishop of Salzburg and his court organist, ending in the latter's resignation. His brother Michael, the archbishop's *Kapellmeister*, must have heard all the Salzburg rumours that the young man had actually been kicked down the steps of His Grace's Vienna residence by one of his courtiers; but Michael —a prey to inertia and drink since his baby daughter's death ten years earlier—was no letter-writer. And so Joseph Haydn probably never heard of the incident which decided that the ten remaining years of Wolfgang Amadeus Mozart's short life should be lived out in Vienna.

Haydn first met him in the winter of that year, during the whirl of court festivities with which the Emperor Joseph II (now sole ruler since his mother's death in 1780) was entertaining the Grand Duke Paul of Russia and his wife and the Duke and Duchess of Württemberg, whose daughter Elisabeth was to marry the Archduke Francis. Mozart was summoned to court to engage in a contest of skill on the clavier with Clementi before the royal visitors, and Haydn attended a concert consisting largely of his works in the grand duchess's apartments on Christmas Day, at which his old friends Tomasini and Weigl took part in a performance of a quartet from his new set dedicated to the grand duke.[1] But Mozart was at the same time intensely absorbed in work on his opera *Die Entführung aus dem Serail* (*The Seraglio*), in the complicated negotiations for its production and in the still more complicated business of piloting his engagement to Constanze Weber (whom he married the following August) through the cross-currents of his future mother-in-law's intrigues and his father's disapproval. So there was little opportunity, just then, for the acquaintanceship to ripen.

They probably met again once or twice in the two following years, although, to Haydn's disgust, Prince Nicholas normally spent only a few weeks at the turn of each year in Vienna. It was not until 1784, when the prince spent a longer time than usual in the capital, that their regard quickened into friendship. Mozart's numerous engagements that winter with the cadet branch of the Esterházy family were probably not due to Haydn but to already existing Masonic connections (indeed Haydn, as a comparative stranger to Vienna, could do little to help Mozart in his increasingly hard struggle for a livelihood); but they may have provided an additional point of contact. Mozart invited him frequently to his house to play quartets, or took him round to his friend Stephen Storace, whose sister Nancy was to play

[1] Hence the nickname of 'The Russian' quartets given to the Op. 33 set.

Susanna in the first performance of *Figaro*. Michael Kelly (Don Basilio in the same performance), who the previous summer had paid his respects to Haydn at Esterház,[1] recalls such a party at Storace's lodging, at which Haydn and Dittersdorf played first and second violin, Mozart the viola and Wanhal the cello.

Mozart, as Kelly observed, 'felt a thorough contempt for insolent mediocrity,' and was quick to express it; but he recognized genius with unerring perception and touching humility. Besides, he found in the older man not only genius but fatherly kindness, a capacity for laughter and enjoyment to match his own, and a steadfastness and strength to which his restless spirit could turn for refreshment and comfort, as Hamlet to Horatio. For years already he had known and studied Haydn's music, and especially his quartets, and now acknowledged his debt with the dedication of the magnificent set of six, K.387, 421, 428, 458, 464 and 465—like Haydn's Op. 33 his first for nearly ten years [2]—in a letter full of veneration and affection. It was after a performance of the three last of these at Mozart's home that Haydn said to Leopold Mozart, who in February 1785 came to cast a critical eye over his son's *ménage*: 'I tell you before God, as an honest man, that your son is the greatest composer I know, either personally or by name; he has taste, and moreover the greatest science in composition.'

For Haydn, indeed, the impact of this friendship may well have been sharper than for Mozart, who knew his music before they met and—as the 'Haydn' quartets show—had learned all that it had to teach him, whereas Haydn would have had little chance of hearing Mozart's work before the two met in Vienna. Since his own genius had sprung to maturity in the 1770s he had, moreover, had no contact with any one approaching his own stature, his only companions being his orchestra and a batch of moderately gifted pupils (among them Fritz and Edmund von Weber, Carl Maria von Weber's half-brothers, and Ignaz Pleyel, his future

[1] Michael Kelly, *Reminiscences*, vol. i. He himself says that his visit was to Eisenstadt, but his account of the place, and his erratic spelling of foreign names, make it probable that he meant Esterház.

[2] His last set, K. 168–73, had been written in 1773; K. 387, the first of the 'Haydn' set, was written in 1782.

reluctant rival in London). Now he was brought into electrifying contact with a personality living and moving at a consuming
tempo, contrasting utterly with the slow and steady pulse of his
own life, and with music which he, though less discriminating
because less critical than Mozart, inevitably recognized as being of a
different order from that of their contemporaries.

There was no such inevitability in Haydn's recognition of
Mozart's superiority over himself. Yet he did recognize it, even
to the point of disturbing, for a while, his own artistic balance.
That he, a man in his fifties, was able to assimilate so much of
Mozart's technique and spirit and integrate them with his own
already mature style, to its deep enrichment, is one of the miracles
of musical history. The personal generosity and humility that lay
behind this miracle is shown in the letter he wrote in December
1787, two months after the first performance of *Don Giovanni* in
Prague, to an official named Roth, who had asked him to provide
an opera for the Bohemian capital:

You ask me for an *opera buffa*; with the greatest pleasure, if you would
care to possess some vocal work of mine for yourself alone. But if it is
for performance at the theatre in Prague, I cannot oblige you in that case,
because all my operas are too closely bound up with our own performers
(at Estoras in Hungary), and besides would never make the effect that
I have gauged in accordance with the place. It would be quite another
matter if I had the inestimable good fortune to compose an entirely new
opera for the theatre there. But there too I should still be taking a
great risk, since it is hardly possible for any one to stand beside the great
Mozart.

For if I could impress Mozart's inimitable works as deeply, and with
that musical understanding and keen feeling with which I myself grasp
and feel them, upon the soul of every music-lover, especially those in
high places, the nations would compete for the possession of such a jewel
within their borders. Prague should keep tight hold of the precious man
—but remunerate him too, for failing that, the tale of great men of genius
is a sad one and gives succeeding generations little encouragement to
further endeavour—hence, alas, the collapse of so many hopeful spirits.
It makes me furious that this unique Mozart has not yet been engaged
by an imperial or royal court! Forgive me for breaking out like this—
I love the man too much.

Six years earlier he had complacently assured Artaria, after the success of his *Stabat Mater* in Paris, that:

... the Parisians have heard nothing yet; if they could only hear my operetta *L'isola disabitata*, or my latest opera *La fedeltà premiata*, for I warrant that nothing like them has been heard in Paris, or even, perhaps, in Vienna.

The gulf between these two estimates of his operatic achievement is the measure both of Mozart's impact upon him, and of his own capacity to absorb it.

It may have been the first enthusiasm of his friendship with Mozart that induced him, in 1785, to become a freemason, though his actual choice of the lodge 'Zur Eintracht' ('Unity') was probably determined by his fellow member and patron von Greiner, a court official and minor poet, who had provided the text of several of his songs. Being an intensely sociable man, the prospect of friendly intercourse with so many congenial spirits attracted him as much as the humanitarian ideals of the order, to which many liberal-minded aristocrats and even Church dignitaries belonged; for at that period the emphasis lay rather on its conception of universal brotherhood than on its repudiation of Christian dogma. But unlike Mozart, to whom the ideals of masonry came as a religious revelation more intense than any he had found in the lukewarm and worldly Catholicism of eighteenth-century Austria, Haydn retained to the end of his days a devout simplicity of faith which found all the food it needed in the sacraments and teaching of the Church. Masonry thus had nothing special to offer him, beyond personal friendships with such men as Puchberg (Mozart's friend and helper in the desperate poverty of his last years), and once the novelty had worn off he ceased to practise it actively.

Life in Esterház grew more burdensome as Vienna multiplied its attractions. Prince Nicholas, for whose sake he still turned down all other offers (including the Earl of Abingdon's attempts to secure him for the London Professional Concerts in 1784), was ageing and entertained less; yet he still loved Esterház, and would linger on there till the late autumn 'despite the fact that he has very little entertainment,' writes Haydn to Artaria in 1784, 'as half the performers are ill or absent; so you can imagine I am hard put to it to keep His Highness amused.' Haydn was hoping to get to Vienna in time for the first performance there of his opera *La fedeltà premiata*, in a German version, by Emanuel Schikaneder's company at the Kärntnertor Theatre. It took place on 18th December, and was a great success; but no one knows if he managed to be there.

Into his precious winter weeks in Vienna he crowded all he could of musical experience and friendly society. He heard *Figaro*, for its melodies haunted his dreams in the bleak and windy Esterház nights, and went with Mozart and Puchberg to the rehearsals of *Così fan tutte* in January 1790; Mozart invited no one else. Many houses were open to him—Councillor von Kees, whose musical library and private concerts were alike famous, the wealthy merchant Tost, a fine violinist, for whom he wrote no fewer than twelve quartets (Opp. 54, 55 and 64),[1] and Baron Gottfried van Swieten, court librarian and amateur composer (Griesinger said that his symphonies were 'as stiff as himself') into whose circle he was probably introduced by Mozart, who rescored Handel's *Messiah* for his private concerts. Then there were the musical evenings with the Mozarts and Storaces, and we hear of other friends such as the Neuwirth family, in whose quartet parties he

---

[1] A violinist named Johann Tost, a member of the Esterházy orchestra from 1783 to 1788, appeared in Paris in 1789 as a soloist, and sold the MSS. of two Haydn symphonies (with one by Gyrowetz falsely described as by Haydn) to the Paris publisher Sieber; the name Tost appears also in 1788 in Haydn's correspondence with Artaria, the composer inquiring whether Artaria has acquired his 'latest quartets' and two symphonies from Tost or elsewhere, and again in 1789, when he asks whether Artaria has acquired the symphonies from Tost direct or from Sieber. No more is heard of the violin virtuoso after 1789, but in 1790 a wealthy merchant named Johann Tost appears on the Viennese scene, newly married to a rich bride, and quickly acquires fame as an amateur violinist. This sequence of events leads Larsen to suggest that Pohl's warning against confusing the two Tosts is unnecessary and that they are in fact identical.

would play the viola.[1] But it was with Dr. Peter Leopold von Genzinger and his wife Marianne that he found—for the first time since he set out from Rohrau on his adventures fifty years before—everything that a real home has to offer.

Genzinger was Prince Nicholas's physician, and his wife was a gifted pianist and a great admirer of Haydn, whom she received as an honoured guest and family friend. But for Haydn, Marianne von Genzinger was almost as much of a revelation as Mozart. Never before had he known a woman whose beauty was matched by such culture, such understanding, such goodness and warmth of heart. Here was someone to whom he could speak without reserve—

Oh, if I could only be with Your Ladyship, even for a quarter of an hour, pour out my troubles and be comforted. . . .

whose society in Vienna made his yearly uprootings more painful—

to-morrow I return to my sad solitude. God keep you and your dear husband and your lovely children—

and Esterház itself drearier, lacking not only the happy companion-ship but also the creature comforts which Frau von Genzinger's motherly nature provided:

Now, here I sit in my desert, forsaken, like a poor orphan, almost without human society, sad, full of the memory of the glorious days gone by— gone, alas, and who knows when those pleasant days will come again? Those happy gatherings when the whole circle is united heart and soul, all those lovely musical evenings . . . ? . . . I found everything upside down at home, for three days I did not know if I was *Capell-meister* or *Capell-*servant, I was inconsolable, my rooms were all in a mess, my forte-piano, which I used to love, was refractory, disobedient, and exas-perated instead of soothing me, I could hardly sleep, even my dreams harried me, for when I dreamed I was happily listening to the opera *Le nozze di Figaro* the inexorable north wind woke me up and almost blew my nightcap off my head. I lost twenty pounds in three days . . . here in Estoras nobody asks me 'do you take your chocolate with or

---

[1] According to Mandyczewski's Supplement to the library Catalogue of the Gesellschaft der Musikfreunde in Vienna (quoted by Larsen, p. 42) to whom the family gave the autograph of the Op. 17 quartets.

Marianne von Genzinger

without milk, will you have your coffee black or with cream, what can
I pass you, my dear Haydn, will you have a vanilla or a pineapple ice?
If only I had a piece of good Parmesan cheese, especially for Lent, to
help down the black dumplings and noodles! . . . Forgive me for
taking up your time, the very first time I write, with such stupid outpourings and such a wretched scribble . . .

It is pleasant to know that in reply to this letter Marianne sent him
a box of biscuits.

Part of the attraction for Haydn, as always, were Marianne's
'lovely children,' and his letters are full of affectionate messages
and good advice about voice production to the two eldest,
Josepha ('my good Miss Pepi') and Franz. But it is easy to see
that he was, in a deeply respectful way, half in love with Marianne
herself; though he anxiously assures her, when one of his letters
to her had been lost on the way, that it contained nothing dishonour-
able for the inquisitive to seize on, and that

my friendship and esteem for Your Ladyship, tender though it is, can never
become culpable, because I always keep before me the reverence due to
Your Ladyship's lofty virtues, which not only I but every one who knows
Your Ladyship must admire.

His deep anxiety was that she, to whom he had 'so much to
say . . . , so much to confess, from which Your Ladyship alone
can absolve me,' should take fright and break off their correspondence 'which is so essential to me in my desert, to comfort my
heart, often so deeply hurt.'

On 23rd February 1790—only a fortnight after his first lament
from his 'desert'—Princess Nicholas Esterházy died. It was the
beginning of the end of Haydn's half-willing bondage; but at the
outset it seemed just the reverse.

'The Prince is so overwhelmed at the death of his lady,' wrote
Haydn to Marianne,

that we have had to strain every nerve to charm His Highness out of his
sadness, I arranged a big programme of chamber music for the first
three evenings . . . but the poor Prince fell into such profound melancholy on hearing my favourite Adagio in D that I had my work cut out
to chase it away again with other pieces.

Throughout the summer the sad old prince would not let Haydn out of his sight, or even let him slip off to Vienna for twenty-four hours during his own absence. A flattering invitation to visit his aristocratic admirer Prince Oettingen-Wallerstein had to be turned down, and Haydn grew almost desperate with worry and work and loneliness—the harder to bear because he could see no term to it.

Now I'm caught yet again and have to remain here: Your Ladyship can imagine what I'm losing by it, it is a sad thing always to be a slave, but Providence will have it so, poor wretch that I am! Constantly harassed with much work and all too little leisure; friends—what can I say?—one real one? There are no real friends left—perhaps just one, a woman? But she is far away. Ah well, I'm just talking to myself, God bless you and keep you from forgetting me.

It was not to last much longer. On 28th September 1790 Prince Nicholas Esterházy died at his Vienna residence, aged seventy-six. He left Haydn a pension of 1000 florins a year. His son and successor, Prince Anton, cared little for music and disbanded his orchestra, retaining only the wind band, Tomasini and Haydn himself. Haydn's only obligation in return for his salary of 400 florins was to retain his title of '*Kapellmeister* to Prince Esterházy'—an arrangement which gave his master a stake in his fame and a lien on his services, but which left him free to do what he liked with his time.

Dazed with his release, he rushed up to Vienna and took lodgings with a friend of his, one Johann Nepomuk Hamberger, on the Wasserkunstbastei. Almost at once offers began pouring in. Count Grassalkovicz, Prince Nicholas's son-in-law, tried to secure him as his *Kapellmeister*, but he refused. King Ferdinand of Naples, who was in Vienna for the triple wedding of his daughter Maria Theresa to the future Emperor Francis II and another daughter and son to a Habsburg prince and princess, ordered music from him for his own peculiar instrument, the *lira organizzata* (a form of hurdy-gurdy), and offered him a post at the Neapolitan court. Here at last was the chance to go to Italy for which he had been longing all his life, and he nearly accepted. Then, one December morning, a stranger was announced, and walked in declaring 'I am Salomon from London and have come to fetch you.'

Johann Peter Salomon, a native of Bonn, had been in London for the past nine years as an active and successful violinist and concert promoter. Like his rival Cramer,[1] and Lord Abingdon, Cramer's backer, he had unsuccessfully tried to secure Haydn in the 1780s. Now, as luck would have it, he was at Cologne when the news of Prince Nicholas Esterházy's death reached him and set off at once for Vienna to try the efficacy of personal contact in securing his prize.

The terms he offered Haydn were tempting: £300 for an opera for the impresario Sir John Gallini, who also owned the Hanover Square rooms where his concerts were held, £300 for six new symphonies and £200 for the copyright of these, £200 for twenty new pieces of different kinds which he was to conduct at as many concerts, and £200 guarantee for a benefit concert. Salomon deposited 5,000 florins with a Viennese banker as security for payment.

Haydn was not only eager for a change of scene; he longed for personal independence and a release from the binding routine of court life. London's concert world offered him such a release, and Salomon's persuasive impetuosity and the excellent material prospects clinched his decision. His friends thought him crazy to undertake such a journey at his advanced age; but, briskly retorting that he was 'still fresh and vigorous,' he accepted Salomon's terms, made his excuses to the disgruntled King of Naples, and set about his preparations.

Even Mozart was against the plan, though he himself had been promised an engagement by Salomon for the following season and had just refused an offer from the director of the Italian Opera to come to England in 1791; perhaps he still hoped that something would turn up in Vienna. In any case he felt that such expeditions were all very well for a man of the world like himself, but quite another matter for his unsophisticated old friend who, he urged, knew too little of the great world and too few languages. Haydn

[1] From Haydn's correspondence with Forster's publishing firm it seems that he almost agreed to appear with Cramer in 1788.

imperturbably replied: 'But all the world understands my language.'

The day of departure came—15th December 1790. Haydn had spent his last day with Mozart; both were strangely shaken at the parting and shed tears. Mozart, desperately anxious for his friend's safety, cried out: 'I fear, father, that this will be our last farewell.' It might have been a flash of that obsession with death that was to give such sinister meaning in his eyes, six months later, to the strange commissioning of the Requiem. But the sudden dread that clutched at his heart cast no prophetic shadow on the older man as he set forth on the journey, not towards death but towards an undreamed-of intensification of creative vitality— 'the last of life, for which the first was made.'

CHAPTER VII

ENGLAND (1791-2)

SALOMON must have enjoyed the seventeen days' journey with Haydn from Vienna to London. There are few things more pleasant for a seasoned traveller than a companion to whom travel itself is a new experience, and who, in addition, possesses that lively and fascinated interest in everything and everybody reflected in the odd assortment of facts, descriptions, recipes, 'anectods' [sic] and statistics collected by Haydn in his travel note-books.

Their way took them through Munich, where they met Christian Cannabich (conductor of the first performance of Mozart's *Idomeneo*), and on Christmas Day they reached Bonn, Salomon's native town and residence of the Elector-Archbishop of Cologne, the cultured Austrian Archduke Maximilian Franz. Next day they attended the elector's chapel and were greeted with a performance of one of Haydn's Masses, after which they were graciously received by the elector and introduced to choir and orchestra. Among his old acquaintances there Salomon may have had difficulty in recognizing, in the deputy organist, a little boy born twenty years earlier in the back premises of the house where his own family lodged and who, when he had last seen him, was being cuffed along the path of a child prodigy by his unsatisfactory father, the court tenor Johann van Beethoven.

Six more days of hard going through bad weather brought them to Calais, 'somewhat thinner owing to fatigue, irregular sleep and unaccustomed diet'—so Haydn writes to Frau von Genzinger—and on New Year's Day 1791,

. . . at half past seven in the morning, after hearing Holy Mass, I went on board ship . . . at first we had hardly any wind for four hours on end and the ship went so slowly that in those four hours we only covered a single English mile . . . our ship's captain was in the worst of tempers and said that if the wind did not change we should have to spend the

whole night at sea. But luckily at about half-past eleven such a favourable wind rose that by four o'clock we had covered twenty-two miles.
But as our big ship could not come alongside the quay owing to the falling
tide, two smaller ships came out to us, to which we transferred ourselves
and our luggage and—though a slight squall was blowing—landed
safely at last. Some of the travellers were afraid to climb down into the
smaller ship and stayed on board, but I joined the larger party. During
the whole crossing I stayed on deck to gaze my fill at that vast monster,
the sea. As long as it was calm I was not afraid, but towards the end,
as the wind grew stronger and stronger and I saw the great stormy waves
bearing down on us, I was seized by a touch of fear, and a touch of
sickness too. But I fought it all off and came ashore without (excuse me)
actually being sick. Most of the passengers were sick and looked like
ghosts.

The first night in London he spent at 45 High Holborn with
the music publisher Bland, whose enterprise in seeking him out
at Esterház in 1789 and good luck in surprising him in the throes
of shaving had secured him—among other things—the manuscript
of the 'Razor' Quartet, Op. 55 No. 2, in exchange for a pair of
English razors. Here he enjoyed Mrs. Bland's hospitality and
excellent pea-soup and the two days' rest which the accumulated
fatigues and excitements of the journey had enforced upon him;
after which he was ready to launch out into the surge of London's
social and musical life.

The London of George III and the future Prince Regent,
of Pitt, Fox and Burke, of Sheridan and Mrs. Siddons, Reynolds
and Hoppner, was as strange and new to Haydn as the sea itself.
Mercantile and colonial expansion had given material wealth a
broad basis outside the landed and titled classes, though the
squalor and destitution so ruthlessly depicted by Hogarth still
co-existed with a high standard of middle-class living. The
established Church, though torpid spiritually by comparison with
the dissenting bodies, impressed Haydn on several occasions by
its buildings and ceremonies; of his own religion, in a London
to whom the Gordon riots of 1780 and the cry of 'No Popery'
were still a vivid memory, there was little trace, beyond a few
chapels where foreigners, including many of his fellow musicians,
and the handful of English Catholics, could unobtrusively hear

Mass. Politically, London was the centre of a unified and lively national consciousness as well as of the nation's commercial life. The nobility and ruling classes exercised their functions through Parliament and found their social life in London's clubs, theatres and drawing-rooms; their country residences were not places to hold court, but purely for sport and relaxation, hunting and shooting and the exercise of a landowner's duties and privileges.[1]

Musical life, in consequence, was a more broad-based and commercial affair than on the Continent, and the publicly organized concert, with its accompaniment of press publicity, played a far larger part, both in London and in provincial cities throughout the eighteenth century, than did aristocratic patronage. Subscription concerts such as Salomon's and the rival organization, the Professional Concerts, vied with undertakings like the Academy of Ancient Music, with its merchant patrons, and the Concerts of Ancient Music, founded by a group of noble lords and later honoured by the patronage of that ardent Handelian King George III.[2] Such clubs as the Nobleman's and Gentlemen's Catch Club and the Anacreontic Society, which usually met in taverns, provided a meeting-ground for professionals and performing amateurs, while the Viennese Tonkünstlersocietät had its counterpart in two organizations for the support of needy musicians and their dependants—the New Musical Fund and the Society of

---

[1] Burney crystallizes the situation with his usual clarity in his letter to Haydn of 19th August 1799, in which he explains that at that time of year three months is insufficient notice for soliciting subscriptions to *The Creation*. He writes: 'I wish it were possible to postpone the delivery of the book in England till next winter. The operas, oratorios and concerts, public and private, seldom begin in London till after Christmas, nor do the nobility and gentry return thither from the country till the meeting of Parliament about that time. Now, three months from the date of your letter, my dear Sir, will only throw your publication to the middle of October, the very time in the whole year when London is the most uninhabited by the lovers of field sports, as well as music.'

[2] It was one of the rules of the organization that no composer's work could be performed until he had been dead twenty years. Even Haydn, with his enormous reputation and popularity, was not exempt from this regulation.

Musicians, which received the prefix 'Royal' after it had success-fully organized the gigantic Handel commemoration festival in Westminster Abbey in 1784. In church music, oratorio took the place of the liturgy as the main aesthetic outlet and stimulus, though here the gigantic figure of Handel successfully barred the way to would-be followers until challenged by Haydn himself.

All this, together with the rival opera undertakings—English opera at Covent Garden and Drury Lane and Italian opera at the Pantheon [1]—provided a vast bulk of musical entertainment, and employment for innumerable foreign musicians, to whom London was the hub of the financial if not of the artistic universe. And in this busy concert world, as well as in private music-loving circles such as Burney's, Haydn's music had been played and loved for nearly twenty years before he appeared in person and, as Burney himself said, 'had been distinguished by an attention which we do not remember to have been bestowed on any other instrumental music before.'

Thanks to all this, and to Salomon's excellent advance publicity, Haydn was a celebrity from the very outset, and between them Salomon, Gallini and his brother-in-law Lord Abingdon [2] saw to it that the initial advantage was followed up. From the 'charming and comfortable but very expensive' lodgings at 18 Great Pulteney Street, where Haydn had joined him, Salomon produced him in the right musical circles—the Academy of Ancient Music (where he himself was first violinist), the Anacreon-tic Society and social reunions like that dinner-party given by the famous Handelian soprano Madame Mara, at which the guests momentarily put Haydn out of countenance by giving him three cheers—a novel and incomprehensible form of greeting. Mean-while he presented his credentials to the Austrian and Neapolitan

[1] The Pantheon, an adapted entertainment hall, was opened in Feb-ruary 1791 with Italian opera, homeless since the burning down in 1789 of the old King's Theatre in the Haymarket (on the site of the present His Majesty's Theatre). It was in the rebuilt King's Theatre that Gallini had hoped to hold his Italian opera season.

[2] Gallini had married a sister of Lord Abingdon's, but they after-wards separated.

ambassadors, and Lord Abingdon introduced him to society to such good purpose that a week after his arrival he had dined out every night. Social recognition reached its climax with a courteous bow from the Prince of Wales at the court ball given for the queen's birthday at St. James's Palace on 18th January, whither Salomon and Gallini had astutely escorted him, and which resulted in a command to attend His Royal Highness at a chamber concert at Carlton House the following evening.

In the intervals of all this compulsory sociability there were personal friends to look up—the Storaces and Michael Kelly, Giornovichi and Gyrowetz (two old violinist acquaintances from Councillor von Kees's concerts; Gyrowetz prided himself on having smoothed Haydn's path by useful introductions), and one with whom he had been in touch for years by letter but had yet to meet in the flesh—Dr. Charles Burney.

Burney was at this time organist at Chelsea Hospital. The author of the highly successful *General History of Music* was an ardent and enlightened champion of contemporary music, who had known and loved Haydn's work for many years and hailed his arrival with an exquisitely bad ode of welcome and an anonymous criticism of his own poem in the *Monthly Review*, which gave him the pretext for a further panegyric. At the evenings of chamber music at Chelsea which followed their meeting—and which must have recalled to Haydn the 'happy gatherings' in the Genzinger household—Burney 'was as much pleased with his mild, unassuming yet cheerful conversation and countenance as with his stupendous musical merit,' and reported to his friend Arthur Young: 'I have had the great Haydn here, I think him as good a creature as great musician.'

Work was not forgotten amid all these social eddies, and from the outset Haydn, true to his lifelong habit, set himself a daily routine which could conserve his energies for the important task of preparing the new symphonies he had engaged to produce for Salomon's concerts. But there had been a hitch in the launching of the series; it was to have opened on 11th February, but Salomon's leading tenor, Davide, was under contract to make his first appearance at the Italian opera season planned by Gallini at the

King's Theatre, Haymarket. Difficulties over the licensing of the theatre for Italian opera (which arose through the strained relations between the Prince of Wales, Gallini's patron, and the king, who supported the rival Italian opera at the Pantheon) caused a double postponement of Davide's appearance [1]—and ultimately the collapse of Gallini's undertaking and the non-performance of Haydn's last opera, *Orfeo*, or *L'anima del filosofo*. In consequence, Salomon's rivals of the Professional Concerts were able to open their series on 7th February, over a month before Salomon. On this occasion they treated Haydn with diplomatic courtesy, presenting him with a free pass for the whole series and opening with an excellent performance of one of his symphonies, but they were not above circulating surreptitious rumours that Haydn was too old to shed the hoped-for lustre on their competitor's undertaking.

But here they reckoned not only without Haydn's vitality, but also without his vast experience in directing orchestral music and his scrupulous attention to fine details of performance, which in the end made the delay (since it gave more time for rehearsal) pure gain for Salomon's orchestra. Supplementing his scanty English by practical demonstration,[2] he soon won their liking and regard by his friendliness, courtesy and profound knowledge and competence, so that as Dies relates, 'their affection stimulated them to that pitch of inspiration that the performance of a Haydn work demands.'

It was this inspired fervour that communicated itself irresistibly

[1] In the end he appeared on 11th March although the opening of the opera season was still held up.

[2] Dies relates that on hearing one of the cellists complaining, in German, about a hold-up over the opening bar of a symphony, Haydn courteously asked permission to illustrate his meaning and, borrowing a violin, was able to convey his wishes perfectly. The trouble arose over a threefold repetition of the same note, *piano*, so the work was probably the 'Oxford' Symphony, whose first bar answers this description. So, too, on his second visit, he demonstrated the correct way of playing the drums to the youthful George Smart, then a violinist in the orchestra, who had volunteered to take the absent drummer's place. On being shown, Smart replied: 'Oh, very well, we can do so in England, if you prefer it.'

to both orchestra and audience when at last, on 11th March 1791, the great day of Salomon's opening concert came. Haydn's latent fires were normally hidden by his deceptively equable manner, but when conducting a performance he was transformed. The clarity and vigour of his movements (so his Viennese contemporaries tell us) communicated his meaning at every point to the performers, while the audience, watching the play of his features, would even use his expressions as a guide to their own applause. And so it was that night at the Hanover Square Rooms. 'Haydn himself presided at the piano-forte,' writes Burney, 'and the sight of that renowned composer . . . electrified the audience' and awakened 'such a degree of enthusiasm as almost amounts to frenzy.'[1] His new Symphony, No. 96 in D,[2] opened the second

[1] *Memoirs of Dr. Burney* by Madame d'Arblay and *Monthly Review*, June 1791 (in Burney's anonymous review of his poem on Haydn).

[2] Mr. Oliver Strunk, in a talk given at the New York Public Library on 25th January 1947, argued conclusively that the first of the Salomon series was not No. 93, as is generally assumed, but No. 96, closely followed by No. 95; No 93 (the symphony promised to Frau von Genzinger in Haydn's letters of 1790) did not receive its first performance till 17th February 1792, the opening concert of Salomon's second season. Mr. Strunk pointed out that Nos. 95 and 96 always appear as a pair: the autographs are together in the possession of the Royal Philharmonic Society, and they are the only London symphonies in von Kees's catalogue, listed as 'von London gekommen.' And in fact Haydn sends to Frau von Genzinger, on 17th November 1791, two 'new symphonies' for transmission to von Kees, apologizing for troubling her—which he hardly would have done if one of them had been the symphony promised to her, with many delays and excuses, since 1790. It is not until 2nd March that he refers to 'her' symphony again, and then again with apologies, for despite its successful production a fortnight earlier he considers the finale weak and wants to alter it before sending it. Mr. Strunk also remarked that the undated reference in Haydn's diary (as quoted by Krehbiel) to the performance at the 'first concert' of a 'new symphony in D' cannot refer to the first London season, because it refers in the same sentence to 'the Chorus' (i.e. *The Storm*), which was not composed until 1792.

I am most grateful to Mr. Strunk for allowing me to make use of his notes on this point.

half of the programme, and—an unprecedented event—the slow movement was encored.

After this triumph—the first of its kind, as Karl Geiringer truly remarks, that Haydn had experienced—London took him completely to its heart. The Prince of Wales attended the second concert (at which a Mozart symphony was played) and at the concerts that followed at weekly intervals throughout March and April the 'grandeur of subject and the rich variety of air and passion' in his new symphonies were acclaimed with delight by press and public.

This was indeed living at high pressure—a pressure very different from that of the detailed routine work at Esterház, and making demands on him at higher level. He responded magnificently in human and creative vitality, but after a couple of months of it he inevitably began to feel the strain. Only a week after his arrival he was finding the noise of London's streets 'insufferable' and planning a move to the outskirts in search of quiet, and by the middle of May he had found a suitable retreat in the rural seclusion of Lisson Grove.[1] Here, with the help of the piano-forte lent by the kindly Dussek, he worked away at his ill-fated opera, with the young John Baptist Cramer—whose father's position as leader of the Professional Concerts did not prevent Haydn from taking a strong liking to him—hovering in respectful attendance. *L'anima del filosofo* received its *coup de grâce* when officials arrived to stop the first rehearsal, and Gallini was forced to compensate himself by arranging bi-weekly 'Entertainments' of music and dancing, with Haydn's music as the chief attraction in many of the programmes.

[1] Marion M. Scott ('Haydn in England,' *Musical Quarterly,* April 1932) shows good grounds for believing that he took rooms at the farmhouse just north of the Manor House which formerly stood at the corner of Lisson Grove and 'New Road,' now Marylebone Road. He was installed there before 18th May, for on the occasion when he was forced to break his engagement to appear at a concert at the Music Room at Oxford, owing to a prolonged rehearsal, the coach which was to have brought him to Oxford called for him that morning at 'Lisson Green.'

The close of May was to bring Haydn a new and unforgettable experience. He attended the series of Handel concerts—the fourth since the great Handel Commemoration of 1784—held in Westminster Abbey on 23rd, 26th, 28th May and 1st June, and was shaken to the depths by the overwhelming power of the music; his only previous encounter with Handel—if any—had probably been the small-scale performances at Baron van Swieten's. On the last day *Messiah* was given and at the 'Hallelujah' chorus he broke down completely and cried 'He is the master of us all'—an opinion which he repeated to Carpani, years later, in Vienna, adding that Handel's music had sent him back to his studies as if he had learnt nothing till then. Further acquaintance with Handel on his second visit—during which the composer Shield 'observed his countenance expressing rapturous astonishment' at a performance of extracts from *Joshua*—only served to strengthen his admiration and quicken that renewed interest in oratorio which bore fruit in *The Creation*.

The concert season was drawing to an end. Salomon's twelfth and last concert was on 3rd June. A fortnight earlier Haydn's benefit concert had brought in £350 (£150 over the guaranteed sum). He wrote his successful 'Italian Catch' for Gallini's benefit on 2nd June, and gave a helping hand to the youthful prodigy Clement (whom Beethoven made immortal by the dedication of his violin Concerto) by appearing at his benefit on 10th June to conduct a symphony and the *Seven Words*. After this the tempo slackened somewhat, and Londoners took their music in the open air, at Ranelagh—where again Haydn appears on the programme with a symphony.

All this time Burney had been busy behind the scenes, and the result of his well-directed activities was the decision of the University of Oxford to confer an honorary D.Mus. on Haydn at the forthcoming Commemoration ceremonies in July. An accompanying festival of three ' Grand CONCERTS of VOCAL and INSTRUMENTAL MUSIC, calculated to raise in the Minds of the Hearers the most pleasing and exalted Sensations that the Powers of Harmony alone are capable of effecting,' was announced in the local press, and the town was crowded with visitors.[1] Haydn himself arrived too late to rehearse his new symphony for the first concert on 6th July, so an already familiar work—known ever since as the 'Oxford' Symphony—was performed instead; the new work—unfortunately unidentified, though it 'was generally deemed one of the most striking compositions ever heard,' was played the next day. Finally, on 8th July, 'a splendid procession of Noblemen, Baronets and other honorary graduates . . . all in their proper habits . . . entered the Theatre' and 'the honorary degree of Doctor in Music was voluntarily and liberally conferred on Joseph Haydn, esq. . . .'[2] The final concert that evening was a good-humoured occasion; Haydn appeared in his doctor's robes of cherry-and-cream-coloured silk and was greeted with roars of applause, which he acknowledged by grasping the lapels of his gown and calling out 'I thank you.' The audience jovially shouted back 'You speak very good English,' while Nancy Storace and his other friends waved greetings from the orchestra. Haydn confessed to mixed feelings about the gown, which, as he noted in his diary, he had to pay half-a-guinea to hire; he said he felt very foolish parading around in it, but wished none the less that his friends in Vienna could have seen him. About the doctorate itself—which he acknowledged by sending a three-part *canon cancrizans* to the words 'Thy voice, O Harmony, is divine'—Haydn had no such doubts. 'I have that doctorate to thank for much, indeed I may say all my success in England: it brought me the acquaintanceship of the most prominent men and the *entrée* into the greatest houses.' This observation, typical both of his modesty and his worldly wisdom, was hardly true of England, where every one, from the Court downwards, was ready to acclaim him from the outset; but in his own country, where social and academic distinction counted for so much, the honour of being 'Doctor of Music at Oxford' not only (as Geiringer remarks) silenced pedantic criticism, but also

[1] *Jackson's Oxford Journal*, 11th June, 2nd July. Oddly enough, Salomon's name does not appear in the lengthy list of performers, which included Nancy Storace and young Clement. The orchestra was led by Cramer, of the Professional Concerts.

[2] *Gentleman's Magazine*, July 1791.

commanded the respect of those circles of society which he had hitherto served.

With the close of the London season Haydn had the best part of five months ahead of him in which to draw breath, prepare for the winter ahead and, with the help of his new-found friends, to see something of England. An excursion by river from West-minster Bridge to Richmond and a 'magnificent' lunch on an East India merchantman showed him the Thames in a twofold light. Then he was carried off into the country by the father of one of his pupils,[1] Mr. Brassey, a Lombard Street banker, who once had broken out into a fury of self-disgust at the contrast between Haydn's early poverty and his own affluence.[2] Here, twelve miles out of London, he lived 'as if in a monastery,' with a family as warm-hearted as the Genzingers (so he described them to Marianne),

working hard, and thinking every morning, as I wander in the woods alone with my English grammer [*sic*], of my Maker, my family and all the friends I have left behind me, of whom you and yours are the dearest.

But even here his peace was not untroubled. Just before setting out for his country retreat—so tired that he confessed to 'days of depression without knowing why'—the news of Antonio Polzelli's death had reawakened all his old restless hopes of marriage with Luigia and longings for 'the time . . . when two pairs of eyes will close'; and he implores her to write, as 'your letters are a com-fort to me however sad I am.' Then in September, Prince Anton Esterházy wrote urgently demanding that he should return at once and compose an opera for the emperor's forthcoming visit to Esterház. But he was pledged to Salomon, who had al-ready announced his plans for the coming season; so he resignedly awaited his dismissal, which he dreaded 'for my poor family's

[1] Taking fashionable pupils was part of the price of success; Haydn had dreaded the extra burden, but to his relief he found that the lessons were mostly nominal.

[2] Haydn told Dies that Brassey had demanded pistols to shoot himself; in his diary he simply says that he 'cursed.' Perhaps the story grew with telling.

sake, 'hoping by God's help to offset this loss by hard work.' Fortunately the prince was too well aware of what he would lose in dismissing his famous *Kapellmeister*, and let the matter drop.

These were not the only troubles. The managers of the Professional Concerts were badgering him to break his agreement with Salomon, outbidding their rivals by £150 for his services. To his undying credit he refused, although these offers came just at the time when he was facing the prospect of dismissal and loss of salary. Then it began to be rumoured in Vienna that his trip was a financial failure. While his patron von Kees very sensibly wrote to him for the facts with which to refute the story, his wife chose the moment to demand money and to tell him, 'only I cannot believe it, that Mozart has been crying me down. I forgive him.' He could not draw on his Vienna bank balance, so, to his intense mortification, he had to beg Frau von Genzinger to advance his wife 150 florins; but he could, and did, ask her at the same time to send Mozart to his bankers for information about the sums to be earned in England. Eager for his friend to share his own success, he did not know that as he wrote— mid-October 1791—Mozart was already in the grip of mortal illness.

The late autumn brought him an odd assortment of experiences —a London fog 'so thick you could spread it on bread,' a puppet show in Savile Row, Guy Fawkes night (on which, as he somewhat confusedly records, 'the boys celebrated the day when the Guys set fire to the town'), and, that same evening, the Lord Mayor's banquet, which he attended as guest of one of the aldermen, a Mr. Silvester;[1] his outstanding impressions were of splendid robes, bad music, fug, deafening noise and much drinking of healths—of which, he observed, none was more loudly acclaimed than Mr. Pitt's. The musical world was coming to life again, and he heard Madame Mara at her farewell concert and the beautiful and notorious Mrs. Billington in Shield's opera

---

[1] Probably the Mr. Charles Silvester to whom, nine years later, he asked Artaria to forward a copy of *The Creation*.

The Woodman at Covent Garden. He went twice to Cambridge (after visiting his friends in Suffolk, Sir Patrick and Lady Blake of Langham Hall), where, with Salomon, he heard and engaged the violinist Peter Dahmen, with his son J. A. Dahmen the cellist, for their forthcoming concerts.[1] Haydn was not too preoccupied to remark on the loveliness of the Backs and of the carvings in King's College Chapel, 'so delicate that nothing more beautiful could have been made of wood.'

With the reopening season royalty once more took notice of Haydn, and at the end of November he was invited to spend a couple of days at the Duke of York's country seat at Oatlands, near Weybridge. The duke himself was sufficiently interested in music to remodel and enlarge the Coldstream Guards band, and his little bride, Princess Friederike (daughter of the royal cellist Frederick William II of Prussia, for whom Mozart had written three quartets and Haydn six, his Op. 50), sat for hours by Haydn's side at the keyboard as he directed the orchestra, humming the tunes she had heard so often at her father's court. On his left sat another royal cellist—the Prince of Wales, later King George IV. Of him Haydn writes that he 'is the handsomest man on God's earth, is extraordinarily fond of music, has a great deal of feeling but little money.' His debts and his love affairs were indeed common knowledge, but he was musician enough to admire Mozart (and acquire the score of *La clemenza di Tito*) at a time when London knew him only by an aria or two— a sure claim on Haydn's regard. He loaded Haydn with friendly attentions, gave him his recipe for punch and had his portrait painted by Hoppner.

From this portrait (now in Buckingham Palace) and from the splendid portrait by Hardy at the Royal College of Music, we can picture Haydn as England saw him. They do not show us his build—square and sturdy, with legs disproportionately short— and they are flattering to his brown and pock-marked complexion;

[1] O. E. Deutsch, 'Haydn in Cambridge' (*Cambridge Review,* p. 312). J. A. Dahmen played in the Salomon concerts of 1792 and again in 1794, when he also took the cello part in Haydn's *Sinfonia concertante* at the singer Ludwig Fischer's benefit.

but they do show the bony strength of the face—though the wig conceals the fine proportions of the forehead—the long, shrewd, humorous mouth, the beaky nose (lengthened at the tip by the polypus that gave him so much discomfort) and the 'fiery and animated' dark grey eyes described by his contemporaries, alight with ardour and inspiration while performing and with friendliness in personal intercourse.

In spite of his social successes he was homesick at times—though there were more disquieting reports from Vienna. 'I do not hate London,' he wrote to Frau von Genzinger, five days before Christmas,

but I could never spend the rest of my days here, even if I could earn millions. . . . I am looking forward like a child to being home again and embracing all my old friends, my one grief is that the great Mozart will be missing, if indeed it is true, which I hope it is not, that he is dead. The world will not see a talent like that again in a hundred years!

News in those days travelled no faster than the bearer of it. Mozart had died in the early hours of 5th December 1791, and the journey from Vienna to London took at least a fortnight. Haydn can barely have heard the first whispers of the rumour as he wrote, on 20th December, and—having himself been reported dead thirteen years back—only half believed it. When, early in the New Year, there was no longer any room for doubt, he wrote to Puchberg, their fellow mason and Mozart's faithful friend:

For some time I was quite beside myself over his death, and could not believe that Providence should so quickly have called away an irreplaceable man into the next world, my one regret is that he could not first come and win over the benighted English, to whom I preached him day in day out . . . please, my dear friend, be good enough to send me a list of his works which are not yet known here, and I will make every effort to push them in the interests of the widow; I wrote to the poor soul myself, three weeks ago, telling her that as soon as her dear son is old enough I will teach him composition to the best of my ability, without charge, so as to replace his father in some measure.

He was as good as his word. Burney recalls that when Haydn was consulted about the purchase of a batch of Mozart's works by the publisher Broderip (whose firm, Longman & Broderip, was among the chief publishers of Haydn's music) he exclaimed emphatically: 'Do buy it by all means. He was truly a great musician. Friends often flatter me that I have some genius, but he stood far above me.' And to another friend, the clergyman Latrobe, he said of Mozart that 'in *him* the world has lost a much greater master of harmony than I am.'[1]

To this sorrow the approaching concert season provided a counter-irritant if not an antidote, threatening to bring what Haydn called 'bloody harmonic war' in its train. For the Professional Concert management, having failed to capture Haydn, had secured the services of his former pupil Ignaz Pleyel, from Strasbourg, and were conducting a vigorous press campaign insinuating that Haydn, old and spent, was past producing anything of interest, whereas Pleyel (who had in fact brought with him a trunkload of old but unperformed works) would provide a 'new' composition for each concert. Haydn felt obliged to announce publicly that he would do the like,

and so, in order to keep my word and uphold poor Salomon, I must be the victim and work incessantly, and I really am feeling the strain, my eyes give me most trouble and I have many sleepless nights, but with God's help I shall get on top of it all.

Personally the situation might have been a painful one, but that Pleyel, who was innocent of any desire to harm his old master, quickly realized what was afoot, and

behaved so modestly since he arrived that he has regained my affection, we see a great deal of each other, and that does him honour, he knows how to value his old father; we will share our renown and both go home content.

On Christmas Eve—which, in continental countries, is the family's Christmas feast—the two exiles dined together, and they saw the old year out with dinner and an opera.

[1] Related by the Rev. C. J. Latrobe to Vincent Novello in his letter of 22nd November 1828, printed by Marion M. Scott in her article 'Haydn: Relics and Reminiscences in England' (*Music & Letters*, April 1932).

By 17th February, when the first concert of the new Salomon series was held, the season was well under way. The musical world had been shocked by the burning down of the Pantheon (a severe loss to the Professional Concerts) and was beginning to be invaded by a swelling stream of refugees from revolutionary France, hoping to offset their poverty by putting their amateur talents to professional use. Gallini, still forbidden to use the King's Theatre for opera, had launched a new series of 'Enter-tainments,' and the Professional Concerts had opened on 13th February—decorously heading the programme, as before, with a Haydn symphony, a gesture which Salomon reciprocated by leading off with a work of Pleyel's. Haydn's own new symphony (No. 93) opened the second half of Salomon's first concert, and the second wound up with a four-part chorus entitled *The Storm*, Haydn's first setting of an English text; the words were by the satirist John Wolcot, *alias* 'Peter Pindar.' At the fourth concert on 9th March the endearing *Sinfonia concertante* for violin, cello, oboe and bassoon 'was performed for the first time with admirable effect,' and the B flat major Symphony, No. 98, first performed the previous week, was repeated by request, and the first and last movements were again encored. The sixth concert saw the first performance of the 'Surprise' Symphony, No. 94. Haydn later disavowed any intention of waking the audience from its after-dinner slumbers, and declared that he had inserted the 'surprise' (which is not in the original score) [1] purely for artistic effect; but Gyrowetz in his Memoirs [2] gives him away by relating that Haydn showed him his new idea and said: 'That will make the ladies scream.' Perhaps it did; at any rate one of the critics declared that

the surprise might not be unaptly likened to the situation of a beautiful shepherdess who, lulled to slumber by the murmur of a distant waterfall, starts alarmed by the unexpected firing of a fowling-piece.

---

[1] According to the facsimile of the autograph of the *andante* repro-duced in the *Musical Times* of May 1909 and formerly in the possession of Felix Moscheles.

[2] Quoted by Pohl, *Mozart und Haydn in London*.

It was the same story as last year: life at high pressure calling out from Haydn reserves of incredible energy ('never in all my life have I written so much in one year as I did in the past twelve months,' he writes to Marianne von Genzinger). But this time the pressure, and the corresponding strain, were intensified. Every one knew him now, and people would even stop him in the street, look him up and down and say 'You are a great man.' He was in incessant demand to shed lustre on private parties, new friends in rivalry with old for his company—among them an M.P., Mr. Shaw, whose handsome wife paid him the odd compliment of embroidering his name on her own and her daughters' hair-fillets, and Dr. John Hunter, the famous surgeon, who on one occasion forcibly attempted to relieve Haydn of the nasal polypus he had inherited from his mother, and whose wife wrote the text of a number of his English songs.

This feverish existence was exhausting enough in itself. But there were emotional complications as well. Constant reports reached Haydn from Vienna that Luigia Polzelli had been speaking ill of him, and had even sold the piano he had given her. His wife (who had even less reason to love Luigia now that she was a widow) joined in the chorus with such acrimony that his patience broke and he wrote that he would never come back—which shook her into holding her peace. For Luigia, on the other hand, he has hardly a word of reproach, though by now the hope of union with her, rekindled by her husband's death the previous summer, had died in his heart, and he humbly asks that if she remarries she will let him know 'the name of the man who will be so happy as to possess you.'

Then suddenly a new flame blazed up on the dying embers of the old. Eight months earlier he had received a formal note from a Mrs. Schroeter, dated from James Street, Buckingham Gate, stating that she had just returned to town and would be happy to see Mr. Haydn whenever it suited him to give her a lesson. His new pupil was the widow of the pianist and composer Johann Samuel Schroeter, who had succeeded John Christian Bach as Queen Charlotte's music master, but who had been driven off the concert platform—so it was rumoured—by his wife's wealthy

family as a condition of their consent to the marriage.[1] She appears
to have continued her music lessons with 'Mr. Haydn' throughout
the winter, but there is no record of the progress of their intimacy
save that in her next recorded letter, dated 8th February 1792, he
has significantly become 'My Dear.' Nor do we know what
passed between Haydn and Rebecca Schroeter on the evening of
6th March, though we can guess something of it—Mrs. Schroeter
silent and tongue-tied, struggling to express her feelings, Haydn
(also none too articulate in a strange language) anxious lest she
had some trouble on her mind, unable to fathom her speechlessness
and at length departing, baffled and hurt. So much she reveals
in the letter she wrote him the following day, protesting that she had
'a thousand affectionate things to say,' that it was 'nothing but
being indisposed with a cold occasion'd my stupidity . . . if
anything had happened to trouble me I would have open'd my
heart,' and that 'no language can express half the Love and affection I feel for you, you are Dearer to me every Day of my life.'
Throughout the spring her letters continue to reflect her tenderness
and solicitude for his health, her anxiety to please and be of use—
now by presents of soap, now by buying blocks of tickets for his
concerts, now by copying music for him ('If my H. would employ
me oftener to write Music I hope I should improve, and I know I
should delight in the occupation'). No letter from him has been
preserved to record his feelings towards the woman who declared
that she felt for him 'the fondest and tenderest attachment the human
heart is capable of.' But there is an isolated and undated entry in
his diary, which reads: 'My friend, you think I love you; in truth
you are not mistaken'; and years later, when the old man was

[1] Her husband's will reveals that her Christian name was Rebecca,
and from the rate books of St. Margaret's, Westminster, it appears
that they lived from 1786 in the house, 6, James Street, Buckingham Gate
where Haydn used to visit her. The latest trace of her is in 1806, when—
eighteen years after her husband's death!—she was granted probate of his
will. I have been unable to discover her age, but the 'sixty' given by
Haydn is clearly a mistake (accidental or deliberate) on his part or Dies's.
Her husband was born in 1750, so that even if they had been the same
age, she was not more than forty-one when she met Haydn.

rambling on to Dies about his time in England, he pulled out his note-book and showed the painter her letters, twenty-two in all, carefully copied into the back pages, telling him that they were from 'an English widow in London who loved me, who although she was sixty at the time, was still a beautiful and lovable woman, whom I would very readily have married if I had been free then.' With her last, undated, letters written in the summer of 1792 the records of their relationship cease. A few fleeting indications point to their having seen each other again on his second visit, when he dedicated a set of Trios to her. More than that we do not know.

Salomon's series meanwhile had ended in May, so successfully that he gave an extra concert on 6th June. There had been a short break in April, as his leading soprano, Madame Mara, had not returned from her European tour; in the end he started again without her, on 20th April, the day on which war broke out between Austria and revolutionary France. May was a crowded month, for beside the regular concerts Salomon and Haydn had held their benefits, and Haydn had been at the keyboard for those of various other artists, including the violinists Janiewicz and Barthélemon and Madame Mara herself, whom, as he records, he accompanied 'quite alone on the pianoforte' in a 'very difficult English aria by Purcell' (it was *From rosy bowers*). He had also heard *Messiah* again—this time at St. Margaret's, Westminster—moderately enjoyed himself at Ranelagh, where in his opinion the old Italian violinist Giardini 'played like a pig'[1] and, like Berlioz half a century later, was moved to tears by the massed voices of some six thousand children at the Charity Schools anniversary at St. Paul's Cathedral.

All this while Luigia Polzelli continued to give trouble—now reporting a false rumour that his wife was dying or dead, now demanding that he should find her a job in London, where he quite frankly did not want her; artistically she would have done him no credit, and it would have meant the end of his tender relationship

[1] Giardini had refused to see him when he called, saying 'I don't want to meet the German dog'—which may have affected Haydn's critical judgment.

with Mrs. Schroeter. He firmly fobbed her off with assurances that the English were none too keen on Italian opera and that in any case he was leaving London himself in a few weeks' time.

In fact, less than a month remained for sightseeing and leave-taking. He found time for a trip to Windsor, where he duly admired St. George's Chapel and the 'divine' view from the terrace, Ascot races, of which his description is as racy as a Rowlandson print,[1] and Slough, home of the famous astronomer Herschel and his sister Caroline. He respectfully noted down the measurements of Herschel's giant telescope, and perhaps (as Tovey suggests) stored away at the back of his mind some impression of the vast-ness of the interstellar spaces, which later fired his imagination as he worked on *The Creation*. Then there was a farewell dinner to be arranged at Parsloes for the Musical Graduates' Society, which had elected him to membership the previous summer (Salomon was present as interpreter), and countless personal friends to visit, not to mention Mrs. Schroeter, to whom 'every moment of your company is more and more precious . . . now your Departure is so near.' He made a final appearance in the royal orbit, at a garden party given by the Duchess of York, and at length left London on 23rd June 1792.

[1] 'In the first heat there were three riders who were compelled to go around the course twice without stopping. They did it in five minutes. . . . The second time there were seven . . . when one thinks the one rider who is about to reach the goal will be the first, at which moment large wagers are laid on him, another rushes past him with inconceivable *force* and reaches the winning post. The riders are very lightly clad in silk, each of a different colour, so as to make it easier to recognize them, and all as lean as greyhounds. . . . The horses are of the finest breeds, light with very thin feet. . . . As soon as they hear the sound of the bell they dash off with the greatest *force*. Every leap of the horses is twenty-two feet long . . . in spite of a heavy rain there were 2000 vehicles, all full of people, and 3 times as many people were present on foot. Besides this there are all kinds of puppet plays, *Ciarlatanz* [*sic*] and conjurors, and buffoons performing during the races, and in a multi-tude of tents food and all kinds of wine and beer . . .'

(Translated by H. E. Krehbiel in his extracts from Haydn's diary in his *Music and Manners in the Classical Period*, New York, 1896.)

CHAPTER VIII

ENGLAND AGAIN (1794–5)

A GLITTERING concourse of kings and princes was converging
on Frankfort-on-Main for the coronation of Francis II of Austria
as emperor of the Holy Roman Empire, and Haydn was to join
Prince Anton Esterházy there. His route accordingly lay once
more through Bonn. The Elector Maximilian had already left
for Frankfort, but the orchestra, delighted to have Haydn to itself,
gave him a festive breakfast at Godesberg, and young Beethoven
snatched a favourable moment to show him a cantata of his and
ask his advice about his further career. Haydn may have heard
Mozart speak four years earlier of the seventeen-year-old Rhinelander
who had visited him in Vienna and startled him by the power and
originality of his keyboard improvisation; in any case he probably
heard something of his story from Salomon after their break of
journey at Bonn on their way to England. Impelled by the merits
of the cantata and his own unfailing interest in the young—especially
where, as in this case, there was poverty and family responsibility
to reckon with—Haydn offered to take Beethoven on as a composition pupil as soon as he could obtain the necessary leave of absence
from the elector.

After the coronation Haydn travelled back to Vienna in Prince
Anton's suite, arriving on 24th July. The general public,
preoccupied with the comings and goings of princes, and with the
agitating news from France (the Tuileries was stormed and the
king made prisoner on 9th August), took little enough notice
of Haydn's return, but the absence of fuss must have been welcome,
for he was tired and longing for peace and relaxation and leisure
to visit all his old friends and delight their hearts with the needles
and nail-scissors, penknives and cornelian cameos he had brought
them as fairings from England. By the autumn he had settled

85

down to work, arranging and revising pieces for his master's wind-band, which had survived the dissolution of the orchestra, incubating the E flat major symphony (No. 99) and the two sets of three quartets for Count Apponyi (Opp. 71 and 74) which saw the light the following year, and giving lessons to three new pupils —one Peter Haensel, Pietro Polzelli and Beethoven.

It must be placed to the credit of the much-abused Frau Haydn that when her husband brought young Pietro Polzelli to live with them, to save his mother money and give more time for lessons, she received her rival's son as kindly as Haydn himself admits that she did; perhaps, starved of motherhood as Haydn was of fatherhood, she became really fond of the delicate, lovable boy. Haydn got him the post of piano teacher in the family of Countess Weissenwolf (a connection of his late princess, Prince Nicholas's wife). As a dutiful son, he asked Haydn to send his entire earnings to his mother—and in return passed on her repeated demands for money to his long-suffering host.

Beethoven arrived in Vienna in November, about the same time as Pietro Polzelli. He was less easy to help, being nearly five years older than young Polzelli, and proud into the bargain. Haydn taught him for a nominal fee of about ninepence a lesson, and let his independent pupil work off his sense of obligation by taking him out to coffee.

Beethoven soon grew restive. It is often a characteristic of great power that it desires to be set exacting tasks, to be subjected to the discipline, the *askesis* that formed the Greek athlete, gave its name to the asceticism of Christian spirituality, and will always be an essential part of the athlete's training, whether physical, mental or spiritual. Beethoven wanted to be put through a course of strict counterpoint: Haydn left his grammatical errors uncorrected. Haydn was no disciplinarian. He had given himself just such a training, and might have been expected to see the need of it; but again, it often happens that those who have attained mastery by being hard on themselves are almost too gentle with others. Besides, he freely confessed that in a choice between correctness and what satisfied his ear he 'would rather let a small grammatical howler stand.' Soon Beethoven was taking counterpoint lessons,

HAYDN (?)

From a portrait attributed to Fuseli, probably 1794–5

unknown to Haydn, first from Schenk, then from Haydn's old friend Albrechtsberger. His concealment was probably due to his anxiety not to hurt or offend Haydn, who was not only a valuable connection but also a good friend who took a steady, if sometimes puzzled interest in his queer pupil. He took Beethoven with him to Eisenstadt, thereby securing him the patronage of the Esterházy family, which resulted, years later, in the commissioning of the Mass in C by Prince Nicholas II, Haydn's fourth, last and least congenial master. When, just before he set out once more for England, Beethoven dedicated to him his three Trios, Op. 1, and Haydn advised him to withhold from publication the third of the set, in C minor, Beethoven, whose nature had a suspicious streak, smelt jealousy in the advice. But, apart from the fact that Haydn was singularly free from that particular fault, it was unthinkable that he, in the security of an international reputation, could have imagined he had anything to fear from a composer thirty-eight years his junior. He had seen, however, what the incomprehension of the imperial capital had done to Mozart, and must have been genuinely anxious lest Beethoven—to whom financial success was essential—should label himself irrevocably as a 'difficult' composer with his first published work.

It was not only Mozart who was missing. Early in 1793 Marianne von Genzinger died, aged only thirty-eight. Her death took the heart out of that life in Vienna which only three years earlier had seemed an unattainable dream of happiness; the protracted negotiations for the purchase of the little house in the suburb of Gumpendorf (of which his wife had written to him while he was in London that it would be so suitable for her to live in as a widow) which he finally bought in August 1793, show no very keen enthusiasm. His wife was 'ailing most of the time, and always in the same bad temper' [1]; Luigia's insatiability appeared more glaring by contrast with his dead friend's disinterested kindness. The *coup de grâce* to his infatuation probably came from

---

[1] Letter to Luigia Polzelli, 20th June 1793 : '. . . mia moglie sta maggior parte male di salute, ed è sempre di medesimo cattivo umore, ma già io non mi curo de niente, finiranno una volta questi guai.'

a certain 'Signor Molton,' who, in bringing Pietro Polzelli a watch from his mother, boasted of having installed himself as her protector and of his intention to marry her. Small wonder that his thoughts were turning towards England once more, though with some misgivings as to whether war conditions would prevent the journey; the alternative—Naples and Luigia—was by now considerably less attractive. In the end he decided for Salomon and England. He had thought of taking Pietro Polzelli or Beethoven with him, but nothing came of either plan; his companion, when he set out (in a carriage given him by Baron van Swieten) on 19th January 1794, was his godson Johann Elssler, who from that time until his death was to serve him, devotedly if not always quite disinterestedly,[1] as valet, copyist and secretary.

He arrived in London a day late for Salomon's first concert, which had been announced for 3rd February; he had allowed a bare fortnight for a journey which even in 1790, under peacetime conditions, had taken seventeen days. The London which welcomed him once more was now the capital of a country none too successfully at war. Toulon, seized by the English forces six months earlier, had been recaptured by the French, and his old patron the Duke of York was in Flanders leading the British contingent of an allied army that should, but for its slowness and divided counsels, have been in Paris the previous summer. Instead, Paris was in the grip of the Reign of Terror.

Haydn's lodgings this time were at 1 Bury Street, at its junction with King Street, St. James's, a bare ten minutes' walk across St. James's Park to Mrs. Schroeter's house in Buckingham Gate. Perhaps it was for this very reason that there are no letters to record the continuance of their association. Be that as it may, the dedication of a set of Trios (in G major, F sharp minor and D major, Nos. 1, 2 and 6 of the Peters edition), and the fact that six years later she was among the subscribers to the original Viennese edition of *The Creation*, are the only signs that they remained in touch with each other, thought it has been surmised that she

[1] Larsen gives details of his trafficking with Haydn manuscripts after and even before his master's death.

was the lady with whom he left the manuscripts of the six symphonies he wrote in the course of his visit.[1]

On 10th February, six days after Haydn's arrival, Salomon
opened his series—this time undisputed master of the field, for the
Professional Concerts had been given up in 1793. Haydn too
was now not a sensational novelty, but an old and welcome
friend, and as such, no longer 'news'; the *Oracle*, adroitly excusing
itself for its brief notice of the concert, hailed him prophetically
with a quotation from Thomson's *The Seasons*: 'Come then,
expressive Silence, muse his praise.' The concerts followed at
weekly intervals, two of his recently composed quartets appearing
in the fourth and seventh concerts. The slow movements of his
symphonies were still invariably encored. Through it all Haydn,
as a German journalist records, 'bears himself always with great
modesty and is loved and esteemed by all.' Salomon's series
closed on 12th May, but until early June he was kept busy taking
part in the benefit concerts of various artists, especially those who
had taken part in his own benefit on 2nd May (at which the
'Military' Symphony, No. 100, was first performed): the violinist
Viotti, the soprano Miss Parke, and Ludwig Fischer, the bass for
whom Mozart had written the part of Osmin in *Die Entführung*.
At Salomon's own benefit, on 28th May, Viotti led the violins
and two of Haydn's symphonies were played.

Ten days after Fischer's concert came the news of Lord Howe's
naval victory of the 'Glorious First of June,' celebrated, as Haydn
remarked, with illuminations and much rowdyism; he also jotted
down with some amusement the punning toast to the old admiral
('Psalm 3'—of which the opening words are 'Lord, how . . .')
which went the round of London's dining-rooms. Four weeks
later, visiting the Isle of Wight as guest of a Mr. Orde, he noted the
number of battle casualties at Gosport Naval Hospital, saw at
Portsmouth one of the captured French ships, 'pitifully shot to
pieces' and, fascinated by the sight of England's navy at close
quarters, filled his note-book with nautical technicalities, even to

[1] Marion M. Scott, 'Haydn in England' (*Musical Quarterly*, April 1932),
and C. F. Pohl, *Mozart und Haydn in London*, part II, p. 262.

sketching the grappling-irons of a fire-ship. On this same trip he saw Winchester Cathedral and Hampton Court, of which the garden reminded him of the one at Esterház.

August was again a month of travel. On the 2nd he went to Bath, with 'Mr. Asher and Mr. Cimandor [*sic*]'[1]; the journey took fifteen hours. His host was the old singer Venanzio Rauzzini, now profitably engaged in teaching and concert management. He entertained Haydn at Woodbine Cottage, his summer residence, where Haydn returned his hospitality by setting the epitaph on his dog's tombstone ('Turk was a faithful dog, and not a man') as a four-part canon. Haydn was welcomed enthusiastically by the local press and notabilities, including the well-known physician and amateur composer, Dr. Harington, and was fascinated by the beauty and individuality of the place; Royal Crescent in particular swept him off his feet, as well it might. After three days' stay he went on to Bristol, as guest of a Mr. Hamilton, of Rodney Place, Clifton Hill. Then at the end of the month Sir Charles Rich, an amateur cellist, invited him to Waverley. There is always a certain poignancy about the beauty of monastic ruins; but to Haydn (who took the trouble to practise his religion in the indifferent if not actively hostile atmosphere of eighteenth-century London[2]), it was sharpened, as he confessed in his diary, by the thought that once it had all belonged to his own faith.

With his old admirer the Earl of Abingdon he visited one or two aristocratic amateurs such as Lord Aston, whose home was

[1] The latter was Giambattista Cimador, an Italian singing-master and composer, an acquaintance of the Bartolozzis, with whom Haydn had also struck up a friendship—probably on his first visit, when Francesco Bartolozzi engraved the highly flattering portrait of him by Ott. Not even Dr. Scholes has been able to find any evidence to substantiate Dies's and Pohl's assertion that Burney went to Bath with him.

[2] The Rev. C. J. Latrobe, in the letter to Vincent Novello quoted by Marion M. Scott in her article 'Haydn: Relics and Reminiscences in England' (*Music & Letters*, April 1932) describes Haydn as being 'of a religious character, and not only attentive to the forms and usages of his own Church, but under the influence of a devotional spirit.'

near Hitchin, shared a kindred sense of humour[1] and competed in setting to music an improper quatrain on the morals of David and Solomon. 'Lord Avington [*sic*] set it, but miserably,' notes Haydn dryly; 'I did it a little better.' In more serious moments Lord Abingdon tried to persuade him to tackle an oratorio, but the proposed text—translated by Needham from Selden's *Mare Clausum*—failed to evoke from him more than two numbers.

Among those of his own profession he had made friends with the composer Shield, who took him to Taplow and later declared that he had learned more on this outing than in years of study. Later that year Haydn heard some incidental music of his at a performance of *Hamlet* and Shield introduced a number of Haydn's works into the spectacular pantomime opera which he had composed and compiled on the legend of Hercules and Omphale. Then—perhaps through the Bartolozzi circle—he made friends with the great double-bass virtuoso Dragonetti (who shared his passion for puppets) and with that distinguished pianist Miss Therese Jansen who was the heroine of the 'Jacob's Dream' Sonata episode; he wrote the piece, which he purposely overloaded with passage-work above the stave, as a homoeopathic cure for a violinist friend of hers with a weakness for the upper register of the instrument. For her, however, he wrote, in this year, the glorious E flat major piano Sonata (No. 52 of the Collected Edition), and—probably in the same year—two others, in C major (No. 50) and in D major (No. 51); and later, when she had become the wife of Gaetano Bartolozzi (son of the engraver Francesco Bartolozzi) he dedicated three Trios to her.[2]

---

[1] He notes in his diary Lord Abingdon's riposte to the bishop who rebuked him for installing an organ in his parish church without permission: 'The Lord gave, and the Lord can take away,' and adds with relish 'This has a double meaning but is *very good*.'

[2] This information is contained in W. Oliver Strunk's article 'Notes on a Haydn Autograph' (*Musical Quarterly*, April 1934), in which also Haydn's signature is reproduced as witness to the marriage of Therese Jansen with Gaetano Bartolozzi on 16th May 1795. The trios were Nos. 3 to 5 of the Peters edition.

The coming winter was to be a hard one for England. The queer weather that Haydn faithfully records in his note-book had wrecked the harvest, while France had been saved from starvation —and the war lengthened by twenty years—by the failure of Lord Howe's barren victory to prevent the French grain-fleet from reaching Brest. The Austrians had been driven back across the Rhine, and the French armies were advancing across the frozen Waal to cut off the retreating British. In December 1794 the Duke of York was recalled, and by January 1795 the British army was disintegrated, and Lord Malmesbury, escorting back to England the Prince of Wales's ill-fated bride, Princess Caroline of Brunswick, was nearly captured. In these circumstances Salomon announced, on 16th January 1795, that he was unable to organize another season. Doubtless he could have done so after a fashion, but he was shrewdly aware that it might be preferable to call a halt while his reputation was at its height. He thanked Haydn for his collaboration and set himself to founding a short-lived National School of Music and accepting engagements as soloist at the newly founded and highly successful series of Opera Concerts, held under Viotti's direction at the King's Theatre, Haymarket, which thus inherited Haydn as conductor and composer. Cramer led the orchestra and Clementi was among the other composers. It was for these concerts that Haydn wrote his last three symphonies, No. 102 in B flat major, No. 103 (the 'Drumroll') and No. 104 (first performed at his benefit on 4th May 1795), usually and illogically singled out as 'The London' Symphony. The series opened on 2nd February, and was so successful that two extra concerts had to be given, on 21 May and 1 June, when the series of nine was over.

The Prince of Wales's approaching marriage was meanwhile the occasion of a series of royal functions, at which an atmosphere of forced geniality replaced the previous strained relations between King George III and his dissolute son. On 1st February the Duke of York gave a party at York House, Piccadilly, attended by the king and queen and the Prince of Wales, at which Haydn conducted his own works from the keyboard. It was here that he was formally presented to the king by the Prince of Wales;

the oboe player Parke, who was within earshot, thus records the drift of the conversation:

Among other observations His Majesty said: 'Dr. Haydn, you have written a good deal.' Haydn modestly replied: 'Yes, Sire, a great deal more than is good.' His Majesty neatly rejoined: 'Oh, no, the world contradicts that.'

A few minutes after this prim exchange of compliments he was at the piano surrounded by the queen and a bunch of princesses, singing his own canzonets in the inimitable way that had—according to Gyrowetz—already won him so many friends,[1] even though his voice was, as he laughingly said, only the size of his top little finger joint. Two days later the Prince of Wales entertained his parents with a concert at Carlton House, which Haydn directed and at which, apart from a concerto of Viotti's, only his music was played.

After the royal wedding, which took place on 8th April, he was again engaged at Carlton House on 10th April; he conducted an earlier symphony of his own, sang in German and English, accompanied the princess's singing and heard her play a pianoforte concerto 'tolerably well.' In all, he played at Carlton House twenty-six times. The prince conveniently forgot to pay him for his services, but when, later, the prince's debts were paid by Parliament (the condition of his consenting to part from Mrs. Fitzherbert and marry Princess Caroline) Haydn, on his friends' advice, sent in a bill for £100, which was promptly met.

Queen Charlotte meanwhile was charmed with him, invited him to numerous musical parties, gave him the manuscript of Handel's early Passion oratorio and offered him apartments at Windsor for the summer if he would make his home in England. But Prince Nicholas Esterházy (II), who had succeeded his father Prince Anton on his death in January 1794 (only five days after Haydn had left for England), had written to Haydn in June of that year asking him to return and reconstitute his orchestra. Haydn had asked for a further year's leave in order to fulfil his

[1] Memoirs of W. T. Parke and A. Gyrowetz, quoted by Karl Geiringer.

engagements to Salomon (which, as it turned out, had fallen through); but he had made up his mind to return, and was not to be persuaded. Perhaps he was right in believing that to be the reason why the court lost interest in him; he received no present from the king, and only his old friend the Duchess of York appeared at his benefit on 4th May. But it may well have been the depressing war news that caused him to drop out of the public eye at the end of May; there were few concerts that summer. The spring had been fairly lively. Salomon had written a spectacular opera, *Windsor Castle*, to celebrate the royal wedding, and the court saw it on 20th April; Haydn had written the overture, which he also attached to his unperformed opera of 1791, *L'anima del filosofo*. Haydn remarks of it that the music was 'passable' and that 'all the gods of heaven and hell and all the denizens of the earth turn up in it.' Besides the Opera Concerts he had performed at Cramer's benefit on 1st May and Madame Dussek's on 29th May, though, oddly enough, not at his friend Dragonetti's on 8th May.

It took him over two months to see the last of England, for he did not set out till 15th August. The only recorded leavetaking is a musical one—his setting of the farewell verses 'O Tuneful Voice' written to him by his old friend Mrs. Hunter—a widow since Dr. Hunter's death in 1793. Besides his souvenirs, which included several presentation pieces of plate [1] and a talking parrot, he took home with him a sheaf of works which represented the sum of his creative effort during his two visits to England, the crown and close of his symphonic achievement and the gateway to that last period which brought his chamber music to its final mastery and embodied the inspiration Handel had given him in *The Creation* and *The Seasons*.

[1] Clementi gave him a goblet of coco-nut shell and silver, and another silver cup was presented by Dr. William Dechair Tattersall 'as a small token of esteem for his abilities and gratitude for his services' in the preparation of a collection of metrical psalms entitled *Improved Psalmody*, to which he contributed six numbers.

CHAPTER IX

VIENNA—THE FINAL HARVEST

HAYDN's second homecoming was more of an event than his first. The honour paid him in England had—as he said himself—made his own countrymen take notice of him. Besides, the London symphonies had been introduced to Vienna and were captivating the Viennese as completely as they had captivated the London public; the 'Surprise' Symphony in particular had caught on and was becoming almost hackneyed. A few months after his return, in the autumn of 1795, he was able to see that this recognition had been given a tangible and unusual form two years earlier by Count Harrach, son of his father's overlord, who had erected a monument in his honour on a picturesque spot on his estate where a sharp curve of the river Leitha turned a corner of the park into a promontory. Haydn drove out to Rohrau, with the Count's three brothers and a party of friends and admirers, to see the monument, and visited his old home, where, overcome with emotion and the strength of old and tender associations, he fell on his knees and kissed the threshold. Perhaps some of his relations came to see him thus honoured—simple working people of whom he was so little ashamed that he used to invite them all to a yearly dinner at the best inn at Bruck, and send them away with a gift of money and an invitation for the following year.

Meanwhile he was once more, after five years, a *Kapellmeister* in fact as well as in name, and the reconstituted Esterházy musical establishment celebrated its restoration and the New Year with a festival performance of Draghi's *Penelope*, in January 1796, at the prince's palace in the Wallnerstrasse. But the old days had not returned, and the restoration of the orchestra was only partial. Prince Nicholas II was not a practising musician; his chief interest lay in church music, and he kept for this purpose a highly competent little group of singers and a small string orchestra (supplemented where necessary by members of the wind-band) for which Haydn was expected to write a yearly mass for the princess's

95

name-day. But he cared little for instrumental music, and only employed the wind-band for parades and outdoor functions and to complete the instrumental accompaniment in church; the symphonies and chamber music with which Haydn had delighted his old master and made his name were not wanted any more. The young prince, too, while he had all his grandfather's urge to patronize the arts in a manner befitting his position, had a colder and more arrogant pride, and his outbursts of anger were not followed by the quick and generous gesture of reconciliation that old Prince Nicholas 'the Magnificent' knew so well how to make. He and Haydn were constantly at odds. He may well have found it irksome to have inherited, as a privileged family retainer, an elderly celebrity whom it would have been injudicious to dismiss, but who went his own way and resented criticism when it was merely an exercise of authority and not of expert knowledge (on one occasion he deeply offended the prince by replying to some ill-judged comment of his, 'Your Highness, that is *my* business'). But it is certain that Haydn's warm and loyal nature would have responded to the slightest show of consideration on his master's side, and he should not have had to rely on Princess Maria Hermenegildis, who liked and admired him, to point out to her husband that a Doctor of Music should no longer be addressed in the third person—a form used in addressing servants.

Esterház was now in disuse, to every one's relief, and the prince kept his court at Eisenstadt in the summer and in Vienna in the winter. In the Eisenstadt months Haydn produced his yearly mass—Prince Nicholas may claim our gratitude for occasioning the composition of these half-dozen works of which four at least are among the finest examples of his mature art—and kept a light hand on the musical establishment while delegating much of the work. He moved, easy-going and friendly, in the narrow social circle of the little place, drinking with his staff and the local worthies of an evening, listening to his colleagues' grumbles and even helping forward their love-affairs as he did with the young official Rosenbaum, who fell in love with Florian Gassmann's daughter Therese when she came to Eisenstadt to take part in a performance of *The Seven Words* (in the choral version which Haydn made soon after completing *The Creation*) in honour of an arch-ducal visit. But in the winter season in Vienna he trod a larger stage, on which he was playing an increasingly conspicuous part.

He had already begun to figure on the public concert platform soon after his return, appearing at several concerts and giving one him-self to introduce three of his latest London symphonies to the capital. Then a new phase opened when the Tonkünstlersocietät, in order to do him belated justice and wipe out its ungenerosity of eighteen years earlier, made him an honorary life member in December 1797. In doing so the society broke all its rules and precedents; but its reward was great. Touched and responsive, Haydn flung himself into its affairs, and not only attended its committee meetings as regularly as his duties allowed, but made available to it, first the choral version of *The Seven Words*, and then *The Creation* and *The Seasons* as they appeared, and conducted the performances himself for the society's funds. This brought the Tonkünstler-societät large revenues over the period Haydn was able to direct these performances; but it also brought Haydn himself before the Viennese public, no longer as a casual and little-heeded visitor, but as the vivid platform personality that had taken London by storm. One success led to another, and until he was over seventy he conducted his big choral works again and again with 'youthful ardour,' not only for the Tonkünstlersocietät, but also for theatrical charities, for St. Mark's Civic Hospital for the sick poor of Vienna, and in aid of the wounded in the Napoleonic wars.

Austria's critical situation was not only reflected in the drums of the 'Agnus Dei' in his 'Kettledrum' Mass—the *Missa in tempore belli* written in 1796 when Napoleon's armies had thrust their way into Styria. Early in the following year Haydn's memories of English crowds roused to patriotic enthusiasm by *God save the King* gave him the idea of writing a similar song to rally his countrymen's spirits in loyalty round their sovereign. He discussed the idea with Baron van Swieten, who passed it on to the president of the provincial government of Lower Austria, a certain Count Saurau (who later claimed to have originated the idea). Saurau produced a lamentable text from one Lorenz Leopold Haschka—an Austrian 'Vicar of Bray' who had been in turn Jesuit, freemason, police informer and professor of aesthetics—Haydn set to work on it with more than ordinary care and devotion, and on 12th February 1797, the Emperor Francis's birthday, words and music of the famous Austrian National Hymn, 'Gott erhalte Franz den Kaiser,' were handed out at the Vienna Burg Theatre and sung with fervour, while the emperor bowed his thanks from the imperial box. Austria had gained a magnificent national anthem, but could not escape defeat. Peace negotiations opened at Leoben in April, and by the treaty of Campo Formio, signed in October, Austria retired from the war.

Haydn's contact with the aristocratic music-lovers of the capital bore fruit in the four great sets of quartets with which he rounded off his life's achievement in that field—Op. 71 and Op. 74, dedicated to Count Apponyi; the six Quartets of Op. 76, dedicated to Count Erdödy, published in 1799 in two batches of three each (the third contains the variations on the Emperor's Hymn); and the two—all that he had the strength to complete—of Op. 77, written in 1799 and dedicated to Prince Lobkowitz, Beethoven's long-suffering patron. He wrote one or two occasional pieces as well —including the lively trumpet Concerto (1796) for a virtuoso named Weidinger who later perfected the first valve trumpet— and still did some teaching, though his beloved Pietro Polzelli died of consumption in December 1796. Beethoven had by now shaken off all forms of tutelage, but was still sufficiently respectful, and sagacious, to dedicate his first set of piano Sonatas, Op. 2, to Haydn, and produce his new works at concert after concert of which the success was assured by Haydn's participation. How unfailingly the young could count on Haydn's kindness and encouragement is shown by story after story—of little Jane Gold-smid, the child of Pitt's financial adviser Abraham Goldsmid, whom he comforted for having lost her place while playing for him by saying: 'Any of us may lose our place, but it is not every one who can get in again as quickly as you did'[1]; of the quartet party

[1] Marion Scott ('Haydn: Relics and Reminiscences in England') quotes the story as told to her by Mr. J. Mewburn Levien, a great-grandson of Abraham Goldsmid. Jane herself was born in 1783, so she could not have been more than twelve.

at his house at which he dispelled the nervousness of the youthful first violinist with a cheerful 'No need to be scared of *me*, my boy, I'm a bad player myself'; and of the young composer Andreas Romberg, whose new quartet Haydn launched by producing it with a flourish for performance at a musical evening and, after being showered with praise and appreciation, saying with a shrewd twinkle: 'Did you really like it? I'm delighted—our Andreas wrote it!' Not only his pupils—chief among them Sigismund Neukomm, who came to him in 1798—but many others of the younger generation came to look on him with an almost filial veneration and love.

In the end, it was Vienna's music-loving nobility who launched him on his last venture. His increasing prominence in the city's musical life inevitably brought him into closer contact with the self-important Baron van Swieten, who had now organized a society of titled amateurs which gave concerts periodically, and whose admiration for Handel Haydn now shared to the full. Before long it emerged that Salomon had given Haydn an English oratorio text—prepared, supposedly, for Handel by one Lidley or Linley [1] and based on Milton's account of the creation of the world in *Paradise Lost*; also that Haydn, fired by Handel's inspiration, was longing to write an oratorio himself, and thus ensure himself a more enduring fame, but did not feel equal to tackling an English text. Van Swieten for his part fancied himself as poet, translator and midwife to genius. He produced a translation of the English text, accompanied by a number of hints for setting it, and got twelve of the wealthier aristocrats belonging to his musical society to subscribe fifty ducats each, thus guaranteeing the expenses of the first performance and an honorarium of 500 ducats for the composer. Thus encouraged, Haydn set to work towards the end of 1796, [2] gravely and with a high sense of responsibility. 'I

[1] Prof. Tovey (*Essays in Musical Analysis*, vol. v, p. 119) suggests that 'Lidley is only Linley with a cold in his head,' and that he was the singing-master and concert promoter Thomas Linley whose daughter married Sheridan.

[2] Albrechtsberger, writing to Beethoven on 15th December 1796, says that Haydn 'was here yesterday, he is busy with the idea of a big

was never so devout as when I was at work on *The Creation*,' he said afterwards; 'I fell on my knees each day and begged God to give me strength to accomplish the work successfully.' On 6th April 1798 he was able to announce to Prince Schwarzenberg, in whose palace in the Neuer Markt the first performance was to be given, that the work was completed. Intensive rehearsals were put in hand at once, and on Monday, 30th April, the market stalls were cleared to make room for the traffic as the musical and fashionable world of Vienna converged on the Neuer Markt. Salieri was at the keyboard, the soloists were Christine Gerardi, Mathias Rathmayr and Ignaz Saal, and Haydn himself conducted by giving the beat with his hands, as was even then the custom with choral works. For him it was a crowning moment, and he knew it. He had—perhaps for the first time in his life—written a deliberately 'great' work, meant to outlast the immediate occasion and his own lifetime; as such it had been awaited and was now being received. 'One moment I was cold as ice all over, the next I was on fire,' he said, 'more than once I was afraid I should have a stroke.' The strain of composing the work, and its resounding success—calling for two more performances within a fortnight of the first—did in fact bring about a sharp reaction and he collapsed under the first of a series of feverish attacks, which, partly brought on by nervous exhaustion, in their turn lowered his vitality still more over the next few years. He was, however, well enough towards the end of the summer to take a lively interest in the battle of the Nile (a diagram of which was found among his papers at his death) and to compose the grand D minor Mass, first performed on 23rd September 1798 and later labelled the 'Nelson' Mass after the admiral had heard it on his visit to Eisenstadt two years later. In October Haydn was back in Vienna, enjoying, after so many years, a visit from his brother Michael.

The spring of 1799 found Austria again at war with France and

---

oratorio which he wants to call *The Creation*; he played through some of his ideas for it and I think it will be very good' (A. Weissenbäcker, 'Drei noch unveröffentlichte Briefe Albrechtsbergers an Beethoven,' *Musica divina*, ix, 10–11).

Haydn as active as ever. On 19th March—his name-day—he conducted the first public performance of *The Creation* in the Burg Theatre, before a packed, perspiring and enthusiastic audience; the male soloists, as before, were Mathias Rathmayr and Ignaz Saal, while Saal's daughter Therese took the soprano part (to the intense chagrin of Rosenbaum, who wanted the part for his *fiancée* Therese Gassmann). Despite the amount of rehearsal this must have involved, Haydn conducted *The Seven Words* for the Tonkünstler-societät on the two preceding days. The popularity of *The Creation* grew with every hearing. Haydn conducted it for the Tonkünst-lersocietät's two annual Christmas concerts, and twice more the following Easter, and before that, in March, he was invited to conduct it at Buda before the Archduke Joseph and his Russian Archduchess Alexandra, whose mother, now the tsaritsa, was Haydn's old admirer of 1781.

Soon after his return from this expedition he heard that his wife, who was at Baden—the little spa near Vienna whither Mozart used to send his Constanze—undergoing treatment for her arthritis, had died there on 20th March. Her death did nothing to soften his memories of her, and it is the measure of their profound and miserable incompatibility that in all his recorded conversations after her death he never made a single forgiving or affectionate reference to her. But it could not now bring him, at sixty-eight, the chance to start afresh. Luigia Polzelli, on hearing the news, besieged him with importunities, but all the satisfaction she got was a written undertaking to marry no one else if he should re-marry at all, and to leave her an annuity of 300 florins. He continued to send her money at intervals, but on her marriage to a singer named Franchi he cut the promised annuity by half. So ended, drearily to the last, Haydn's two closest and most lasting relationships with women; of all the great composers he was perhaps the one who could have given and received most in the normal and natural joys of marriage and fatherhood.

Amid all the pressure of work his business letters lay unanswered and young Gottfried Härtel, of the Leipzig publishing firm of Breitkopf & Härtel, decided therefore, in 1799, to ask a friend attached to the Saxon legation in Vienna, Georg August

Griesinger, to see whether a personal approach produced better results. It did, both for the firm and for musical history; Griesinger became a regular visitor and friend, and his letters, and the little memoir of Haydn which he compiled after the composer's death, provide essential information regarding his life. Personal contact—this time through an official of the British embassy—also put him into touch with the Scottish publisher Thomson; for him, and for his rival Whyte, he arranged, in the course of the next few years, more than 250 Scottish and Welsh songs. Work on these arrangements was to provide him with an occupation and a source of income in the years when his failing energies could no longer marshal the creative ideas that still welled up within him.

Work and age were beginning to tell on him increasingly, and in April 1800 he was ill once more with 'rheumatic head fever'—more seriously this time, for at one point his life was thought to be in danger. He pulled round, but was poorly all summer. Composition was becoming an increasing effort; a year earlier he was already writing to Griesinger:

My affairs, alas, multiply with my years, and yet it is almost as though the desire and impulse to work were waxing as my mental powers are on the wane. Oh God, how much is still to be done in this splendid art, even by such a man as I have been! True, the world pays me many daily compliments, even on the fire of my latest works; but no one will believe the trouble and effort it costs me to start it up, for on many days I am so overwhelmed by my feeble memory and unstrung nerves that I fall into the most unhappy condition, and hence for days on end am in no state to produce a single idea, until at last Providence heartens me and I can sit down once again at the clavier and begin to hammer away. Then it comes back again, praise God!

Now—labouring against cross-currents of nervous weariness and repugnance to an uncongenial text—he was struggling to finish *The Seasons*.

Van Swieten, anxious to repeat the success of his earlier collaboration, had this time constructed the libretto himself, with remote reference to James Thomson's poem. If Haydn found the theme less attractive than that of *The Creation*, it was partly because of the baron's insistence that the descriptive elements in the text should

be given their musical counterpart,[1] and partly because his handling
of the subject was sententious without real loftiness or nobility.
Haydn summed up his feelings on this head in two remarks—that
he had been an industrious man all his life but had never thought
of setting industry to music, and that while the *dramatis personae* of
The Creation were angels, in *The Seasons* they were merely peasants.

In September 1800 Nelson, after being fêted in Vienna, visited
Eisenstadt with Sir William and Lady Hamilton; the capricious
Emma alternately ignored Haydn (when cards were afoot) and sat
in his pocket, insisting on singing his *Arianna* and, of course, his
new cantata, a setting of portions of a 'Pindarick Ode' on the
Battle of the Nile, by her friend and companion Miss Knight.
(There appears to be no confirmation of Griesinger's story that
Nelson himself asked Haydn for his pen and gave him his gold
watch in return.)   Three months later the emperor himself was at
Eisenstadt, reviewing the Hungarian militia, and in January of
the following year, 1801, Haydn was back in Vienna, conducting *The Creation* in aid of the wounded in the disastrous
defeat of Hohenlinden and taking part in a charity concert for
the same object organized by Christine Franck-Gerardi (the
soloist in the first performance of *The Creation*).   Poor Michael
Haydn, meanwhile, had felt the pinch of war in real earnest, for the
French soldiery had looted his house on their entry into Salzburg,
and Joseph sent him a gold watch and money to make good his losses.

By April 1801, despite another attack of the old *Kopffieber,*
The Seasons was finished.   Like *The Creation,* it was first performed
under Haydn's direction at the Schwarzenberg Palace, on 24th
April and repeated twice in the following week.   It was then
given at Court on 24th May, followed by *The Creation* on 25th
May, with the empress singing the soprano solos in both works,
and on 29th May he conducted the first public performance in the
Redoutensaal.   He had just entered his seventieth year.

[1] When making the pianoforte score, he wrote to Breitkopf & Härtel
regarding the passage depicting the croaking of the frogs in the 'Summer'
section: 'This frenchified trash was forced upon me'; the remark,
indiscreetly reported in a magazine article, not unnaturally offended
the baron, and caused a temporary quarrel between him and Haydn.

CHAPTER X

'MERE GLIMMERINGS AND DECAYS'

ONE of Somerset Maugham's characters, referring to a fictional 'Grand Old Man' of English letters, concludes that 'longevity is genius.' The aphorism contains this much of truth, that the attainment of old age by a creative artist focuses attention on the sum of his achievement, work upon work gradually accumulating, until at last men become aware of the mountain standing where none was before and transforming the face of the landscape.

In the eight years of life that remained to him Haydn was treated as a landmark in European music. Musical societies and academies vied with each other to load him with medals and diplomas—spanning the earthquake-fissures of war, for France was enthralled with *The Creation* and bestowed more distinctions on him than any other country, while for music-loving visitors to Vienna the quiet little house at Gumpendorf became a place of pilgrimage.

He still occasionally conducted his own works for charity; his last appearance was on 26th December 1803, when *The Seven Words* was performed in aid of St. Mark's Hospital. But at Eisenstadt he was able to do less and less, and history repeated itself as Prince Nicholas appointed one Johann Fuchs as Vice-*Kapellmeister*[1] to do for him what he had done for old Gregor Werner over fifty years ago. Fuchs's task was easy by comparison, for Haydn was on the friendliest terms with him during the two years he still remained in nominal charge. But in 1804, when a long spell of ill health kept Haydn in Vienna all the summer, the last traces of active control over the Esterházy musical establishment slipped from his unresisting hands.

---

[1] Prince Nicholas had offered the post to Michael Haydn, who visited Joseph and Hansl at Eisenstadt in the autumn of 1801—the last time the three old brothers were together; but Joseph's account of the petty cliques and intrigues of life in a small court—for which he thought Michael unfitted—probably put him off, for he never took the post.

He led a quiet and regular life, enjoying his garden and the neighbours' children in the daytime and his card-games with the servants
of an evening, and receiving his visitors with a certain amount of
ceremony and ritual. Outwardly his life was peaceful, in spite
of the war situation, which, as the French occupied Vienna after
their victory at Ulm in 1805, caused him intense depression—though
he was cheered by several visits from his ardent admirer Cherubini.
He might indeed have been tolerably happy if he had been less
inwardly alive; but the creative surge of his genius, breaking against
the walls of his failing body, gave him no rest. He had been
full of plans after finishing *The Seasons*—a set of six quartets for
Count Fries, and a new oratorio, possibly on the Last Judgment.
But his mind and nerves were by now too spent to shape and evolve
and commit to paper the ideas that still teemed in his brain. At
first he kept hoping that the incapacity would pass, and made all
sorts of plans and promises; slowly he was forced to recognize
that he would never carry them out. When, in 1806, he let
Griesinger send to Breitkopf & Härtel the two middle movements
of his last, unfinished quartet, begun in 1803 (it was to have been
one of the set for Count Fries) it was the gesture with which he
admitted his defeat, sealing the admission by attaching to it his new
visiting card, printed with a quotation from his song 'The Old Man':

> Gone is all my strength,
> Old and weak am I.

How dreadful the torment of his 'weak memory,' as he called
it, was to him, is shown in the incident movingly related by the
landscape painter Dies, who, introduced by their mutual friend,
the sculptor Grassi, had been visiting him to collect material for
his vivid little volume of biographical notes. He had been obliged
to send to Dies to ask him for the name of a friend of his—Zelter—
which he had forgotten and whose letter he had lost. Apologizing
to Dies for having troubled him, he went on:

Musical ideas pursue me to the point of torture. I cannot get rid of them,
they stand before me like a wall. If it is an *allegro* that pursues me, my
pulse beats faster, I cannot sleep; if an *adagio*, I find my pulse beating
slowly. My imagination plays upon me as if I were a keyboard.

'Then,' Dies continues, 'Haydn smiled, the blood suddenly flamed in his cheeks as he said "I really am a living keyboard."'

His one relief from this oppression was to play over his Emperor's Hymn; 'then it gets easier—that helps me.'

He was not actively ill, though his polypus made him 'grumpy and uncomfortable,' and he was subject to sudden attacks of giddiness; but the sense of incapacitation and weakness was horrifying and unaccustomed, making him, as old people so often are, a trifle valetudinarian. Slowly his enfeeblement, which at first had co-existed with a perfectly clear mind, slipped into something much nearer senility. He was quick to tears—at a stimulating interview, an appreciative letter, the mention of Mozart's name. The fear of not having enough to live on and leave his relations at his death (a regular obsession of age) sent him burrowing through his shelves for unpublished works to sell and made him fret about his doctor's bills (which Prince Nicholas Esterházy paid, to his intense gratitude) and accept small presents of food with pathetic and undignified eagerness. Most piercing of all to those who loved and honoured him were the touches of childish vanity in one who had always borne himself with the dignity and humility begotten of the knowledge that his genius was the gift of God. Only his faith was as strong as ever. He spent hours with his rosary in his hands, and was calmly and even eagerly ready for death; 'I am no more use to the world,' he said to Griesinger, 'I have to be waited on and tended like a child; it is high time God called me to Himself.'

He was to know one last moment of glory. On 27th March 1808, as the last of a series of subscription concerts, a performance of *The Creation* was arranged in the beautiful hall of the old university, and he was persuaded to come. The three soloists were from the Court Theatre, Salieri conducted and the violinist Clement, now a grown man, led the orchestra. A fanfare of trumpets sounded as he was carried into the hall, poems of homage were presented to him and, as he shivered a little, Princess Esterházy put her wrap around his shoulders; other noble ladies followed suit till he was swathed like a cocoon in shawls. The performance began; at the great C major blaze of 'And there was light' the audience, as usual, broke into applause; in the midst of it he was heard to say, with trembling hands uplifted: 'Not from me—it all comes from above.' He was clearly too overwrought to sit through the entire performance, and was taken away at the interval. All knew that this was the end and crowded round him to say a last good-bye; Beethoven knelt among them to kiss his forehead and hands. As he reached the door he signed to his bearers to stop. With wordless gestures he thanked the company; then, 'turning to the orchestra with an expression impossible to describe, he suddenly raised his eyes and hands heavenwards and blessed his children with tears.'[1]

In the following year, 1809, the war again flooded Austria and for the second time engulfed Vienna itself. Haydn was very much alone. Both his brothers were dead—Hansl in 1805, Michael in 1806; so were many of his friends—Dr. von Genzinger, Grassi, old Albrechtsberger. Neukomm had gone back to his job in St. Petersburg, and early in May Griesinger (who had continued his visits out of affection long after their original reason had ceased to exist) had to leave the threatened capital. On 11th May the French began to bombard the city (Beethoven, to whose diseased hearing the noise was a torment, was wrestling with the 'Emperor' Concerto in a cellar, his head muffled in pillows). Four shots fell close to Haydn's house as he was getting up. Above the crash and the vibration his terrified servants heard his voice ring out: 'Don't be frightened, children, where Haydn is no harm can come to you.'

But the shock had done its work. He was seized with a violent fit of trembling, and from that day could no longer walk unaided. The French, chivalrous and respectful as always, posted sentries at his door, and a young French officer, Sulémy by name, called and asked to be allowed to sing to him. He sang 'In native worth' from *The Creation*, with moving beauty, and his tears flowed with those of the dying old man as they embraced across the barriers of war.

Slowly and steadily he grew weaker and failed to respond

[1] Carpani, *Le Haydine*.

to stimulants. He would creep to the pianoforte and play the Emperor's Hymn to comfort himself; on 26th May he played it three times over, with so much depth of expression that he himself wondered at it. That evening he felt worse and asked to be helped to bed. He never left it again. Another doctor was called in for consultation; but there was nothing to be done. He let himself be tended (so Elssler wrote to Griesinger) 'so readily and peacefully that we were all amazed . . . and when we asked him how he was, he kept answering, "Cheer up, children, I'm all right."' Only Elssler and the servants were with him as his strength slipped away and, speechless by now but still conscious, he pressed his old cook Nannerl's hand. Ten minutes later he died, on 31st May 1809, aged seventy-seven years and two months.

He was buried the next day, after a funeral service at Gumpendorf parish church, in the Hundsturm cemetery (whence his body was later taken to the Bergkirche at Eisenstadt). Communications were disorganized, and the notice was short—doubtless owing to the stifling weather—and only a handful of people were present. But a fortnight later, on 15th June, French and Viennese soldiers took turns to guard the catafalque as the crowds poured into the Schottenkirche to honour his memory, and it was to the music of Mozart's Requiem that the prayer of the Mass for the Dead, 'et lux perpetua luceat eis,' commended his soul to the presence of the uncreated Light.

CHAPTER XI

MUSICAL CHARACTERISTICS

THERE is no great composer (save perhaps Sibelius) whose creative lifetime spans greater changes, both in emotional climate and in technique and means of expression, than does Haydn's. In 1759, the year of Handel's death, he was already in his late twenties, just entering on his first full-time post with a Mass and a sheaf of small instrumental works to his credit. By 1801, when *The Seasons* appeared, Beethoven had written his first symphony, three piano concertos, eleven of his piano sonatas and the Op. 18 quartets. And between these two poles lies the world of Mozart's creation.

The changes which Haydn lived through, and did so much to bring about, may be crudely summarized as being the discovery of the formal and dramatic possibilities inherent in key relationships, and—inseparably linked with this—the attainment by instrumental music of equal rights with the voice. But for most of his life Haydn was hardly conscious of the part he was playing. To him (as to his contemporaries) opera—the performance of other men's, and the composition and production of his own—was the most important and exacting part of his work. Instrumental music was thought of either in terms of home performance by the talented amateurs for whom he wrote his sonatas and chamber works, or as a form of entertainment to grace a banquet or other social occasion—hence his symphonies and divertimenti; or again as a vehicle for display by professional virtuosi—hence the concerto, which, being no virtuoso himself, and remote from the city life which fostered such displays, he did not cultivate. The extensive sales of his instrumental works in the 1780s doubtless led him, shrewd as he was, to value them more highly; but it was not until London focused on the Salomon concerts an attention which Dr. Burney 'did not remember to have been bestowed on any other instrumental music before' that he could look back and begin to realize what he had done. Even then he could hardly have guessed the full extent of his achievement.

That achievement was not—as was formerly claimed—the 'invention' of the symphony and the string quartet. In both these categories he had his forerunners and models—though it is hardly possible to speak of categories when in Haydn's young days symphony and quartet were barely distinguishable, and their eventual differentiation was one aspect of his mastery. But it is true to say that at one end of the scale there were the *quadri* of such Italians as Tartini and Sammartini who, by occasionally dropping the continuo, broke away from the older type represented by Dall'Abaco and Pugnani (which was simply a *sonata da chiesa* for four stringed instruments and continuo) and whose lead was followed by a handful of composers in Vienna and southern Germany. At the other end were the symphonies or 'overtures' of the Viennese composers—Reutter, Monn, Wagenseil—whose music Haydn would have heard in the great houses where he came and went as a choirboy or music-master. Here, and in the *quadri* also, the forms of opera—the lively Neapolitan overture with its slow central episode, the *da capo* aria with its statement, contrasting middle section and restatement—had left their mark; and these early symphonies (mostly in three movements, but occasionally incorporating the minuet) abound in primitive examples of 'sonata form' with scarcely a glimmer of the drama and tension which are the essence of the fully developed sonata style. Between these two types lay the vast, undemarcated field of partita and serenade, divertimento and cassation, with any number of movements, in which the suites of the older period lived on, and into which both *quadro* and *sinfonia* tended to merge whenever they shook off the continuo.[1]

As for individual influences, Haydn himself admitted a

[1] Haydn's own earliest quartets illustrate this tendency, for all but No. 5 of Op. 1, and the entire Op. 2, are five-movement divertimenti with two minuets apiece, and Nos. 3 and 5 of Op. 2 were published as such, with the addition of two horns, in a French edition with the title *Six Sinfonies ou Quatuor* [*sic*] *dialogues*; and Op. 1 No. 5 is a three-movement symphony. And yet in early editions of all his first four sets of quartets—such was the force of tradition and habit—the cello part is described as 'basso' and figured accordingly.

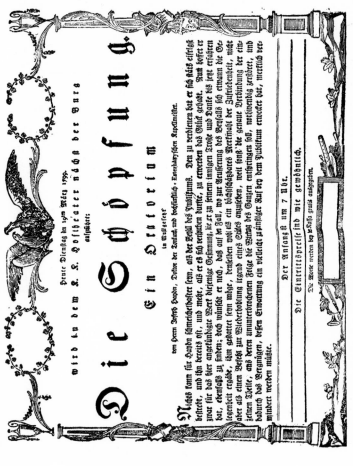

FACSIMILE OF THE ANNOUNCEMENT BILL OF THE FIRST PERFORMANCE OF 'THE CREATION'

profound debt of gratitude to Carl Philipp Emanuel Bach, while
in the same breath expressly repudiating the influence of the
Milanese Sammartini, whom he called a 'dauber.' Sammartini's
music was for some reason antipathetic to him, but the Italian's
effervescent, lively instrumental style was part of the background
furniture of his mind, whether he liked it or not. C. P. E. Bach,
on the other hand, satisfied the emotional needs of his lonely youth,
strongly influenced his keyboard style and gave him the key to the
world of romance and drama conjured up by remote modulations,
though he probably found his structural models nearer home.

But there was one feature common to all the instrumental
music to which he was exposed in his formative years: the decline
of counterpoint that characterizes this fluid period. The older
instrumental music—the *concerti grossi* of Handel and Vivaldi,
the sonatas of Corelli and his followers, to whom contrapuntal
writing was the natural language—was by the middle of the eighteenth century looked upon as archaic: its rolling periods were
being broken up into the short phrases of Italian aria and French
chanson, its inner parts reduced to a mere accompaniment to the
melody and thus impoverished, both melodically and harmonic-
ally. By 1760, when Haydn entered the service of the Esterházy
family, the distinction between the 'learned' contrapuntal style
and the newer, so-called courtly (*galant*) style—tuneful, episodic,
full of the 'sensibility' that was becoming fashionable in the current
literature—was consciously made and their separation virtually
complete.

It is indeed not without reason that the third quarter of the
eighteenth century is, for the present-day music-lover, a curiously
blank period. Bach is dead, Handel soon falls silent; Mozart is a
youthful prodigy, but his full glory is yet to come. Numberless
shadowy and forgotten figures flit across the stage; but only two
familiar faces detach themselves—Gluck, whose operas, for all the
advanced theories behind them, have the austere nobility of that
earlier age whose defects of stiffness and artificiality he denounced
—and Haydn himself. And with a growing fascination we
watch Haydn's solitary figure moving through this twilight inter-
regnum, laying his hands on one isolated strand after another—

galanterie, the old 'learned' polyphony, folk melody, Italian opera—and gradually drawing them together into a new style of incredible resilience and adaptability.

Haydn in fact was interested in structure for its own sake, and it was this, more than any other single quality, that enabled him to achieve what he did. From the child improvising a drum to the man of sixty fascinated by Herschel's telescope and the rig and tackle of the British Navy, the trait persists throughout his life. He may not have invented forms—except perhaps his characteristic alternating variations; but he could never let his models alone, and by pulling them this way and that, taking them to pieces and putting them together again in odd and sometimes unsatisfactory shapes, he gradually discovered their potentialities. It was he who, retaining the older tradition of the fast minuet alongside the newer 'courtly' type, used it to open up a new range of humorous and dramatic expression. It was he who, after at first following his contemporaries in merely allowing the themes of his first movements to wander sequentially through their development sections in a chain of related keys, began to break them up into their rhythmic and melodic components and, with these smaller units, to weave a far more intricate and close-knit fabric. The fact that some of his finest sonata-form movements are mono-thematic—that their so-called 'second subject' in the complementary key is merely a modification of the first—is the strongest evidence of his ability to see the full range of possibilities latent in a single theme. And, having begun to 'develop,' he could not stop; his recapitulations begin to take on irregular contours, sometimes sharply condensed, sometimes surprisingly expanded, losing their first tame symmetry to regain a balance of a far higher and more satisfying order.

Lastly, it was he who brought out of its religious enclosure the strict counterpoint he had encountered in the polyphonic church music of his choirboy days and taught himself in solitary discipline, and, by wrestling to draw it into use as a framework on which to build his structure of key changes and melodic transformations, began the reconquest of counterpoint for instrumental music. He did not complete it alone. The Op. 17 and Op. 20

112

quartets show the extent of his unaided achievement; even here, the pure contrapuntal writing is largely localized in the finales. But he had put the fusion within reach of Mozart's hands, and from them received it back again, to transfigure the works of his last years. It is indeed significant that it was the Op.20 quartets, of which four have fugues as finales, that first caught the seventeen-year-old Mozart's eye and inspired the fugal last movements of two (K. 168 and 173) out of the set he wrote in 1773. But it is also characteristic of their relationship that while the first of the set he dedicated to Haydn—that in G major, K. 387, written in 1782 —has a contrapuntal finale, it already shows that complete integra-tion of counterpoint with the sonata style which it was to take Haydn another five years to attain.

This fact crystallizes two elements in the polarity of Haydn and Mozart—the vast difference in their maturing-rates, and the fact that, whereas Haydn was fundamentally interested in structure, Mozart was not. Mozart was twenty-seven when he wrote the G major Quartet; by the time he died, at thirty-five, he had ex-pressed, in music of almost unbearable perfection, a whole world of human experience. If Haydn had died at the same age—in 1767—he would have been just at the beginning of that creative outbreak which brought his genius to power and self-realization—though not even yet to maturity—by the time he was forty; and to-day we should hardly remember his name. Again, while Haydn was the constructor *par excellence*, Mozart (like J. S. Bach, to whom he turned towards the end of his life as the one musician from whom he could still learn) was a supreme example of that other type of artist—those who accept the forms they find ready to their hand, and whose energies, thus husbanded, are released to charge those forms with an infinitely richer content. It was largely due to Haydn that the forms Mozart did find were strong enough to take the weight of his passion and poetry and give scope for his breathtaking technical accomplishment.[1]

---

[1] What Mozart owed to Haydn and to his many lesser forerunners may be seen by comparing his achievement with that of one who shared his precocious genius and early death but, unlike him, was 'born out of due time'—Henry Purcell. For all his genius, Purcell

Never, indeed, have two such widely differing musical personalities stood in so close a relationship, their music reflecting their differences with astonishing precision. Mozart, with his mercurial and Hamlet-like complexity, explores (as both Dr. Alfred Einstein and Sir Donald Tovey point out) the subtleties of the closer key-relationships with unparalleled delicacy, and his melody and harmony alike are shadowed by chromatic nuances. Haydn—his Horatio in music as in life—reflects in his remote and plunging modulations, made the more effective by his diatonic harmony, the adventurous spirit, the virility and depth of a strong and ardent but essentially uncomplicated nature. His music, has, moreover, none of the two-edged ambiguity of mood that is so piercing in Mozart, of whose music one can often say:

> But whether note of joy, or knell,
> Not his own Father-singer knew.

Haydn's movements, whether solemn or comical, overflowing with tragic passion or sheer *joie de vivre*, declare themselves from the outset, and express one mood at a time.

Einstein further observes, with acute insight, that the remote keys which Haydn so often chooses for his slow movements serve him as a kind of springboard into poetic inspiration.[1] Mozart needs no such springboard; poetry with him is instinctive and habitual. No one who knows the full range of Haydn's work can agree with Michel Brenet and Teodor de Wyzewa that, although 'an admirable "prose-writer,"' he was no poet. But the poetic vision, with him, was a transitory visitant, needing the touch of mystery and strangeness in his remote keys to evoke it.

Haydn's use of folk melody has made him the object of much ethnological theorizing, and while it now seems to be proved beyond doubt that he himself was of German extraction, it is no

---

lacked the constructive ability to make for himself the forms which his transitional age failed to provide; and so his inspiration was all too often diffused, or seeped away through inadequate vessels.

[1] *Mozart: his Character, his Work*, p. 159.

less certain that in his music he draws freely on Croatian and Hungarian traditional tunes. As he was of peasant stock, and spent most of his life in that eastern borderland of Austria and Hungary where so much intermingling of peoples has taken place (and in addition, so Carpani tells us, actively collected folk tunes), it is not remarkable that he spoke that musical language as naturally as he did the cultivated musical language of his training, and that not only do Croatian and Hungarian folk tunes appear in his work from early to late,[1] but that his own melodies also frequently bear the same imprint. What is indeed remarkable is the racy twist with which he not only lifts them out of the commonplace but also gives them the stamina to move symphonically. In the alternating variations that make up the Andante of the 'Drum-roll' Symphony (No. 103), the minor melody (a Croat tune from Sopron, near Eisenstadt) is originally a symmetrical affair, subsiding on to its tonic; by the time Haydn has finished with it, it has become a sinewy, free-modulating creature, able to carry some of his finest scoring and contrapuntal ornament, while in the major tune (another folk melody) he has only to sharpen the F in the ascending scale (matching the minor tune) to give it that spark of originality which, in the coda, kindles into an incandescent blaze of poetry:

Ex. 1
(a)1.

FOLK SONG "Na Traviknu"

---

[1] The Croatian sources of a number of his themes are traced by Hugo Conrat in his article 'Joseph Haydn und das Kroatische Volkslied' (*Die Musik*, vol. xiv, 1904–5) and by Sir W. H. Hadow in his book *A Croatian Composer: Notes towards the Study of Joseph Haydn*. (London, 1897.)

(a)2. HAYDN. Symphony No. 103.

Andante

(b)1. FOLK SONG "Jur Postaje"

(b)2. HAYDN. Symphony No. 103.

So, too, he opens the last movement of the 'London' Symphony (No. 104) with the popular Eisenstadt ballad 'Oj Jelena'; but he quickly trips up its heels when it shows an inclination to sit down on its cadences and repeat itself, and whirls it away on its own rhythm into one of the most close-knit as well as one of the most exhilarating of all his finales. Haydn, in fact, triumphantly refutes Constant Lambert's famous dictum on the unsuitability of folk melody for symphonic treatment, that 'once you have played it through there is nothing much you can do except play it over again, and play it rather louder.'

Child of his time as Haydn was, it is the more significant that his creative span abuts on the nineteenth century. And though at first it appears strange that Beethoven derived so little conscious benefit from his teaching, it is not really surprising: their qualities were similar, not complementary, and their temperamental kinship too strong for them to have much to give each other. What Beethoven learned from Haydn by the process of unconscious assimilation is written all over the music of his early and middle periods; he shared Haydn's powerful architectural sense and could not but be influenced by his freedom of form, though, being himself slow to mature, it was some time before he achieved the like. This kinship of theirs shows itself in their melodic habits—though Haydn's melody is on the whole more elastic and full of odd phrase-lengths, and its upward flow and downward plunges are even more purposeful—and, most markedly, in their harmonic traits. Their sense of mystery and unfathomableness—a quality also shared by Schubert—appears in their love for Rembrandtesque major-minor contrasts of dark and light and in their sudden modulations into remote keys; Beethoven and Schubert alike follow Haydn both in his abrupt plunges into the key of the flat sixth and in his exploration of the sharp, 'bright' side of the harmonic spectrum. Haydn, however, is more apt to choose such a contrasting key for a movement in the course of a work such as the F sharp major *largo* of the Quartet in D major, Op. 76 No. 5), besides modulating with equal freedom during a single movement.

Humour is yet another trait common to Haydn and Beethoven. Wit they shared with Mozart; but, unlike Mozart's, their instrumental music is often downright funny as well. Their explosive dynamics, both in their orchestral and their keyboard writing, reflect their storms at one end of the scale and their love of practical joking at the other. Pranks with tempo, such as the gradual emergence of the little ascending scale which opens the last movement of Beethoven's first Symphony, and the portentous slowings-up near the end of the fourth, are paralleled a dozen times in Haydn's work, though Haydn goes even farther in his fooling with actual instrumental timbres.

To his contemporaries Haydn's instrumentation was remarkable for the way in which he realized the peculiar qualities of the different instruments and gave them their independence. This is indeed one of his supreme merits, and in achieving it his youthful experience of serenading in Vienna's streets was of decisive influence. In the salon or church, where harpsichord or organ invariably accompanied every musical performance, the continuo provided the harmonic backbone, held the bass line, intervened actively in the melodic action above it and made a uniform background of tone-colour. Without it, in the open air, the wind instruments were, on the one hand, obliged to perform some of its harmonic functions, supporting the movement of the strings by sustained or rhythmically repeated chords, and on the other hand were free to enter into the thematic working-out of the music, bringing to bear on the discussion their own individual tone-quality. Though Haydn never abandoned the keyboard and, as Dr. Burney tells us, 'presided at the piano-forte' at the Salomon concerts, he had by then given the instruments of the orchestra such freedom that his presidency must have been purely nominal. And, but for the disappearance of the continuo, the string quartet as we know it could never have flowered under Haydn's hands.

But his scoring, brilliant though it often is, has not Mozart's uncanny inerrancy. In his piano trios, which are virtually piano sonatas with *obbligato* accompaniment for violin and cello, he never transcended the convention of the time, as Beethoven was to do, by creating a new interplay between keyboard and strings; and his quartets, though they give the viola freedom and interesting occupation, rarely exploit its distinctive tone. In his orchestral works passages where the woodwind instruments are treated with the utmost imaginative boldness are matched by others in which they are doubled by the strings, which blur or obliterate their characteristic colour. In this case it is obvious that Haydn was forced time and again, by the limitations of his performers, to play for safety. The advantages of having an orchestra always at his elbow for experiments are obvious; but it was not all pure gain, and the visionary scoring of Schubert's great C major Symphony (written without hope of actual performance) will show what heights an inspired but not infallible imagination can reach when writing for ideal and not for actual conditions.

Here we must also reckon once more with Haydn's exceptionally slow maturing-rate. He himself said 'I have only just learned in my old age how to use the wind instruments, and now that I do understand them I must leave the world'; and indeed a comparison of even the last and ripest of the London symphonies with *The*

Creation shows an extraordinary heightening of both imaginative and technical mastery in the scoring of the later work.

This slowness must never be forgotten when forming a picture of the complete Haydn. The gaiety, serenity and prevailing major mode of his latest and best-known works have gained him a reputation for unclouded optimism. But, though no attempt should be made to read into his music a pessimism which it does not contain, a glance at a few of the symphonies and quartets written when his genius was in ferment between 1767 and 1773, and again at some of the curiously unsettled symphonies of the early 1780s, will show that passion and sorrow were at work within him, but that, at the time, his technique was inadequate to express them. Here is the opening of his G minor Symphony, No. 39:

Ex. 2. **Allegro assai**

Its resemblance to Mozart's G minor Symphony (K. 550), in mood, key-scheme, even melodic figuration, is remarkable; but even more remarkable is the contrast between Haydn's abruptness and crudity and Mozart's unattainable perfection. Only in a handful of works—the C minor piano Sonata No. 20 (1771) and the G minor and F minor Quartets, Op. 20 Nos. 3 and 5, dating from 1772—does his technique begin to draw level with his emotion. And when, in his fifties, he had attained his full technical mastery, it was too late: he had moved on long ago. To the end of his life he could have said of his medium what T. S. Eliot says of his:

> . . . one has only learnt to get the better of words.
> For the thing one no longer has to say, or the way in which
> One is no longer disposed to say it. And so each venture
> Is a new beginning. . . .

CHAPTER XII

VOCAL WORKS EXCLUDING OPERA

IN past centuries, when, as Paul Hindemith has observed, performing amateur musicians accounted for a good nine-tenths of
the musical world, a very high proportion of music was written
with their needs and tastes in mind, ranging in quality from the
equivalent of the current ladies' magazines to that of the finest
contemporary work in literature and art. If Haydn's keyboard
sonatas and chamber music belong to this category, so also do his
songs. And if he came to solo song only in middle life, the
reason was that in Vienna itself, as Einstein writes, 'the history of
the song had been even shorter than in other German centres,
because Vienna was a city of instrumental Italian music and
Italian opera'; indeed, it only began in 1778, with the publication
of Josef Anton Steffan's first *Sammlung deutscher Lieder für das
Klavier*, whereas in northern Germany the theory and practice of
song-writing had been occupying the minds of composers for the
past forty years (hence the young and cosmopolitan Mozart had
been composing songs on and off since 1768). Haydn's first set
of twelve songs was published in 1781, followed by a second in
1784. Haydn brought to them a rich and vigorous keyboard
style and a mind at once symphonic and operatic but unexercised
in the problem of relating text to music in the fine detail required
in an intimate lyric. Thus—discounting the mere melodious
trifles among the two sets—it is not to be wondered at that certain
songs (the *Liebeslied* in the first set, or, in the second, *Das Leben ist
ein Traum*) have something of the character of operatic arias, while

others are not so much songs as finely wrought keyboard pieces, notably the moving but curiously unvocal G minor *Gebet zu Gott*. The wonder is rather that Haydn so often achieves a real fusion of voice and accompaniment, of structure and feeling, as he does in the *Abschiedslied*, with its touching tenderness, the passionate *Die Verlassene* and the gentle, Schubertian *Trost unglücklicher Liebe*—or, at the other end of the emotional scale, in the enchantingly funny *Lob der Faulheit* or in *Die zu späte Ankunft der Mutter*, with its melodic line shared, in delightful interplay, between voice and keyboard.

In his English songs Haydn uses three staves throughout, and the accompaniment attains greater independence and a marvellous translucency of sound. But the inner life of an imperfectly mastered language eluded him. *Recollection*, for all its pensive charm, is an object-lesson in the deadening effect which even a fine, flexible musical phrase can make on words which it shapes mechanically, and even *The Wanderer*, with its fine romantic gloom, uses verbal repetitions to carry the big curve of the melody to an extent that lessens the impact of the words themselves. The one Shakespeare text, *She never told her love*, he rightly treats in the manner of an accompanied recitative, but brings to it a purely static dignity instead of the moving expressiveness that he normally commands in that idiom. But in his two English songs separately published, *O Tuneful Voice* and *The Spirit's Song*, Haydn at last achieved a true integration of words and music. The first of these is a setting of the farewell eulogy addressed to him by Mrs. Hunter, but (as Marion Scott finely suggests) its rhythmic impetus and inner fire transform it into a paean in praise of music itself.[1] Even here verbal repetitions are used to support its compressed sonata-form design; but in *The Spirit's Song*, at last, the design, for all its strength and freedom, is shaped to carry the text, so that the whole song becomes both musically and emotionally alive and moving.

Apart from the songs, there are a few longer pieces with

---

[1] In her absorbing article 'Some English Affinities and Associations of Haydn's Songs' (*Music & Letters*, January 1944).

keyboard accompaniment: one or two charming duets, and the splendid cantata *Arianna a Naxos*. Here, in an alternating sequence of two expressive accompanied recitatives and two arias, Haydn carries his heroine from her first loving reverie, through the dawning realization that she is alone and deserted, to the desolation of her last F minor outburst. Its counterpart, among the handful of fine concert arias for professional performance, is the superb *Scena di Berenice* which Haydn wrote for Mrs. Billington in 1795. The design is the same, even to the final despairing F minor aria, but the power and passion of the recitatives, with their astonishing modulations, rank it with the greatest of Haydn's vocal works.

A word must be said here about his arrangements of Scottish and Welsh songs. His first set of a hundred, with accompaniments for piano, violin and cello, was made in the summer or autumn of 1791 (perhaps at Mrs. Schroeter's instance—he had been her husband's publisher) to save the publisher Napier from bankruptcy, and a second set of fifty was published in 1794. Interested as he was in folk melody, the idea caught his fancy, and in his old age he drew pleasure and material profit from making over two hundred similar arrangements—with added ritornelli— for the two Scottish publishers Thomson and Whyte. But the scientific study of folk melody and its appropriate harmonization was a thing of the future, and for all his enjoyment of these songs, it never occurred to him to adapt his musical idiom to theirs. His settings (like those which Beethoven later made for Thomson) thus give them an alien charm—though the Celtic beauties are often very attractive in their period costume.

England's glee clubs and her thriving native tradition of concerted singing may have stimulated the composition of many of his rounds and canons, and Karl Geiringer suggests that this impetus, carried over into his last years, inspired his last thirteen three- and four-part songs, composed between 1796 and 1801 for pure pleasure (by his own account) and not on commission. Some, such as *Die Harmonie in der Ehe* (*Wedded Harmony*) and *Beredsamkeit* (*Eloquence*) are delightfully funny; but *Der Greis* (*The Old Man*) has a gentle pathos, and the *Danklied zu Gott* (*Thanksgiving to God*) and

Abendlied zu Gott (Evening Hymn) are among his noblest inspira-tions.

Unique and unclassifiable stands his great melody 'Gott erhalte Franz den Kaiser,' one of the most glorious of all national anthems.[1] Students of Haydn's sources in folk melody have unearthed Croat matrices for the tune, and the last line but one is a current melodic formula which occurs repeatedly in both Haydn's and Mozart's earlier works. But a phrase is understood in its context, and Haydn's power and originality are nowhere better illustrated than in the melodic and harmonic preparation by means of which this formula is made the climax of his tune and given the force of revelation. His sketches, preserved in the Vienna National Library, show the self-denial and economy with which he struggled to achieve this seemingly inevitable climax, pruning the earlier and more obviously interesting version of the fifth and sixth lines, which would have anticipated, and so lessened, its over-whelming effect:

Ex. 3.

(a) Draft

(b) Final Version (from Haydn's ms.)

Haydn's masses were criticized, even during his lifetime, for their cheerfulness, and he himself apologized for them by saying that

[1] It is one of history's minor tragedies that the use of the tune in Germany as the melody of *Deutschland über Alles*, has, in the light of recent events, caused Austria to abandon her own great national hymn.

'at the thought of God his heart leapt for joy, and he could not help his music's doing the same.' Many of his contemporaries thought his brother Michael's church music better and more devotional, and he may have agreed with them; he thought highly of Michael's abilities.

None of this should mislead us. Haydn's church music is deeply sincere and essentially religious in character, and no greater mistake could be made than to look upon his or Mozart's masses as frivolous and secular because they are written in an operatic idiom. The operatic idiom was simply the musical language of their time, and neither then nor earlier were music, or life, divided into sacred and secular compartments, as they have been later, to the detriment of both. Bach and Handel freely adapted their secular pieces for their religious works, and in the sixteenth-century polyphonic period, regarded as the golden age of pure church music, the greatest writers—Palestrina, Lassus, Byrd— wrote their masses and motets in the same style as they did their madrigals.

Haydn's religious style is rooted firmly in the seventeenth-century southern German and Austrian tradition (derived in its turn from northern Italy) in which solo voices and choir were contrasted and woven together (like the *concertino* and *ripieno* instruments of a *concerto grosso*) in the course of each number. The Neapolitan 'cantata mass' in which each section of the text is divided into choruses and solo arias (exemplified by Mozart's C minor Mass) is not represented at all in Haydn's work, though he approaches it in the 'Great Organ Mass' of 1766 (Novello 12) and the 'St. Cecilia' Mass of the 1770s (Novello 5), with their florid solo parts. Two of his other early masses—the F major Mass of the 1750s (Novello 11) and the *Missa Sancti Joannis de Deo* or 'Little Organ Mass' of about 1775 (Novello 8)—show the reverse tendency, being drastically telescoped by the procedure, common at the time, though repeatedly forbidden, of setting several clauses of the text simultaneously in different voices. (This device occurs more frequently in the *missa brevis*, written for ordinary use, than in the *missa solemnis*, in which the deliberate ritual of a solemn high mass allows of considerable musical development.)

The 'St. Nicholas' Mass (Novello 7) was written in 1772 for the prince's name-day—6th December. Perhaps it was the approaching Christmas feast that gave this Mass its idyllic mood, akin to the Christmas pastoral cantatas of Alessandro Scarlatti and the 'pastoral symphonies' in *Messiah* and Bach's Christmas Oratorio—in all of which the prevalent classical vogue translates the shepherds of Bethlehem to Arcady. The 'Kyrie' strikes this lyrical note at the outset, and it returns to round off the noble G minor 'Agnus Dei,' as an appropriate setting to the words 'dona nobis pacem':

Ex. 4.

Soprano and Alto Soli

Ky - ri - e   e - lei - son   Ky - ri - e   e - lei-son, e - le - i - son.

The 'St. Cecilia' Mass is a big ceremonial work probably written about 1771 for performance by a Viennese musicians' guild. Less attractive than its successors, it may well serve as an example of the current traditions and the extent to which Mozart's, Haydn's and even Beethoven's masses were not purely personal outpourings but had their roots in contemporary practice. Thus the 'Kyrie' has the solemnly festive character common in almost all masses at this period, and criticized even then, as Einstein points out, on the ground that 'this text is a *textus lamentabilis*'; the defending critic who asked 'May not the communicant be full of devotion even though he be splendidly attired?' might have had the 'Kyrie' of Beethoven's Mass in D prophetically in mind. In the 'Credo,' the florid repetition by the soloist of the words 'credo, credo' before each article of faith is a common device used by Michael Haydn and the youthful Mozart, and again seized upon by Beethoven with heightened intensity. Lastly the 'Dona nobis pacem,' a *presto* movement of the kind frowned on by nineteenth-century critics, is paralleled in the masses of Michael Haydn; the 'Dona' was in fact regarded as being in legitimate contrast to the frequently solemn and minor-mode 'Agnus Dei' and was given something of the note of relaxation of a symphony finale. Even here the heavenly release of tension after the preceding anguish in the 'Agnus Dei' of Beethoven's great Mass had its source in a contemporary custom to which he gave an eternal significance.

The best of Haydn's earlier masses is the 'Mariazell' Mass of 1782 (Novello 15), commissioned as a votive offering by a recently ennobled government official, one Anton Liebe von Kreutzner. Particularly beautiful are its solemn opening and the tenor solo at 'Et incarnatus est'—the choir entering with dramatic power at the 'Crucifixus.' Any one who is seriously disturbed by the knowledge that Handel's 'For unto us a Child is born' was originally an Italian love duet may, however, be permitted to harden his heart against the melting loveliness of the 'Benedictus,' for Haydn has simply adapted for the quartet of soloists an aria from his opera *Il mondo della luna*:

Fourteen years elapsed before Haydn wrote another mass. Prince Nicholas's increasing age and loss of interest may have partly accounted for this, as also the Emperor Joseph II's regulation of 1783 restricting the use of musical instruments in church, which left both Haydn and Mozart (neither of them interested, as Michael Haydn was, in attempting the ancient polyphonic style) without the stimulus of performance. Both emperor and prince died in 1790, but then came the English journeys, and it was not until 1796 that the younger Prince Nicholas's interest in church music set the springs flowing again. That year saw the composition of two masses, the C major *Missa in tempore belli* or 'Kettledrum' Mass

(Novello 2) and the *Heiligmesse* in B flat major (Novello 1), so named because the melody of the traditional hymn 'Heilig, heilig' ('Holy, holy') is used in the inner parts of the 'Sanctus.'

The C major Mass, as Haydn's Latin title implies, was written in time of war; Napoleon's armies were across the Styrian border and were pressing towards Leoben. How closely, in Haydn and Beethoven, stimulus and response were matched, may be seen by comparing the 'Agnus Dei' in this Mass and Beethoven's Mass in D. Here are the same broken interjections, interrupted by the drum-rolls which give the work its nickname, the urgent cry above the trumpet calls, the following entreaty; though in Beethoven's 'Prayer for inward and outward peace' the warfare is also timeless and elemental. The same sense of urgency is felt when the choir breaks in with its repeated 'suscipe' on the tranquil bass (and cello) solo of the 'Qui tollis,' and in the sombre yet tender 'Et incarnatus est' (see below).

This fugal writing, in this and in the *Heiligmesse* alike, is noble and spacious, though in the *Heiligmesse* the solo parts are less closely interwoven with the choir, except in the 'Et incarnatus est' and 'Crucifixus,' in which soloists and chorus, E flat major and E flat minor, alternate with poignant effect.

Ex. 6.

The D minor 'Nelson' or 'Imperial' Mass of 1798 (Novello 3) again draws soloists and choir purposefully together. Contrapuntally, too, this Mass is outstanding, with its grand fugue on 'In gloria Dei Patris,' and its 'Credo,' in which the entire opening section is a canon at the fifth:

The 'Theresa' Mass in B flat major (Novello 16) of the following year (probably named after the Emperor Francis II's consort, another Maria Theresa) is a singularly inspired work, from the noble *adagio* opening of the 'Kyrie' to the powerful G minor— B flat major 'Agnus Dei.' The depth and tenderness of the 'Et incarnatus est' and 'Crucifixus' are particularly moving; so too, in a

different way, is the masterly treatment of the doctrinal clauses on a single theme swinging from voice to voice and from key to key (see p. 131); and the magnificent 'Et vitam venturi' fugue, in which the great theme is restated by the basses beneath a high tonic pedal to form an electrifying climax. And the operatic nature of his idiom is seen to perfection in the exquisite ensemble writing of the G major 'Benedictus.'

The 'Creation' Mass (Novello 4) of 1801, also in B flat, is so called because the 'Qui tollis' quotes the melody of the *allegro* section of Adam and Eve's duet from *The Creation*. Despite fine moments, it is inferior both to its predecessors and to the 'Wind-band' Mass (*Harmoniemesse*) of 1802 (Novello 6), again in B flat. Written at the age of seventy, this is his last large-scale work, and no isolated quotation can do justice to its breadth of design, shown in the radiant 'Kyrie,' which is virtually a great sonata-form slow movement, or to the power of the contrapuntal writing, notably in the 'Benedictus,' and in the 'Gratias' and 'Qui tollis,' bound into one vast section by the recurring cadential figure from which the orchestra weaves, round the slowly moving vocal parts, an elaborate counter-theme, transmuting their opening lyricism into an almost Bach-like majesty and inevitability. Its amazing vigour is tempered by the autumnal serenity of his last years, especially in the 'Agnus Dei,' in which he seems to say 'Hail and farewell' both to Mozart's genius and his own.

Ex. 9.

Lack of space precludes discussion of his smaller church works. The 'Stabat Mater' (1767–8), for all its floridity, is deeply felt and at times highly dramatic. Of his two settings of the

'Te Deum,' both in C major, the first (1764) is a comparatively early work; the second, a fine straightforward piece of choral writing, was composed in 1800.

When, in 1775, Haydn first ventured into the field of oratorio with his *Il ritorno di Tobia,* the vigorous native tradition of the seventeenth and early eighteenth centuries had been broken by the wars and distresses of Maria Theresa's early years on the throne, and by the time the Tonkünstlersocietät revived the form in its public concerts of the 1770s the field lay vacant for the Italians and for such purely Italianate composers as Hasse.[1]   Thus Haydn's *Tobia* is also in the Italian vein and has a mediocre Italian text. It is heavily overloaded with formal *da capo* arias, though there are a few fine ones among them; but almost all the choral numbers are splendid.   One of them has survived in another form—the 'storm' chorus, better known with its Latin text as the offertory *Insanae et vanae curae.*

Haydn's experience with *Tobia* was discouraging, and it was not until he had enjoyed the success of his first attempt to handle an English text—Wolcot's *The Storm,* most effectively set for chorus, soloists and orchestra—that he returned to oratorio.   Even then his first project, the *Invocation of Neptune* cantata, was never completed.   But after his return to Vienna, the clumsy effort of a cleric at Passau to add vocal parts to his *Seven Words* stimulated him to transform the work himself into an oratorio, adding to it an austerely majestic new intermezzo in A minor for wind instru-ments.   This adaptation was most skilfully done, and only the uniformity of mood and tempo imposed upon the music by its origin as a set of meditations for a Good Friday three-hour service prevents this beautiful work from being more frequently performed.

But oratorio—essentially dramatic and rhetorical—had become alien to the spirit of the late eighteenth century, with its deliberate rejection of artificiality and its cult of reason, morality—and nature. How strange and providential, then, that the much-abused libretto

---

[1] Hasse's *Santa Elena al Calvario,* it will be remembered, supplanted *Il ritorno di Tobia* at the Tonkünstlersocietät's concerts in 1781.

of *The Creation*—adapted from Milton's *Paradise Lost*, rejected (it is said) by Handel, translated and remodelled by van Swieten and retranslated by him into English with frequent absurdities—should, by treating of the manifestation of God's glory in nature, provide a meeting-point for Haydn's robust medieval devoutness and the prevailing temper of the age, and so provide what Hans Schnoor calls 'an exceptional example of complete musical interpenetration of the social and the individual *psyche*.'[1]

It is also a magnificent sustained flight of the imagination. The orchestral 'Representation of Chaos' which serves as prelude combines apparent irreconcilables—terseness with spaciousness, a sense of formlessness and lawlessness (produced by purely musical means, distant modulations and the cancelling out of an implied tonality by contradictory harmonies) with a strong inner unity and design. Here his inspiration is indeed working on a Miltonic plane. Equally inspired is the hushed entry of the chorus after the opening recitative, over a slowly pulsating orchestral accompaniment, on the words 'And the Spirit of God moved upon the face of the waters,' and their C major *fortissimo* on the word 'Light'—simplest, most inevitable and most elementally moving of all strokes of genius. But the brightness of the A major of the following number, 'Now vanish before the holy beams,' in relation to C major, and the changes of harmony at the recurring entries of the phrase 'A new-created world,' though more subtle, are no less telling.

The choruses, in which the angelic hosts give praise after each day of creation, all share the brightness and clarity of this first one, partly because of their extreme, and obviously deliberate, harmonic simplicity (making their occasional bursts of colour all the more dramatic) and partly because of the brilliance with which —as in his masses—Haydn used soloists and choir in combination. Particularly lovely examples of this gay and delicate interplay are 'The marv'llous work behold amazed,' for soprano and choir,

[1] Adler, *Handbuch der Musikgeschichte*. See also vol. v of Sir Donald Tovey's *Essays in Musical Analysis* for a full and illuminating discussion of both *The Creation* and *The Seasons*.

and the trio 'Most beautiful appear,' followed without break by the chorus 'The Lord is great,' in which all three soloists participate; but the principle is carried out most majestically in 'The Heavens are telling' and in the great C major duet and chorus near the end, 'By Thee with bliss.'

The narrative and descriptive numbers are entrusted to the soloists (representing the archangels Gabriel, Uriel and Raphael) and orchestra. It would require pages of quotation to show how completely musical, throughout the work as in the prelude, are the means by which each descriptive passage makes its point, drawn with the directness and loving precision of Fra Angelico's flowers or Giotto's ox and ass. Only a profoundly experienced, as well as profoundly inspired, musician could have endowed the recitative 'Be fruitful all' with the shrouded depth and richness suggested by its accompaniment of divided lower strings alone, or conceived the perfect simplicity of the sunrise passage—and chosen the subdominant, with its sense of shadow and withdrawal in relation to the tonic, for the moon's key:

Ex. 10.

(a) **Andante**

Haydn

(b) Più Adagio

With soft - er beams and mild - er___ light steps on the sil - ver

Moon   through si - - - - - - - - - lent night

The Seasons has suffered, by comparison with *The Creation*. both from Haydn's own strictures on it and from the weakening of our musical digestion by comparison with that of an age which could cheerfully swallow two new Beethoven symphonies, his 'Choral Fantasia' and fourth piano Concerto and various vocal items in a single evening. Perhaps, now that the radio has made it possible to broadcast its four self-contained sections in serial form, it will come into its own again. And so it should, for its spontaneous loveliness cuts through van Swieten's stilted adaptation of Thomson's poem to the spirit of the original, with its freshness and fidelity of observation.

In this work soloists and choir are combined as effectively as in *The Creation*, and his choral writing is enriched by a new device, the alternation and contrast of men's and women's voices. Used with poetic effect in the first chorus, 'Come gentle Spring,' it also adds point and colour to the two autumn choruses, 'Hark, the mountains resound' and 'Joyful the liquor flows,' in which Thomson's stag-hunt and inn scene are transplanted from the English countryside to an unmistakably Austrian setting. Here, and in the thunderstorm chorus 'Hark the deep tremendous voice,' Haydn the countryman stands on common ground with the Beethoven of the 'Pastoral' Symphony; while the winter spinning-chorus, 'Let the wheel move gaily,' with its effortless pivoting from D minor to A minor, C major, E minor and back to D minor, and its whirring orchestral accompaniment, points forward through

Schubert to the Wagner of *The Flying Dutchman*. His individual peasants (with whose moralizings he was out of sympathy) are less successful than either his group pictures or the pure nature painting of such numbers as 'Distressful nature fainting sinks' and the enchantingly scored 'O how pleasing to the senses,' from 'Summer,' or the orchestral prelude 'expressing the thick fogs at the approach of winter.' But when the text gives him an opening for nobility he takes it with both hands, as he does in the chorus 'God of Light' that concludes 'Spring' [1] and in the splendid closing numbers of 'Winter,' in which van Swieten's allegorical comparison between winter and man's last end and hope of immortality struck a responsive note in the old man, for whom this work, for all its youthful vitality, was a winter flowering.

[1] As Geiringer points out, this chorus is clearly intended to follow the preceding duet and chorus without break, for only thus can the grand modulation to B flat from the closing D major of the earlier number make its full effect. He also remarks that the idea of a remote modulation at this point was suggested by Van Swieten in a note in the manuscript of his libretto used by Haydn.

CHAPTER XIII

KEYBOARD WORKS

THE distance travelled by Haydn in the course of his creative life could not be more dramatically illustrated than by comparing his last five piano sonatas with his earliest keyboard works—tiny and primitive pieces, called 'partite' in their earliest editions and conforming to the partita or suite type in their uniformity of key throughout all movements. For the most part they are too rudimentary to be interesting, though there are exceptions—the witty finale of No. 14 (11), [1] the minuet of No. 12 (30) in A, with its syncopated trio, and No. 6 (26) in G, in which the trio of the minuet is strikingly chromatic and the pensive G minor *adagio* suggests the ritornello of a Bach aria. In fact they bear the marks of their origin in the blank decades of 1750–1770 and in the mind of a composer a generation older than Mozart, who is still assimilating the influence of the past and of his older contemporaries, chief among them Carl Philipp Emanuel Bach, J. S. Bach's most gifted son.

Born in the same year as Gluck—1714—it was in the 1740s that C. P. E. Bach wrote his first sets of sonatas, which broke upon the young Haydn as a revelation; but his subsequent sets appeared at intervals until as late as 1787, and cannot have failed to influence one who to the end of his life admired him so deeply. From him Haydn took—somewhat uncritically, lacking a virtuoso technique as touchstone—many characteristic features of his keyboard style: repeated notes, profusion of ornament, undulating sextuplet figures; also his massive chordal effects and his vigorous ranging over all five octaves of the contemporary keyboard. It is a style utterly unlike Mozart's (which has the clarity of his

[1] The numbering is that of Van Hoboken's Catalogue, taken over by him from the Breitkopf & Härtel Collected Edition edited by Carl Päsler; the numbering of the second Augener edition (edited by Franklin Taylor and Riemann), which is more accessible, is given in parentheses.

Italian and French models) and at its worst becomes turgid and involved, but at its best it has a noble richness and variety.

But C. P. E. Bach's was not the only influence Haydn assimilated; his Viennese contemporaries, chief among them Wagenseil, provided him with models enough. Their keyboard sonatas, while reducing the number of movements to three or (occasionally) four, retained the minuet—a minuet of a *galant* type which gave rise to Haydn's many *tempo di minuetto* finales. Their harmonies lacked the richness of C. P. E. Bach's, but made great play—especially in their minuets and trios—with the major-minor contrast which, in all the greatest composers of the Viennese school, was to serve such varied ends, from pastoral lyricism to sheer sublimity.

Only the earliest of Haydn's sonatas show, in their crisp answering phrases and their changes of register, the influence of the harpsichord. By the 1760s the pianoforte was beginning to supplant the older instrument, although the harpsichord was still in use as an accompanying instrument in concerted performances. Both Mozart and Haydn expressly mention the *forte-piano* as the instrument on which they played and for which they composed, and it is more of an anachronism to play their mature works on a harpsichord than on a modern concert grand piano. And to hear them—or for that matter any of Beethoven's sonatas—played on a contemporary pianoforte is a beautiful and illuminating experience.

Significantly, it is round about 1767 that Haydn's piano sonatas begin to grow in power and scope; the first movement of No. 19 (22) in D, composed in that year, is more heroic in temper and proportions than any of its predecessors, and the cello-like *cantilena* of its *adagio*, though slightly overlong, speaks with a new accent of noble seriousness, like the superb D flat *adagio* of its neighbour No. 46 (38) in A flat (published in 1789 but dated by Larsen around 1770). They are followed by the C minor Sonata, No. 20 (32). Composed in 1771, it was written in the middle of his period of ferment, and, by a miracle, his technique matches the intensity of his emotion to produce a masterpiece of tragic power. Though he was later to write more highly organized developments than that of the first movement, and weave polyphony far closer than the finale shows, he rarely surpassed the mounting tension of the former, or the inexorable rage with which the last movement, by an inspired structural twist which brings the first subject back a second time in the recapitulation, asserts its sombre tonality and defiant mood to the end. The translucent middle movement in A flat, *andante con moto*, achieves by subtle condensation what the *adagio* of No. 19 attempts—a sonata-form slow movement of perfect proportions.

Six sonatas follow, written in 1773 and dedicated to Prince Nicholas. Two of them, Nos. 21 (33) in C and 23 (13) in F, are elaborate in texture and slight in content, but the delightful No. 22 (10) in E is both simpler technically and warmer emotionally. The last three of the set, Nos. 24 to 26, are not included in current editions of the piano sonatas, and are better known as Nos. 2 to 4 in the Peters edition of his eight violin sonatas, having been published as such in early editions. (The violin sonatas may be dismissed here by explaining that, of the rest, Nos. 5 and 6 were also originally piano sonatas [Nos. 43 and 15], Nos. 7 and 8 are arrangements of the two string quartets in G and F of Op. 77, and the placid No. 1, in G, which appeared in 1794, was originally published as a piano trio.) These three 'violin' sonatas are excellent examples of the contemporary sonata 'with violin accompaniment'; apart from occasional passages where the keyboard subsides into pure accompanying figuration, the absence of the violin would hardly be noticed. Nos. 25 in E flat and 26 in A have fine romantic first movements, rather outweighing the short and mainly contrapuntal movements that follow, but the three-movement No. 24 in D is better balanced; after a sunny opening movement, a dark *adagio* in D minor leads without break into a syncopated *presto* finale, of a peculiar luminous tenderness and grace.[1]

The next set of sonatas, Nos 27–32, appeared in 1776. The *tempo di minuetto* is a feature of this group, appearing three times as middle movement, in Nos. 27, 28 and 32 (9, 34 and 36) and twice as finale, in Nos. 29 and 30 (8 and 35). They are a curiously

[1] The direction *tempo di minuetto* in the violin edition is an error, albeit of early origin, and wholly misleading.

uneven bunch, with No. 32 (36) in B minor standing head and shoulders above the rest. Less tragic than the C minor, there is a sardonic streak in it (which we shall meet again in the quartets), rising to almost demonic rage in the short but pithy development of the first movement, and in the *fortissimo* octaves with which the *presto* finale, with its furious repeated quaver rhythm, storms to its end.

The set published by Artaria in 1780 is dedicated to the sisters Franziska and Marianne Auenbrugger, and consists of Nos. 35–39 (5–7, 21, 12), with the C minor, No. 20, to complete the half-dozen. Their octave passages and ornate *adagio* slow movements gave full scope for the ladies' virtuosity, and the twofold use of the same melodic idea in Nos. 36 and 39 (to which Haydn calls attention in a foreword) must have fascinated them. Unfortunately the idea is not a very inspired one; in No. 39 (12) in G it is the theme of the variation-form first movement and in No. 36 (6) it is the weak *scherzando* middle movement of an otherwise fine work in C sharp minor. Nos. 37 (7) in D and 38 (21) in E flat are both on the same pattern, for in each of them a deeply felt slow movement in the tonic minor leads without break into the finale. The E flat is the stronger work, but its energetic first movement and finely passionate *adagio* outweigh the minuet-finale; the popular D major, with its short and highly original *sarabanda* interposed between two sparkling light-weight movements, has the better proportions.

Of those which appeared in the next few years, easily the best is the E minor, No. 34 (2), published in 1785 or 1786.[1] In the first movement the rhythm of its opening phrases persists almost unbroken, giving it a wonderful unity. The *adagio* in G major is of a florid type Haydn has often essayed less successfully before; but here the elaborate ornamentation is made the servant and medium of a dreamlike poetic quality. No. 44 (4), the two-movement G minor, has a certain pensive charm, though it lacks the power of the E minor. The set of three dedicated to the younger Princess Nicholas Esterházy in 1784, Nos. 40 to 42 (16, 19, 20), are trivial works made for a lady's light relaxation.

[1] Larsen (*Die Haydn-Überlieferung*, p. 301) has corrected the publication date of 1778 given in the Collected Edition.

With the last five sonatas, Nos. 48 to 52, we are in another world. In every one of these his poetic and constructive imagination alike are working at full strength. No. 48 (15) in C was contributed by Haydn to a 'Musikalisches Pot-Pourri' published by Breitkopf & Härtel in 1789. It is a boldly original design in two movements—an *andante con espressione* consisting of alternating major and minor variations on the same lyrical and intricate theme, and a brilliant rondo of the calibre of his late symphony finales. No. 49 (3) is the Sonata in E flat which he started to compose for Marianne von Genzinger in 1788 and completed in the trying and lonely months of 1790 with that slow movement which he told her was 'full of significance.' In this Sonata, as in No. 48, his piano writing has lightened and simplified, possibly under Mozart's influence, though the current Viennese style shows similar features in its clear texture and lavish use of the Alberti bass. Haydn, however, took to the Alberti bass too late in life to make it a mere habit. His use of it is sparing and flexible, lending resilience to a forward-moving theme or romantic urgency to a *cantabile*:

Ex. 11.

(a) SONATA No. 49. 1st Movement

(b) SONATA No. 48 1st Movement
Andante con espressione

The last three sonatas were all written for Therese Jansen, the brilliant pianist whom he met in London on his second visit.[1] If these sonatas reflect Miss Jansen's own style of performance—

[1] Oliver Strunk, in his article 'Notes on a Haydn Autograph' (*Musical Quarterly*, April 1934), argues convincingly that these three sonatas constitute an opus, composed in 1794, the date of No. 52, and that their numerical order should be reversed.

There is a fine article on the E flat Sonata, No. 52, in Sir Donald Tovey's *Essays in Musical Analysis: Chamber Music,* edited by Hubert J. Foss.

as the lyricism of No. 49 probably reflects Marianne von Genzinger's—she must have had a technique of masculine strength,
so well controlled as to be capable at the same time of great delicacy
and warmth. All these qualities are present in the great E flat
Sonata No. 52 (1), in which, despite its compactness, the heroic
massiveness of Haydn's keyboard style, his range of modulation
—the sharp contrast of the E major *adagio* with the E flat of the outer
movements, and the remote excursions of the first movement—and
even such little strokes of genius as the plunge on to the first
inversion of the subdominant near the opening, with its effect
of stepping off into fathomless depths, shows his power to be
'bounded in a nutshell and count himself king of infinite space':

By contrast with the rich variety of the E flat, the D major, No. 51 (18) with its two fiery movements in the same key, is drastic-ally concentrated. Its *presto* finale is built on a curious and original plan—two sections of unequal length, each with repeats written out, the second of which recalls the first after a modulatory passage, but with the same thematic and rhythmic idea persisting without contrast throughout: a kind of resimplification of the sonata-form pattern. The upsurge of its opening figure, its relentless crotchet movement, its ardent and swift-moving harmonic progressions, dramatically illustrate the Haydnishness of Beethoven. The C major No. 50 (23) has three movements, of which the opening *allegro* is austerely monothematic, and the second (a revision of an earlier *adagio* published separately) is hardly warm enough in tone to offset the intellectuality of the first; the finale has the same structure as that of the D major, but the mood here is one of whimsical banter.

Of his other works for solo piano the most remarkable are the Fantasia in C (1789), humorous and bewilderingly free in structure, and the piece which he composed in 1793 and misleadingly called 'Un piccolo divertimento scritto e composto per la stimatissima Signora Ployer.' Barbara Ployer, to whom Mozart dedicated two piano concertos (K. 449 and 453), was still further honoured by this dedication, for the work is no trifle, but the splendid F minor Variations, one of his finest alternating-variation works.

The grouping of Haydn's piano trios with his piano sonatas in a single chapter is not purely arbitrary. Alfred Einstein sums up the position by pointing out that

a work for piano, or for a group of instruments including piano, was . . . usually not taken so seriously as a quartet or quintet for strings. . . . A work for quartet or quintet of strings had four movements, while a piano sonata had only three. A string quartet was for connoisseurs [*Kenner*]; a piano sonata, a sonata for piano and violin, a piano trio or piano quartet, was for amateurs [*Liebhaber*], masculine or feminine. 'For piano and violin,' not 'for violin and piano': the striking fact, from the point of view of the nineteenth or twentieth century, is that in these works the keyboard instrument has the dominant role, and thus is responsible for their lighter character.[1]

---

[1] *Mozart: his Character, his Work*, pp. 238–9.

So it comes about that in these works the cello is still yoked to the bass line of the piano part, and although the violin has more independence, and often carries the melody over a keyboard accompaniment, the action is mainly in the hands of the pianist. Professional performers thus find little to interest them, with the result that the concert-going music-lover is cut off from one of the most beautiful and intimate aspects of Haydn's art.

The piano trios are unique among his works in that they belong almost entirely to the latter part of his life; only four of the thirty-one (Nos. 1, 2, 4 and 5 of Van Hoboken's Catalogue) [1] were written earlier than 1780. Of these, No. 1 in G minor (written before 1769), with its complicated polyphonic texture strongly recalling C. P. E. Bach, is the most interesting. Doubtless it was Prince Nicholas's incessant demand for new baryton works that took up Haydn's energies: he wrote 126 trios for baryton, viola and cello between 1761 and 1775. But by 1780 the prince's advancing age (he was then sixty-six) and Haydn's new connection with Artaria, and later with the English publishers Forster and Bland, led to a new phase of productivity and to the composition of a dozen trios—Nos. 6–17—for his competing customers, before he went to England. The last group, Nos. 15–17, are the pleasant works for piano, flute (or violin) and cello acquired by the importunate Bland in 1789 and 1790. The best of the rest are No. 12 in E minor, with its fiery and closely worked-out opening movement; No. 14 in A flat, in which a beautiful song-like *adagio* in the remote key of E major leads back by an enharmonic modulation from G sharp minor into a witty rondo in the home key, and the group of two-movement trios Nos. 9, 11 and 13. No. 13 in C (minor and major) has a fine set of alternating variations, the major theme being a free derivative of the minor, and in No. 9 in A the florid opening *adagio* shows for once a real interplay between keyboard and strings.

There is no evidence that Haydn composed any new piano music during his first visit to England, and thus his last trios (four sets of three, and two single works) belong, like Therese Jansen's

[1] The numbering of the Peters edition is given for reference in the Catalogue of Works, Appendix B.

sonatas, to his ripest phase of instrumental composition. Like his last four sonatas, too, they are dedicated to women to whom he was bound by ties of professional admiration or personal affection and gratitude.

Therese Jansen (later Mrs. Bartolozzi) received, besides the sonatas, the set of trios Nos. 27–9. No. 27 in C is brilliant and powerful; the first movement is on the grand scale and full of romantic ardour. Like the quieter No. 29 in E flat, it has a delicately lyrical slow movement in a remote key—A major, while that of No. 29 is in B major (enharmonically C flat, the flat sixth)—and an exuberant finale. No. 28 in E, on the other hand, remains soberly in the same tonality, and its mysteriously archaic E minor *allegretto* is a passacaglia in spirit and almost in fact.

In Rebecca Schroeter's set, the G major (No. 25) has a middle movement in a contrasting key, E major (and the famous *rondo all' ongarese* as finale), but the F sharp minor (No. 26) and the D major (No. 24) are single-tonality works. The middle movement of the first has a dreamy magic even without the wonderful scoring which Haydn added when he transposed it down a semitone (and repeated the opening section) to form the *adagio* of the B flat Symphony No. 102 [1]; the finale is a crisp and original *tempo di minuetto*. The D major is, in a way, the most beautiful of all the trios. Others are more immediately impressive, but this work is irradiated by that sunset calm that is so peculiarly his, pervading the fine monothematic first movement, clouding over in the D minor *andante* and, as this leads without break into the finale, *allegro ma dolce*, shining out again with the tenderest poetry.

His kind friend and champion, the younger Princess Nicholas Esterházy, received Nos. 21–23, of which No. 23 in D (minor and major) is an excellent double-variation work. To another Esterházy princess, the widow of the short-lived Prince Anton, he dedicated Nos. 18–20, of which No. 19 is the best, with its subtly chromatic double variations and exquisite *adagio* middle movement.

The Trio in E flat minor (No. 31) is dedicated to the gifted

[1] It is not certain which is the original version, but this is the view taken by Tovey and Larsen.

HAYDN'S SILHOUETTE
By Lavater

MEDALLION
By N. Gatteaux, Paris, 1800

young pianist Magdalene von Kurzböck, whose visits and whose playing cheered him in his last years.[1]   The first movement, again a set of alternating variations, is unusual in that the two major 'variations' have different themes, and are thus more like rondo episodes; but the first is a fine free variant of the minor theme, reversing the rise and fall of its opening figure and making play with its rhythm:

Ex. 13.

His last trio of all, No. 30 in E flat, bears no dedication.   A certain gravity of mood pervades its finely built first movement and its solemn *andante con moto* in C major.   A wonderful bridge passage leads back, through A flat and C minor, to the original tonic and the impetuous *presto* finale—another of those movements which show that Count Waldstein's injunction to the youthful Beethoven to 'receive the spirit of Mozart at the hands of Haydn' was wide of the mark.   The spirit of Mozart was incommunicable; what Beethoven did receive was Haydn's own.

[1] In 1803 the younger Prince Nicholas, then on a diplomatic mission to France, repeatedly importuned him to compose a sonata for the wife of one of Napoleon's generals, Mme Moreau.   But his energies were not equal to the task and he resorted to the subterfuge of sending this work, arranged as a solo sonata, with a dedication to Mme Moreau.

CHAPTER XIV

CHAMBER MUSIC FOR STRINGS

IT is wholly in keeping with the air of paradox and contradiction
that surrounds Haydn's works that while his quartets are rightly
regarded as one of the highest achievements of chamber music,
his first essays in this field were probably not designed as chamber
music at all, but, like his symphonies, seeded themselves out of
doors; while the earliest chamber music which he definitely wrote
as such is for the most part forgotten.

The twenty-one string trios which he lists in his catalogue
belong to this category, for Geiringer, who dates most of them
around 1750, considers that their style takes the presence of the
continuo player for granted; like his earliest piano sonatas, they are
very rudimentary. In this class also must be reckoned his 126
trios for baryton, viola and cello, dating from 1761 to about 1775,
and written for an instrument capable of producing charming
sound effects with its gamba-like tone and plucked metal strings
behind the finger-board, but so complicated that its technical and
expressive range alike were limited. Oliver Strunk, in his article
on Haydn's baryton trios, [1] stresses their importance as a laboratory
for Haydn's forms and procedures during his great maturing
period. A number of them were published during his lifetime
and have since appeared in modern editions as string or flute
trios; one or two of them—notably No. 96 of Haydn's thematic
list, in G minor, and the beautiful No. 74 in D—transcend mere
tunefulness and are among his finest inspirations. [2]

---

[1] 'Haydn's Divertimenti for Baryton, Viola and Bass' (*Musical Quarterly*,
April 1932). Mr. Strunk points out that the instrument's range of
practicable keys—despite Haydn's struggles to prove the contrary—was
in fact very limited.

[2] The baryton trios constitute Series XIV of the Complete Edition

For England, where the flute was highly popular with amateurs including Haydn's patron and friend, Lord Abingdon, he wrote, besides his three keyboard trios, six trios for two flutes (or flute and violin) and cello in 1784, and another set in 1794 for the same combination, comprising three trios and a separate *Allegro* in G. The two flutes combine surprisingly well with the cello and these little pieces sound very engaging.[1]

The six duo sonatas for violin and viola, written early in the 1770s, are disappointing in that the viola is used mainly as an accompanying instrument, with little regard for its individuality; but they contain some fine musical material.

It is a despairing task to attempt to do justice to Haydn's string quartets in a single short chapter; the reader should turn to Sir Donald Tovey's great article in Cobbett's *Cyclopedic Survey of Chamber Music*, where the subject is treated with a breadth and penetration to match its importance. It is equally impossible to date Haydn's first quartets with any certainty.[2] Both 1750 and 1755 have been claimed as the date of his first quartet—the earlier date by his friend Griesinger. The association with Count Fürnberg and Schloss Weinzierl, where—also according to Griesinger

---

published by the Joseph Haydn Institute, Cologne; three volumes, containing Nos. 25–96, have appeared at the time of writing. Other modern editions are listed by Van Hoboken under the trio in question.

[1] Of the 1784 set, one consists of movements from Baryton Trio, XI. 97, while in three others Haydn draws freely on the music of *Il mondo della luna*.

[2] Even the sacrosanct number 'Haydn's 83' is something of a myth, for *The Seven Words* were originally orchestral works (though arranged for string quartet by Haydn himself), Op. 1 No. 5 was originally a symphony and Op. 2 Nos. 3 and 5 were originally sextets with two horns; while the little work in E flat listed in Haydn's Thematic Catalogue as No. 6 of the *Divertimenti auf verschiedene Instrumenten* appeared as No. 1 in a number of early editions of Op. 1. It was edited, with a preface claiming it as the original 'Op. 1 No. 1,' by Marion Scott (Oxford University Press, 1931). Van Hoboken, however, continues to list it as a divertimento.

—the first quartet originated, can hardly have begun before the later date. But the fact that the first thirteen quartets (the twelve of Op. 1 and Op. 2, and the E flat Quartet edited by Marion Scott) are all virtually divertimenti should warn us against attempting a wisdom after the event natural in Haydn's first biographers, but unhistorical in the light of our own scholarly uncertainty as to the origin of string quartets in general and Haydn's in particular. Perhaps it could be tentatively said that, while Haydn definitely and consciously wrote *quadri* for the quartet party at Weinzierl, he had almost certainly, in the previous years, written for stringed instruments—four or five—without continuo. 'Without continuo'— that is the key to the origin of the string quartet as we know it, and the door which that key unlocks leads us once again out into Vienna's streets and courtyards where, away from the salon with its inevitable harpsichord, a bunch of struggling young players are trying over a set of little movements written for them by one of their number to perform under a lady's window.[1] Again and again, listening to Haydn's first dozen quartets, the impression becomes overwhelming: this is open-air music for four players thought of as a tiny string orchestra. The absence of that complex interplay of melodic figures between all instruments that is essential to the developed quartet style, and the actual simplicity of the string writing—with the significant exception of the florid *adagio* movements in which the first violin declaims and sings like an operatic soprano or a concerto soloist above the repeated chords of the lower strings—point in that direction. So, too, does his habit— for which he was promptly criticized by the purists—of octave doubling between first and second violins, viola and cello, producing a bold and highly effective two-part harmony obviously

[1] Griesinger's statement that 'in the evenings Haydn often "went *gassatim*" [i. e. went out to play in the narrow lanes—*Gassen*—of the city] with his fellow musicians; on these occasions some work of his was usually performed, and he remembered having written a quintet for this purpose about 1753' is significant. The quintet is the Divertimento *a cinque*, No. 2 of his list of 'Divertimenti auf Verschiedene Instrumenten' in his thematic catalogue.

designed to sound well in the open. Here is an instance of this device: [1]

Ex. 14.
Op. 1. No. 1. 4th Movement

It was, like so many of his earliest habits, to remain with him to the end, but sublimated into the exquisitely pure two-part writing that appears at intervals in his later quartets, and finally, and most nobly, in the *andante* of his last complete Quartet, Op. 77 No. 2.

Certainly it was in this school that Haydn gained that insight into the potentialities of stringed instruments, and that sureness of touch in handling them, that was his throughout his life. Slight and undeveloped as these first quartets are, sometimes ill shaped and often conventional and trivial—especially in the long-winded slow movements—they have a knack of sounding far better in perform-ance than they look on paper, and the best of them can still charm the listener, and surprise the score-reader, by their melodic freshness and the delight of their sheer sound.

Haydn's early opus numbers, it should be pointed out, are purely publisher's artefacts, not deliberate groupings by the com-poser, and in the case of the quartets all they indicate is the order of publication of the different sets. The quartets of Op. 3, in Geiringer's opinion, originated in the middle 1760s. They represent a step away from the divertimento in that four of them are four-movement works with only one minuet apiece.[2] As in the

---

[1] It also occurs—modified with characteristic subtlety—in the minuet of that most familiar of all serenades—Mozart's *Eine kleine Nachtmusik*.

[2] Of the other two quartets of Op. 3, No. 2, with its opening variations, is in three movements and No. 4 is an odd work consisting of two

quartets of Op. 1 and Op. 2—and in his early symphonies—the minuets are the most attractive feature; that of Op. 3 No. 3 is the famous *Dudelsack* (bagpipe) minuet, but that of Op. 3 No. 6, with its answering *pizzicato* and *arco* phrases, is just as captivating. But there are two slow movements of a type different from those of the earlier works, *andante* in tempo and with new tone-colours: mutes and a *pizzicato* accompaniment. One is the inescapable 'Serenade' of Op. 3 No. 5, the other (with slightly different scoring) is the little-known, but equally charming *andantino grazioso* of Op. 3 No. 1:

Ex. 15. **Andantino grazioso**

Traces of real thematic development appear in the first movements of these two quartets, and in the finales of Nos. 3, 5 and 6 Haydn's ingrained fun writes *scherzando* not only at the head of the score but all through the music.

With Op. 9 and Op. 17 we are on surer ground chronologically: Op. 9 appeared in 1769 and Op. 17 was composed in 1771. In the few years separating them from Op. 3 the spring that was to release the full force of his genius had been touched, and here too a transformation has taken place: these works have become unmistakably string quartets. For most of their length it would be unthinkable to play them with more than one instrument to a part, and it is significant that eight of the ten normal first movements

movements in different keys, B flat and E flat, which do not appear to belong together at all. Perhaps the publisher put together two isolated movements to complete the set.

(the other two are sets of variations) are marked *moderato*; a deliberate tempo is necessary to allow for the more elaborate part-writing, especially in the lower strings.

The neglect of these two sets may be due to the fact that in technique they are still in a sense adolescent, lacking both the serenading simplicity of the earlier sets and the mature richness of their successors. Despite this there are some lovely works among them, notably the two minor numbers, the D minor Op. 9 No. 4 and the C minor Op. 17 No. 4. Both are finely ardent works, bearing the unmistakable stress of his inner conflagration, but bearing it more successfully than the symphonies of the same years. A quotation from the first movement of the D minor will show its affinity with his G minor Symphony No. 39 (and with the Mozart of K. 550):

Ex. 16.

The rising third with which the C minor opens is used—in a manner anticipating his later practices—to pivot on to different triads and into different keys:

1. Beginning of Movement

2. Beginning of Development

More significant is his attempt to assimilate contrapuntal texture in the finales of both works. The entire absence of the complexities of 'learned' polyphony, so integral a part of the older chamber music, from his earlier quartets, is another indication of their possible outdoor origin. But now Haydn clearly feels an irresistible urge to conquer this resource for his quartet style; to such an extent that, although these two finales are fairly successful essays in a combined polyphonic and homophonic style, he abandons that fruitful line in his next set, Op. 20, in order to write four out of their six finales as pure fugues.

That belongs to 1772, Haydn's *annus mirabilis*, and is indeed its crowning achievement. Here, as in no other field, he had attained a technical maturity fully equal to the pressure of his inspiration. Everything that his later works were to bring to fruition is here, not merely in embryo but breaking into flower; even the thematic development regarded as being the special achievement of the Op. 33 quartets, and the essence of the 'new and special manner' in which Haydn declared they were written, is present in the Op. 20

quartets, not so highly evolved as in the best of Op. 33, but the same in principle. The following passage from the development of Op. 20 No. 4 in D, starting with the *fausse reprise* of the first subject, shows it, simply but perfectly clearly:

Ex. 18. **(Allegro di molto)**

The emotional intensity and variety of the Op. 20 set is extraordinary. If Mozart at seventeen was attracted by its four fugal finales, the fierce desolation of the minuet of the G minor, No. 3, must also have found its echo in the darker recesses of his young heart:

Ex. 19.

so, too, must the restless opening of the F minor, No. 5, the pathos
of its A flat major 'second subject' on its return in the tonic minor
(as quoted below) and the strange progressions of the coda based
upon it:

Ex. 19 a

But the four major-mode quartets, too, are all distinct and well-rounded personalities: the sweet and sunny No. 6 in A; No. 4 in D, a many-sided character, serious in its first movement, an elegiac poet in its D minor variations, and exuberantly exotic in its minuet (*allegretto alla zingarese*) and finale; No. 2 in C, rich alike in subject-matter and scoring, spacious and dramatic (especially in its powerful C minor *adagio*, full of the spirit of *opera seria*, the C major of the minuet breaking like a shaft of light from its solemn closing chords); and No. 1 in E flat, whose quietness has the still depth of a Constable landscape. A single quotation will show something of the quality of the incomparable slow movement, *affettuoso e sostenuto*[1] and illustrate his capacity (pointed out by Marion Scott in a broadcast lecture) for laying out his string parts in such a way as to combine the utmost richness with the utmost clarity of sound:

Ex. 20.

---

[1] The direction *sostenuto*, rather than the 3–8 time signature, indicates both the spirit and the tempo of one of the most flawlessly integrated sonata-form slow movements ever written.

After a nine years' gap, the Op. 33 quartets appeared in 1781, heralded by a circular letter to subscribers in which Haydn stated that they were written 'in an entirely new and special manner.' Larsen is surely right in suggesting that this is a selling-point rather than an aesthetic pronouncement. But the hard work of the intervening years had undoubtedly given Haydn a greater mastery of the potentialities of thematic development, and the fugal element is no longer an isolated feature, but has passed into the growing fluency and felicity of the part-writing.

The star of the set is the 'Bird' Quartet, No. 3 in C, which has everything that a lyric comedy should have—lightness and gaiety, just the right amount of emotional contrast, and a technical sureness and poise in which the delicate harmonic changes in the recapitulation of the first movement, and the cross-rhythms in the *adagio*, are entirely effortless and natural. But Haydn is a complete human being, and the works of his sombre and ironic vein, such as the B minor quartet, No. 1 of the set, though rarer, are no less characteristic. Its first movement, minuet (*scherzando*) and finale share the astringency of the piano sonata in the same key written a few years earlier, and its *andante* has a pungent and witty chromaticism that must have delighted Mozart. The first movement of the E flat, No. 2, reflects yet another Haydn, the quiet and profound artist of Op. 20 No. 1; the spirit is the same, though the skill is perfected, as may be seen in the fragment on p. 162 from the complex thematic pattern of the development. The *largo sostenuto* of the same quartet is one of those movements in which the sturdy two-part writing of his youth is transmuted into an art of undreamed-of beauty and refinement. Nos. 4–6 are lighter in weight, but full of adventure, the recapitulations of the first movements of both No. 5 and No. 6 flying off at harmonic tangents and completely changing their contours in the process.

The sense of controlled power which the successful achievement of Op. 33 brought must have been very pleasant, and Haydn used it to produce nineteen works before his first journey to England —the mysteriously laconic single Quartet in D minor, Op. 42, in 1785, the six of Op. 50 for the King of Prussia in 1786, and,

Ex. 21

Allegro moderato cantabile

between 1787 and 1790, the twelve of Op. 54 and 55 (three in each set) and Op. 64, for that enigmatic and ubiquitous person, Johann Tost—in all of which we feel him well within his powers and on the whole free from intense emotional strain. In each half-dozen he includes one work in the minor mode. In the F sharp minor, Op. 50 No. 4, the finely worked-out first movement has a major

ending, but its closing fugue is uncompromisingly tragic; in Op.
55 No. 2 in F minor (the 'Razor') the opening set of minor-
major variations is followed by a prickly monothematic sonata-
form *allegro* in F minor; but it ends in the major, and the finale
is pure hilarity. The powerful opening movement of Op. 64
No. 2 in B minor, like its companion piece, Op. 33 No. 1,
starts ambiguously with a theme that might be major or
minor, but keeps its stormy mood to the end, thus throwing
into greater contrast the cloudless B major of the *adagio*; the
whimsical finale yields at last to good temper and the major mode.

Throughout these sets one is aware of experiment in so far as he
is trying out new types of movement that are beginning to appear
in his symphonies. The extraordinary freedom of his London
symphonies in the recapitulations of their sonata-form movements
already shows itself in many of these works, from the extreme
condensation of both first movement and finale of the immacu-
lately monothematic little Op. 50 No. 3 to the spaciousness of
Op. 64 No. 5 (the 'Lark'), in the first movement of which the
recapitulation restates the opening theme twice, with bland
disregard for the conventions and glorious effect. In the slow
movements he begins to abandon sonata form (of which the only
full-fledged example is the beautiful D minor *adagio* of Op. 50
No. 6) in favour of variations, straight or alternating, and a new
simple A B A type of *adagio*, usually major with a middle episode
in the minor, in which everything is focused on sheer melodic
beauty; the most perfect examples are the slow movements of Op.
64 Nos. 5 and 6, and the strange C minor *adagio* of Op. 54
No. 2, with its stabbing dissonances. His finales also are moving
towards the London symphony type; those of Op. 50 No. 1 and
Op. 64 No. 6 are brilliant examples of his late sonata rondos,
and so is that of Op. 55 No. 1, which has the characteristic feature
of a fugato on the second entry of the main theme.

A concentrated study of these quartets brings, indeed, an overwhelming impression of Haydn's superb mastery as a contra-
puntist. It is not simply in his more obvious *tours de force*, of
which the following, from the first movement of Op. 50 No. 2, is
only one out of many possible instances:

The part-writing throughout has a definition and purity of line all the more remarkable in movements such as the jewel-like *andante più tosto allegretto* of Op. 50 No. 3 (opening with a perfect specimen of his two-part harmony) in which it is implicit and unobtrusive.

The first English visit intervened between these quartets and the half-dozen he wrote in 1793 for Count Apponyi, Opp. 71 and 74, and it was not until after his final return home that he wrote his last eight complete quartets—Op. 76, dedicated to Count Erdödy, which appeared in 1799, and the two quartets of Op. 77 (all he managed to compose of a projected set of six for Prince Lobkowitz), written in the same year.

Count Apponyi's quartets all have the distinguishing feature of a short introduction—a single tonic chord in Op. 71 No. 3, cadential formulae in Op. 71 No. 1 and Op. 74, more extended preludes in the remaining three. Op. 71 No. 2, in D, after its four-bar *adagio*, breaks into a leaping and angular *allegro* in which he seems to be aiming at that almost orchestral sonority of tone which he attains at last, fully within the limits of true quartet writing, in his two great C major quartets: Op. 74 No. 1 in this series (in which the high quality of his themes is matched by that of their contrapuntal treatment) and, in the next set, the 'Emperor' Quartet, Op. 76 No. 3. Of the rest, Op. 71 No. 1 in B flat has an *andante* with Mozartian inflexions but a purely Haydnish repose and gentleness, and the first movement of Op. 71 No. 3 in E flat is as finely serious as its *andante* variations are sparkling. Op. 74 No. 2, in F, is pure and perfect comedy from start to finish; No. 3 in G minor (the 'Rider') has a wild *élan* that lands it up in the major mode both in first movement and finale, but its wonderful E major *largo* is one of Haydn's most solemn utterances. It is matched by the great *adagio sostenuto* of the G major Quartet Op. 76 No. 1. In this work the driving, furious finale, like that of the 'Rider,' begins in G minor; but this is more remarkable in a major-mode work, and is an experiment which he only repeats once, in the noble finale of the 'Emperor' Quartet.[1]

Op. 76 also has its minor-mode work, No. 2 in D minor, its fiery first movement pervaded by the dropping fifth with which it opens. In the third movement he reverts to the octave-doubling of his youth, but this time to produce a masterpiece of weird effectiveness, the famous canonic 'Witches' Minuet.' No. 3 receives its nickname from its variations on his Emperor's Hymn; in these he is content to let his melody speak for itself, merely surrounding it with an aura of accompanying figuration and, in the last variation, treating it chorale-wise, with harmonies that Bach would have been proud to have written. The work as a whole has a symphonic massiveness which makes the wonderful

---

[1] He had tried it once before, in the curious finale of the D major Symphony No. 70 (1779).

opening of Op. 76 No. 4 in B flat (the 'Sunrise') seem the more ethereal by contrast. The grave and heart-searching slow movement of this work is a miracle of subtly condensed sonata-form construction, and the *stretto* on the main theme, near the end, shows to perfection the heightening of emotional intensity by a technical device:

Ex. 23.

The unusual *allegretto* first movement of Op. 76 No. 5 in D is, in fact if not in name, a set of very free variations. Nothing could be more unconventional, or more radiantly beautiful. An equal but more unearthly radiance pervades the F sharp major *largo, cantabile e mesto*; but Haydn comes back to earth in the last movement, which is the apotheosis of all his Croatian-type finales. Variations, spare and contrapuntal, constitute the first movement of No. 6 in E flat and—in effect—its magical trio, all ascending and descending scales.

Of the two great works of Op. 77, the first movement of No. 1 in G major has perhaps more richness of tone and freedom of form, and the modulations of the fathomlessly profound *adagio* in E flat range to the extremes of the harmonic universe. But the diversity of scoring in the crystalline first movement of the F major is as remarkable as the unity of its structure: compare the opening theme, quoted below, with its modified appearance as 'second subject' veiled by a beautiful and dark-toned counter-melody.

The second movement, *presto ma non troppo*, is a pure one-in-a-bar

Ex. 24.

scherzo, with a trio in D flat glowing tenderly in contrast. The
D major *andante*, opening with a magnificent piece of two-part
writing, seems to gather up all his *andante* and *allegretto* movements
in a piece of strange power, turning their light step into a measured
tread, unswerving and inevitable as that of time itself. The finale
gloriously releases the tension—for sheer brilliance in the treatment
of the thematic material there is nothing to choose between it
and that of the G major.

The last, unfinished quartet consists of two movements, an
andante grazioso in B flat and a Minuet in D minor; we may assume

Ex. 25.

that D, major or minor, would have been the key of the work. The *andante* has a touching and valedictory calm, but the passion and ardour of the minuet seem to rekindle the fires of the 1770s, with a mastery then unknown; the rising chromatic figure in the passage quoted on p. 168 raises the pressure to an almost unexampled pitch. Listening to this minuet, it is almost possible to believe that in the old man sitting stiffly in his chair, tormented by the music that he could no longer write, as truly as in Schubert's early grave, music had buried 'a rich treasure, but still fairer hopes.'

CHAPTER XV

SYMPHONIES AND OTHER ORCHESTRAL WORKS

HAYDN was a methodical man, and as early as 1765 he began to draft a thematic catalogue of his works with the help of Prince Esterházy's copyist Joseph Elssler. But even with Elssler's co-operation he was too busy to keep it up consistently, and after 1777 few entries were made. And when, in 1805, his faithful factotum Johann Elssler (the elder Elssler's son) helped him to put his affairs in order by drawing up the 'Verzeichniss aller derjenigen Compositionen welche ich mich beyläufig erinnere von meinem 18ten bis in das 73ste Jahr verfertiget zu haben' ('List of all the compositions which I approximately remember having completed from my 18th until my 73rd year'), his memory was erratic, and the list has many omissions.

This would not have mattered unduly if the musical scholarship of later generations had been quicker in producing the usual collected edition of his works, or even a complete thematic catalogue of them, as Köchel did for Mozart. But successive projects for a collected edition broke down, with the result that for many years great tracts of his output were only available in specialist libraries, or lay forgotten in private collections. Thus, although to countless students Haydn has been held up as 'the father of the symphony,' it has been impossible for them to survey all his known symphonies from start to finish, let alone examine the vast corpus of his lesser instrumental works.

Two publications, however, marked the beginning of a new epoch in the study of Haydn's instrumental music. In 1957 appeared Volume I of Anthony Van Hoboken's Thematic Catalogue, with its systematic grouping of Haydn's instrumental works. And two years earlier H. C. Robbins Landon, in his *The Symphonies of Joseph Haydn*, gave us for the first time a complete study of Haydn's symphonic development. This great and many-sided book, with its important section on Haydn's symphonies in performance, is of inestimable value alike to the student and the practical musician, and throws fresh light not only on the symphonies themselves but on the gradual emergence of Haydn's symphonic style from the unmapped hinterland of small concerted instrumental works for which 'divertimento' is a convenient heading.

The term 'divertimento' was, as we know, a peculiarly elastic one. Haydn himself applied it to anything and everything— piano solos, baryton trios, string quartets and concerted works for any number of instruments. The use of the term is here confined to his numerous little works in four to six movements, for wind instruments or combinations of strings and wind,[1] indiscriminately labelled 'divertimento,' 'cassation,' 'scherzando,' 'notturno' or even 'concertante.' Most of these small works are no more than pleasant, but they form the matrix from which his mature symphonic style developed; and, as we shall see, the *concertante* element in his technique was one which he never abandoned.

The most important of these works are the six *Divertissements à huit parties concertantes*, written about 1775, and the eight *Notturni* which Haydn composed in 1790 for King Ferdinand of Naples. Of the earlier set, five were originally scored for baryton, two horns and strings, the flute replacing the baryton in the published version; they are in three movements and contain some splendid music, notably the passionate Adagios of Nos. 1 and 2. The *Notturni* originally contained parts for King Ferdinand's instrument, the *lira organizzata*, which, for all its imposing name, is simply a variant of the peasant hurdy-gurdy, a kind of mechanical fiddle. While in London Haydn re-scored them for Salomon, replacing the two *lire* by a flute and oboe (or two flutes). In the *Notturni*, Haydn's last works of the divertimento type, the distinction between symphony and divertimento is now complete.

---

[1] Of the works in this category formerly accepted as by Haydn, the six *Feldpartiten* for wind instruments, one of which contains the famous *Chorale St. Antoni* immortalized by Brahms, are now regarded as of doubtful authenticity; they are possibly by Ignaz Pleyel. The 'Toy Symphony' is now thought to be by either Leopold Mozart or Michael Haydn (Landon, *The Symphonies of Joseph Haydn*, Appendix II, No. 26).

For all their close construction they are on a far smaller scale than the symphonies of the same period, and their scoring is of a translucent, chamber-music texture.

It was the practical circumstances of his life, and his own lack of technical virtuosity, which reduced Haydn's contribution in the field of the concerto to such small proportions. Even the best-known of his five keyboard concertos, the D major (1784), is not outstanding, and neither are his violin concertos.[1] His horn Concerto in D (1762) deserves an occasional performance. As for the cello Concerto in D (1783), Haydn's most familiar concerto for that instrument,[2] Larsen had successfully championed its authenticity against an earlier attempt to attribute it to Haydn's pupil Anton Kraft, even before the rediscovery of Haydn's autograph, and although it is not one of his major works, it has a sweetness and dignity, and in the last movement a nursery-rhyme fun, that are characteristic enough.

Two concertos belong to his latest period — the *Sinfonia concertante* in B flat, for violin, cello, oboe and bassoon, and the trumpet Concerto in E flat. The former, written in London in 1792, is a friendly and gracious if not a great work, in which the four soloists are treated as a *concertino* rather than as individual virtuosi. The delightfully gay trumpet Concerto in E flat was written in 1796 for the court trumpeter Anton Weidinger and his experimental E flat keyed trumpet, soon superseded by the valve trumpet which he finally evolved in 1801. The solo part is there-

---

[1] In order to avoid discussion of unsolved problems, only those concertos are enumerated which are quoted by Haydn himself in his thematic list (with the exception of the D major piano Concerto, not listed by him but generally accepted as authentic). Two concertos sometimes attributed to Haydn are now regarded as spurious: the flute Concerto, which is definitely by Leopold Hoffmann, and the oboe Concerto, for the authenticity of which there is no satisfactory evidence. The second of the horn Concertos in D edited by Mandyczewski (and singly by Pottag) is doubtful, though Geiringer believes it may be genuine.

[2] The lost Concerto in C was rediscovered in Prague by H. C. Robbins Landon in 1962.

fore not confined to the natural notes, but is chromatic in all registers of the instrument.

The original orchestral version of *The Seven Words of Our Saviour on the Cross* was commissioned in 1785 to provide interludes between the sermons of a Good Friday three-hour service at Cadiz Cathedral. By his own admission Haydn found that 'the task of writing seven *adagios*, each of which was to last about ten minutes, to preserve a connection between them without wearying the hearers, was none of the lightest.' The deep devotion, and the noble variety of melody and expression in these pieces, show how finely he succeeded; but 'seven *adagios*' on end (eight, including the superb D minor introduction) do not suit the average concert programme, and so the work is rarely given in its original form. Fortunately it is sometimes performed in the string quartet version which appeared shortly afterwards, and is profoundly rewarding to players and listeners willing to attune themselves to its deliberate pace and its mood of sustained and loving meditation.

Turning now to his symphonies, the first impression is one of amazement at the gulf separating his first efforts, so crude and elementary, from the richness and mastery of the latest works. Closer examination, however, reveals no gulf, but an unbroken continuity, formed by the early emergence and steady persistence of Haydn's most characteristic traits. So, from the very outset, counterpoint exerts its magnetism. The finales of four of his first fourteen symphonies are polyphonic in texture: that of No. 40 (the recently discovered autograph dates it in 1763, between Nos. 13 and 14) is a full-blown fugue, and that of No. 13 is a gallant attempt to bring off a fugal movement in sonata form on the contrapuntists' tag which was to serve Mozart, twenty-five years later, in one of his greatest polyphonic triumphs—the finale of the great C major Symphony (K. 551). His bent towards odd phrase-lengths shows itself even earlier: in the finale of No. 1 with its six-bar opening, in the three-bar phrases of the minuet of No. 9 and the trio of No. 13—all of which show, in crude and sprawling form, his inherent melodic spaciousness—and the seven-bar phrases of the *andante più tosto allegretto* of No. 40—another delightful piece of two-part harmony:

repeated with
Violins and Violas
an octave lower

So, too, in his very first phase, he shows his tendency to construct
sonata-form works on a single theme and to modify his recapitulations—a tendency seen in such contrasting types as the second
movement of No. 11, a fine monothematic *allegro* in polyphonic
style, and the first movement of No. 8, a *galant* movement of
slight achievement but prophetic potentialities.

This symphony is the last of the set of three entitled 'Le Matin,'
'Le Midi' and 'Le Soir,' Nos. 6–8, which Haydn wrote in
1761, a few months after his appointment, at the behest of Prince
Paul Anton Esterházy. They are on a larger scale, and more
richly scored, than their predecessors, and are clearly designed
to show off the orchestra's paces—and incidentally those of its new
Vice-*Kapellmeister*. Of the three, No. 7 in C, the five-movement
'Le Midi,' is the most immediately impressive, with its stately slow
introduction and its strange and imaginative second movement
in C minor, entitled *Recitativo* because of its eloquent recitative
passages for solo violin; but the following *adagio*, for all its charming
scoring, is entirely conventional, and the colour effects and gay
bustle of the outer movements cannot disguise their lack of real
thematic development. It is No. 8 in G, 'Le Soir,' a less satisfactory work in itself, which holds the key to the future, for in the
first movement the composite 'second subject' opens with a

derivative of the main theme, there is a real attempt to develop it, and the recapitulation, sharply modified, by-passes this derivative by way of a sudden plunge on to E flat, the flat sixth of the key. And while the minuets of all three symphonies are their best movements, that of No. 8 breaks away from the courtly dignity of the first two, and in its nimbler movement and fresh melody we hear for the first time Haydn's friendly and familiar country accents.

This early triptych does in fact canalize many of the springs from which Haydn drew: the *galant* style; the opera, which offered him overture, aria, recitative and its amusing Neapolitan *buffo* finales; the symphonies of his Viennese forerunners, whose first movements gave him that well-defined dualism of key and subject-matter which he soon began to worry into different shapes; the *concerto grosso* with its interplay of *concertante* and *ripieno* instruments; and the serenades of his youth, often played by such small groups that each player was a soloist. In the twenty odd symphonies which followed in the next few years—a few, such as Nos. 11, 13, 40 and 22 ('Der Philosoph'), still capable of giving real delight in performance, but many of them elementary and conventional— we see him finding out, by laborious trial and error, what to use and what to reject of these diverse elements. Recitative he discards, except for occasional special effects;[1] the display aria he uses and outgrows—the symphony is not the place for exhibitions of sustained virtuosity by single instruments. The occasional *concertante* use of solo instruments, however, runs like a continuous thread throughout Haydn's work: witness the cello solo in the trio of Symphony No. 95 and the solo violin entries in three of the first London symphonies (95, 96 and 98) and in the *andante* of No. 103 (the 'Drum-roll'). And the speed, eventfulness and humour of the *buffo* finale were completely congenial to him, and on to them he grafted the alternating *forte* and *piano* of *galanterie* (originally

[1] His use of it in Symphony No. 7, in the *adagio* of the Quartet, Op. 17 No. 5, and in the introduction to the finale of the *Sinfonia Concertante* points to the source of Beethoven's far more pregnant and purposeful use of the same device at the opening of the finale of the ninth Symphony— historically, the opera, temperamentally, the sense of drama common to both composers.

intended—as many of his inferior early slow movements show—
for the expression of modishly delicate susceptibilities, but diverted
by him to the perpetration of explosive practical jokes), and also
its scrappy little phrases, which lend themselves admirably to
instrumental fooling of the kind carried to perfection in his best
finales, from early to late.

These tendencies find expression in the piquant finale of Symphony No. 35 in B flat (1767):

In this elegant little work Haydn shows that he has at last learned
to speak the language of comedy with skill and fluency, and use
it to express his own thoughts as well.

But now, suddenly, comes the language of tragedy. Save for a
premonitory shiver in the opening *adagio* of No. 34, there is nothing
in his earlier work to parallel the sombre intensity of utterance
found in the D minor Symphony, No. 26 ('Lamentatione'), or
the F minor, No. 49 ('La Passione'), of 1768. Both are Passion-
tide symphonies, No. 26 containing actual quotations of the
plainsong melodies of the Holy Week Liturgy.[1] The F minor
contains no direct quotation, but its unrelieved sorrow, and
its key (always, for Haydn, the key of pain and dereliction),
bear out the implications of its title; the leaden-footed opening
adagio (see p. 177) might well depict the *via crucis*. And Haydn's
newly won facility vanishes under it. The thematic development is inferior to that of No. 35, and its archaic instrumental
lay-out almost demands a continuo, unthinkable in the earlier
work. It is indeed a problem whether his technique has

[1] H. C. R. Landon, *The Symphonies of Joseph Haydn*, pp. 285–93.

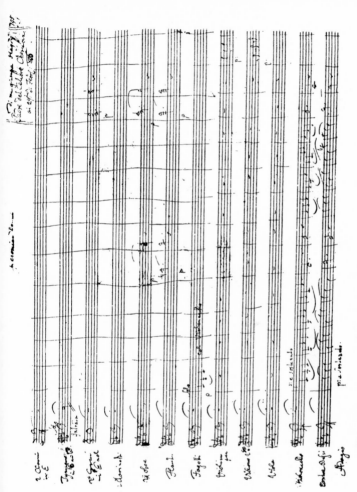

FIRST PAGE OF MANUSCRIPT OF SYMPHONY NO. 103, IN E FLAT MAJOR

given way under emotional stress, or deliberately reverted to archaism as part of his violent and conscious effort to bring the older contrapuntal style within his instrumental range; perhaps a little of both.

Then, probably within the same year, comes the equally passionate G minor, No. 39, quickly followed by the E minor ('Mourning') Symphony No. 44. Technically this is an advance on the other two; the minuet, eerily and effectively contrapuntal, is in canon, offset by a warm and flowing E major trio:

and the finale, fiercely energetic, is well and unusually constructed. The first movement, despite a repetitive development, is kept tense and unified by its persistent opening figure.

The 'Farewell' Symphony, No. 45 in F sharp minor (1772), owes its fame rather to the romantic story of its origin than to any intrinsic superiority over its predecessors; but it has its own personal merits—a tense opening movement, in which the first note of relief comes with an entirely new major theme in the development, and an *adagio* in A major of the utmost delicacy. Its finale really consists of two movements—a sonata-form *presto* in F sharp minor leading into an *adagio* (during which the instruments fall silent one by one), also in sonata form, but shifting from the A major of its opening to F sharp major, the tonic major of the piece, for its recapitulation. No. 52 in C minor, probably written in 1773, is no less fine a work, though its technique again shows archaic features and there is little real thematic development; but it has a beautifully fashioned *andante* and its minor-major minuet and trio, both based on the same melody, are magnificent.

The major-mode symphonies of this period are on the same small scale as No. 35. One or two of them show the same charm and accomplishment, notably No. 43 in E flat ('Mercury'), No. 46 in B major, with its delightful *poco adagio* in the minor, and No. 47 in G—much preoccupied with contrapuntal technique, for it contains the 'reversible' minuet which also appears in the piano Sonata No. 26, and its slow movement consists of variations on a pair of invertible themes.

Then, with No. 48 in C major, the 'Maria Theresa,' performed during the empress's visit to Esterház in 1773, comes another large-scale and glittering *pièce de circonstance*. It is very nearly

first-rate. Its opening movement has a complex and promising
exposition and works up to a fine imbroglio on its transitional
material, and the 6–8 *adagio* in F is a supple and flowing sonata-form
movement with a much-subdivided beat. But something is
wanting; and, as with the G minor Symphony, the trouble is
that the same thing has been better done elsewhere (see below).
That the difference is one of technique rather than of spirit is
shown in the passage from the *adagio* quoted below; it ought to
sound enchanting, but, in performance, melody and accompaniment
run into one another with curiously inept effect.   So the youthful,

Ex 30

(a)   HAYDN   Symphony No 48 ('Maria Theresa')

(b) MOZART. Symphony in C major, K.551.

keen-edged loveliness, which Mozart captures in the slow movements of his two C major symphonies, slips through the clumsier
fingers of the forty-year-old Haydn, never to return:

Ex. 31

(a) HAYDN. Symphony No. 48 (Maria Theresa)

(b) MOZART. Symphony K.425 ('Linz')

No. 51 in B flat (1773) is a more modest but more satisfactory work, and the presence of a virtuoso horn player has inspired him not only to fireworks in the trio of the minuet, but to the noble melody of the finely wrought slow movement:

After this the tide recedes. But there is no sign of any slackening of effort, for even in the period of inevitable reaction after such an outbreak of creative energy Haydn continues his architectural struggles. The 'Schoolmaster' Symphony, No. 55 in E flat, shows how far sheer craftsmanship will take him even when his emotional voltage is low, and the first movement of No. 56 in C is splendidly constructed. So is that of No. 53 in D (which for some reason became enormously popular in England and was nick-named the 'Festino Overture') and of No. 63 in C ('La Roxo-lane'). These two symphonies also provide the first examples of Haydn's double variations on alternating themes, major and minor (or vice versa); the minor theme of No. 63 is the traditional French air which gives the Symphony its nickname. No. 64 in A is on a far higher plane, a lovely little work with a *largo* of startling emotional power.

All this time his scoring is growing more assured. The special effects which, in his earlier symphonies, he reserves for the trios of his minuets, are beginning to pervade the other movements, and the works of this period are full of original and imaginative orchestral touches—even bizarre effects, such as the *col legno* passage in the F major symphony No. 67, which with characteristic good judgment he abandons after a single trial.

Meanwhile a new wave of energy and inspiration has been gathering strength, and by the early 1780s it is upon us with No. 75 in D. The development of the first movement has a magnificent tension, and in the recapitulation the second group of subjects is entirely omitted and replaced by a canon on the opening theme (a procedure splendidly employed, a few years later. in several of his quartets):

Ex. 33. **Presto**

Even more impressive is the powerful concentration of the first movement of No. 78 in C minor. In both these works the other movements, though attractive in themselves, suffer a little by comparison with the first; with No. 77 in B flat, on the other hand, the cream of the work is the F major *andante sostenuto*, exquisite alike in construction and scoring.

From now until the end there is hardly a single symphony that lacks power and significance. In some—notably Nos. 82 in C ('L'Ours') and 85 in B flat ('La Reine'), the first and fourth of the six commissioned by the Concert de la Loge Olympique in Paris—we find him vigorously exploiting all the resources of his own rich comic vein. In others he seems to give himself up to the impact of Mozart's genius, letting it react on his strong and well-matured style with disturbing effect. No. 80 in D minor (1783-1784), a stormy, unsatisfactory yet fascinating work, gives a curiously unsettled impression, especially in the *adagio,* in which his efforts in pursuit of his friend's subtleties only succeed in creating a chaos of apparently different tempos by the use of a multiplicity of rhythmic patterns. In the last two movements the fire and tension are better controlled; the syncopated finale is a masterpiece of wit and vitality. The splendid No. 83 in G minor ('La Poule') shows the same dualism, but here it is between the two halves of the Symphony, its vehement first movement (far more closely developed than that of No. 80) and the intensely personal emotion of the E flat *andante* contrasting sharply with the comedy of the minuet and finale. And Mozart's fingerprints are clearly visible in the *largo* of No. 86 in D; here is one of them:

The marvel is that with all this disturbance there is no blind surrender, but eventual assimilation. Moreover, he continues to work out his own lines of exploration: ambiguities of tonality such as he tries out in the first and third movements of the charming No. 81 in G and the first movement of No. 86, and which eventually reach their peak of subtlety in the first movement of No. 94 (the 'Surprise'):

Ex. 35.
SYMPHONY No. 94 1st Movement
(a) *Beginning of Exposition*

(b) *End of Exposition and beginning of Development*

(c) *Return to opening Theme and Recapitulation*

and also his other type of variations, that with a single minor episode almost too free to be reckoned as a variation, as found in the variation movements of Nos. 82 and 91 in E flat, and also in the two ravishing sets of variations in 6-8 time in Nos. 81 and 84.

No. 88 in G ('Letter V')—and the wonderful *adagio* of No. 87—show that the process of absorption is almost complete; and the three symphonies Haydn wrote in 1788 for the Comte d'Ogny,[1] Nos. 90 in C, 91 in E flat and 92 in G (the 'Oxford') show an intricacy of polyphony and a sparkling delicacy of orchestration that are truly Mozartian, allied with Haydn's most individual humour, warmth and modulating adventurousness.

With the London symphonies Haydn reaches the summit of his art as a symphonist. His freedom and variety of form is amazing, and each work is unique and unpredictable. There are first movements like those of No. 94 or No. 99 in E flat, in which the thematic material, already complex, is yet further reshaped and expanded in recapitulation, prompting Tovey's aphorism that 'Beethoven's codas are Haydn's recapitulations'; others, like No. 95 in C minor, in which the recapitulation is sharply telescoped; and others where, though apparently regular, it is full of subtle changes, like the austere No. 98 in B flat, or the ardent and spacious No. 104 (the 'London') in D.

His finales are equally varied. Eight of the twelve may, for convenience, be labelled 'sonata rondos'; but no two of them are exactly alike in construction. Perhaps the most intricate is that of No. 93 in D, and the most exciting that of No. 100 in G (the 'Military'), with its meteoric modulations, but those of Nos. 95 in C minor and 101 in D (the 'Clock'), are outstanding both in their mellow and serene gaiety and in their extensive use of *fugato*—shared with the finales of No. 97 in C and No. 99 in E flat, but performing different functions in each work. In No. 101 it takes the place of recapitulation, in Nos. 95 and 97 it acts twice as an energetic transition—but to varying destinations—and in No. 99 it

[1] The Library of Congress in Washington possesses the dated autograph of No. 90 and photostats of the title-page, also dated, and *incipits* of No. 91. Both are stamped with the Comte d'Ogny's name and No. 91 bears the words 'Pour Mon^r. le Comte D'ogny' in Haydn's hand. These, with No. 92, as Larsen has shown, were the symphonies he delivered as 'new' to Prince Kraft Ernst von Oettingen-Wallerstein in 1789: one of his less justifiable deceptions. I have been unable so far to trace any details about the Comte d'Ogny's connection with Haydn.

constitutes the development of a movement so absurdly funny that its perfect construction is hardly noticed. Of the three finales in sonata form only No. 98 is even approximately normal, No. 103 is regular as regards tonality, but its monothematic web is so completely seamless that it defies subdivision, and No. 104, despite its two distinct thematic groups, is entirely unorthodox in its recapitulation.

Even in his minuets—a relatively simple form—Haydn's variety is endless. They range in speed from the leisurely *moderato* of No. 100 to the *allegro* of No. 104, from which it is only a step to the one-in-a-bar pulse of Beethoven's scherzos. The minuets of Nos. 98 and 101 are specimens of that miniature sonata form which appeared in Haydn's symphonies as early as No. 56, and which was to breed titanic offspring—the scherzos of Beethoven's and Schubert's ninth symphonies. Others are full of harmonic adventures, from the wide modulations of Nos. 98 and 99 to the use of a single note, either as a multiple personality in a succession of different keys, as in the trio of No. 93, or again, as in Nos. 99 and 104, as a point of leverage from which to swing the entire trio into a new and distant tonality. In spirit, too, their scope is equally varied, ranging from the earthy vigour and inimitable country tunefulness of Nos. 94 and 102 and the trios of Nos. 99 and 104 to the dignified sweep of Nos. 96 and 101 and the exultation of the jubilant No. 97 in C.

Between the first and second sets there is a perceptible advance, and it is in the slow movements that this is most apparent. It is possible to feel that in the first set the slow movements are the weakest. Two of them indeed, the G major slow movements of the two symphonies in D, Nos. 93 and 96, are in his most felicitous comedy vein; but the famous *andante* of the 'Surprise' Symphony is no more than a good straight set of variations, and the C minor and C major Symphonies, Nos. 95 and 97, are both so splendid in other respects that their merely charming variation slow movements seem a little inadequate. Only the B flat Symphony No. 98 has an *adagio*, in F; but this makes up for any deficiencies in the others, for it is one of the most heart-subduing—and most completely Mozartian—movements Haydn ever wrote. Here is the return of the opening theme, with its new counterpoint for cellos:

Ex. 36.

Adagio cantabile

The slow movements of the second set have far more variety. Pure light-heartedness is represented in the *andante* of No. 101 (the 'Clock'), with its audacious scoring, and in the high-stepping *allegretto* of No. 100 (the 'Military'), in which he tentatively tries out the clarinets Salomon had managed to produce in the interval between his two visits. There are two *adagios*—the F major of No. 102, its dream-like quality enhanced by its veiled and miraculous orchestration, and the G major sonata-form *adagio* of the E flat Symphony No. 99, with its shining solemnity, in which the bassoon is allowed to drop his clowning and sing out his romantic soul (see below).

Then at last come the double variations of No. 103 (the 'Drum-roll'), at the close of which part-writing and modulations fuse in a white heat of inspiration, and the meditative G major *andante* of the 'London' Symphony, which, shortly after the apparently

Ex. 37.

Adagio

normal return of the opening melody after a modulatory 'middle section,' suddenly floats clear of the earth in an effortless modulation into a remote and luminous region somewhere between A flat and D flat, hovers there for a while, then clouds over enharmonically into C sharp minor, and quietly spirals down again through F sharp (major and minor) into the calm and steady daylight of the home key:

Ex. 38.

Andante of the 'London' Symphony

It is, indeed, tempting to see, in this last of Haydn's symphonic slow movements, with its visionary moment and its tranquil return to 'the light of common day,' an epitome, all the more moving because entirely unconscious, of Haydn's whole relation to his art. Unlike Beethoven, he was no mystic, and any claim to a special, personal and prophetic revelation, such as Beethoven could justly make, would have been repugnant to his sober humility alike as a good Christian and a good craftsman. But he was perfectly aware of his gifts, and at the end of his life, replying to a little group of music-lovers who had banded together to perform *The Creation* in the small and distant Baltic town of Bergen he sums up his underlying attitude:

You give me the most happy assurance that I am often the enviable source from which you and many other families derive pleasure and satisfaction. . . . Often when I was wrestling with obstacles of every kind, when my physical and mental strength alike were running low and it was hard for me to persevere in the path on which I had set my feet, a secret feeling within me whispered: 'There are so few happy and contented people here below, sorrow and anxiety pursue them everywhere; perhaps your work may, some day, become a spring from which the careworn may draw a few moment's rest and refreshment.' And that was a powerful motive for pressing onward. . . .

His was no exalted other-worldly aim, but the daily offering of his work to God typified by the 'In nomine Domini' and 'Laus Deo' with which his manuscripts begin and end, and the modest hope of making his fellow men a little happier: objectives wholly worthy of one who kept to the end, unquenched by disappointment or the slow attrition of years, the capacity for adventure and acceptance and the quality which the French essayist Joubert has called 'le plus beau de tous les courages—le courage d'être heureux.'

CHAPTER XVI

HAYDN AND OPERA

IF any one had told Haydn that, although he was destined for immortality, thousands would remain unaware that he had ever written a note of opera, he would have been blankly incredulous; so central a place did opera hold, both in the eighteenth-century musical world at large and in Haydn's own personal life and work. The completion of the great palace at Esterház, with its opera-house and marionette theatre, brought opera increasingly into the foreground of Prince Nicholas's musical interests and hence of Haydn's responsibilities as Kapellmeister. Indeed he was for nearly a quarter of a century—from 1766, the date of the move to Esterház, until Prince Nicholas's death in 1790—not only a composer of operas but also a full-time operatic director;[1] and from 1775 onwards (when, it seems, the prince lost interest in the baryton) opera loomed increasingly large among Haydn's duties and preoccupations. In the fifteen years between 1775 and 1790 Haydn was responsible for no fewer than eighty-eight new operatic productions. The number of operas staged in a year (mostly new to the repertory, but with a few already familiar) ranged from five in 1775 to the astonishing total of eighteen in 1786; twelve to fifteen was the normal figure. It fell to Haydn to coach the singers individually, conduct all rehearsals and supervise the orchestral material as well as directing the actual performances; the sheer volume of work is such that one marvels that he had time or vitality left to compose a note of his own. And yet it was between 1775 and 1784 that he composed seven of his own operas. Certainly the curious falling-off in the quality of his symphonies in

[1] The extent and scope of Haydn's operatic work have become apparent as the result of recent research on the operatic material formerly in the Esterházy archives and now in the National Library at Budapest. Dr. Dénes Bartha and Dr. László Somfai, who had been largely responsible for this research, have set forth their results in their important book *Haydn als Opernkapellmeister. Die Haydn-Dokumente der Esterházy-Opernsammlung* (1960).

194

the latter half of the 1770s could be accounted for by this alone, even if no other factors were involved; it is not for nothing that the second spring of his symphonic art came after 1784, when he wrote *Armida*, his last opera for Esterház, even though he was no less immersed in the production of other men's work right up to Prince Nicholas's death.

Nor was this a matter of mere performance. The Esterházy operatic archives provide abundant evidence of the extent to which Haydn revised, cut, rescored and even recomposed the works of his contemporaries, to suit the voices and capacities of his singers, Prince Nicholas's taste or his own. An important aspect of this work, moreover, was the composition of extra arias, either to replace an existing aria by one more suited to a particular singer, or to provide singers with additional opportunities. Mozart composed many such arias as by-products of his operatic work; some are among the finest things he wrote. Haydn too poured a wealth of inspiration into this work, and his additional arias range from delicious comedy numbers like 'Son pietosa, son bonina,' for a curious composite production entitled *La Circe*, to Orestes' eloquent 'Ah, tu non senti, amico,' for Traetta's *Ifigenia in Tauride*, from graceful lyrics like 'Quando la rosa' or 'Chi vive amante,' both written for Luigia Polzelli, to the original and elaborate scena 'Son due ore che giro,' a splendid additional complication for the already involved plot of *La Circe*.[1]

Haydn's own operas [2] contain so much fine music that their

[1] 'Son due ore che giro' has been issued in full score by Dénes Bartha & László Somfai as a Supplement to *Haydn als Opernkapellmeister*, and H. C. Robbins Landon has published a number of these additional arias in *Joseph Haydn; Arien für Sopran*, 2 vols. (Haydn-Mozart Press, 1961).

[2] At the time of writing the following are available in modern reprints: *La Canterina* and *Lo Speziale*, both in full score (Joseph Haydn Institute, Series XXV, Nos. 2 and 3), and, in vocal score, *L'infedeltà delusa* (Haydn-Mozart Press, 1960), *Il mondo della luna* (Bärenreiter, 1958) and *La vera costanza* (Henschelverlag and Peters) in a (textually altered) German version entitled *List und Liebe*. The publication of the marionette opera *Das abgebrannte Haus*, rediscovered and edited by H. C. Robbins Landon, has been undertaken by Schott.

failure to achieve that vitality that enables an opera to outlive its generation is the harder to account for. It is indeed true that, as Haydn himself wrote, they were designed for special, intimate conditions and for a team of singers whose capacities Haydn knew how to use to the best advantage; but the same is true, *mutatis mutandis*, of almost all eighteenth-century music. It is also true that many of his libretti were of inferior quality, and while a poor libretto can evoke fine music, it can effectively prevent an opera from becoming viable in performance. But Haydn also lacked that dramatic sense by virtue of which a Mozart or a Verdi can fuse even a mediocre libretto into a convincing unity: the power of grasping and depicting not only isolated situations but the total flow of the drama. He can give utterance to a single emotion or state of mind in an eloquent accompanied recitative or a moving aria, but these remain isolated moments without cumulative effect. Even in his final *ensembles*, often so admirably built up, the situations change, and the character of the music with them, but there is rarely any heightening of musical or dramatic tension. This matters less where the opera is all of a piece, like his two purely farcical comedies written to Goldoni texts, *Lo Speziale* and *Il mondo della luna*, or, in a wholly different way, the little Singspiel *Philemon und Baucis* (originally written for marionettes), with its simple sincerity and tenderness. But in works of the *dramma eroicomico* type, which Prince Nicholas seems to have preferred, such as *Orlando Paladino* and (despite its description of *dramma giocoso*) *L'incontro improvviso*, the heroic and the comic elements fall apart and unity is lost.

It is some measure of the extent to which a good libretto makes a good opera that two of Haydn's best operas are to Goldoni texts. Indeed *Lo Speziale* (1768)—his first full-scale opera for the Esterház theatre, for the gay and amusing *La Canterina*, with its elements of parody, is only a short intermezzo—is a demonstration of the effectiveness of conventions when skilfully and wittily handled. All the characters are stock types: elderly guardian, pretty ward, faithful lover, designing rival. Haydn's music, too, consists largely of formulas. Operatic music was so all-pervasive, and so full of formulas, that they formed a large part of the everyday musical language of the eighteenth century; and Haydn's own musical personality, which by 1768 was already breaking through in his instrumental music, had not yet set its stamp upon his operatic idiom. But formulas can provide deliciously comic effects in an original context, and Goldoni's old Sempronio, by a delightful twist, is a newspaper bore, retailing all the foreign news with an unction faithfully reflected in the pompous flourishes of his big first-act aria. Best of all, and genuinely witty despite their lack of outright melodic originality, are the first- and second-act finales. The first is a terzetto in which the lovers, pretending to work in the dispensary, snatch a flirtation under Sempronio's very nose (buried, of course, in the daily paper). In the second, a variant of the notary-with-marriage-contract situation, Grilletta's two younger suitors appear in rival legal disguises to draft (and deflect to themselves) the marriage contract between her and her guardian; structurally it is a rondo with concluding presto, deliciously scored, with a solo oboe hovering demurely above the imbroglio.

Haydn's second Goldoni opera, *Le Pescatrici* (1769), is semi-serious and, despite imaginative moments, not wholly successful. It is not until 1777 that he rejoins Goldoni in the realm of pure nonsense with *Il mondo della luna*. This is again a type-character opera; the rich and gullible Buonafede, whose passion is astronomy, is tricked by Ecclitico, a bogus astronomer with designs on one of his two daughters, into believing that he has actually made a flight to the moon. After the 'moon' scenes have given scope for various satirical reflections on manners and morals in the sub-lunar world, Buonafede is induced to provide dowries for both his daughters' lunar marriages, upon which follow discovery, fury, penitence and final reconciliation. In this preposterous world of artifice Haydn cannot put a foot wrong. His melody is fresh and vital, and aria follows aria with gloriously spontaneous invention. The scoring is full of imagination (witness the swirling of muted strings as the drugged Buonafede takes his imagined flight), and again and again the music breaks into real poetry, as in the exquisite love duet between Ecclitico and his Clarice, or the G minor aria sung by the other daughter's lover; here the gentle gravity and tenderness of the music so transcend the somewhat prosaic text that it is hardly surprising that Haydn saw a still better use for it and turned it into the 'Benedictus' of the Mariazell Mass without the slightest incongruity.

Haydn's only other really satisfactory libretto was that of *L'Infedeltà delusa* (1773), by the 'reform' librettist Marco Coltellini. Its merits are that it handles stock characters and situations with a certain wit and individuality, and keeps the action all on one plane. All the characters are peasants: the rich and grasping Filippo is trying to marry his daughter Sandrina to Nencio, prosperous, well-meaning and stupid. But she loves the poor but deserving Nanni, whose sister Vespina has been jilted by Nencio, and Vespina (like her immortal near-namesake in *Così*) is enough of a schemer and strategist to achieve her ends by a series of disguises and devices, including the usual marriage-contract, in which, needless to say, she is disguised as a notary. Haydn came to this reasonably promising text in all the vigour of his newly found maturity, and uses the full language of opera, and not merely its conventional formulas, with power and precision. Sandrina utters her gentle, ineffectual agitation, Nanni his indignant dismay (in F minor, Haydn's key of pain, anger and desolation) and the pompous Nencio blusters his way through a splendid 'revenge' aria and is caricatured in his enchantingly funny and flat-footed serenade. The opening evening *ensemble*, 'Bella sera,' has a true sunset poetry, and both the first- and second-act finales are splendid pieces, especially the second, moving purposefully from the mock solemnity of the faked marriage contract through the triumph and anger of disclosure to the resolutely happy conclusion.

If Haydn's other operas are less satisfactory, part (though not all) of the blame can be laid at the door of the libretto. That of *L'incontro improvviso* (1775) is an Italian *opera buffa* version of It is a 'Turkish' opera, its theme virtually identical with that of Dancourt's French text set by Gluck in his *La rencontre imprévue*. *Die Entführung aus dem Serail*: the heroine Rezia is a prisoner in the harem, her lover Prince Ali is in disguise attempting to rescue her, with the aid of a comic servant. He is helped, hindered and

betrayed by the Calandro, the rascally beggar monk, and his comrades, and finally pardoned by the magnanimous sultan. Prince
Ali's arias are eloquent in a conventional way, and the servant
Osmin has two genuinely funny arias, but much of the humour—
topical anti-clerical satire centred on the bibulous Calandro—is
flat and obvious. The two outstanding pieces are the ravishing
dream-terzetto between Rezia and her two handmaids in Act I,
and her love-scene with the Prince in Act II; but these are not
enough to vitalize the whole. In *La vera costanza* (1776), too, the
fatuities of the plot appear to have driven Haydn back on conventional musical utterance, even in the skilfully constructed *ensembles*.
Only in the arias of the emotionally unstable young Count,
unjustly suspecting the fidelity of his peasant bride, are his changing
moods closely matched by changes in the tempo and character of
the music, shaping the arias in a fresh and original manner; and
the wronged Rosina has a despairing recitative and aria—again in
F minor—which splendidly expresses her state of mind. But once
more, isolated situations do not make an opera.

L'isola disabitata was composed in 1779, the year in which fire had
severely damaged the Esterház theatre and its equipment. This
probably accounts in great measure for the choice of this particular
Metastasio text, calling for only a single set and only four characters: Costanza and Gernando, the devoted husband and wife
separated for long years by shipwreck and pirates and finally
reunited, Silvia, Costanza's young sister, who has grown up on
the island and never yet set eyes on a man, and Gernando's friend
Errico, who wins her affections. The outstanding feature of the
opera is the expressive accompanied recitative in which the modest
little drama evolves; there are comparatively few arias and only one
big *ensemble*, the quartet in the second act. Unfortunately neither
plot nor characters are sufficiently alive to call forth Haydn's best
music in the formal numbers, but the recitative affords a tantalizing
glimpse of what he might have done with a more vital libretto.

Haydn was to write two more operas for Esterház, the *dramma
eroi-comico Orlando Paladino* (1781) and *Armida* (1784), described as
a *dramma eroico*, which is a reversion to pure *opera seria*. Neither is
completely successful, and if *Armida* fails by having too little

variety—mainly big solo numbers, very few *ensembles* and (save in one fine recitative and aria for the hero Rinaldo) no accompanied recitative—*Orlando Paladino* falls apart by having too much. It is based on Ariosto's story of the knight Orlando, mad with jealous love for Angelica, who loves not him but the gentle Medoro. These, with the fire-eating Rodomonte and the sorceress Alcina, are the 'heroic' parts, and their music is cast on a large scale and is passionate in emotion and richly scored. But there is also the comic element—Pasquale, Orlando's squire, an engaging braggart-coward, and his peasant sweetheart Eurilla, whose tuneful airs and duets belong to the realm of *Singspiel*. Perhaps the Mozart of the *Magic Flute* could have fused these disparate elements into a convincing unity; but it was outside Haydn's range. Again one is the more tantalized by the quality of the component parts: the big love duet for Angelica and Medoro in Act II, Pasquale's delicious aria demonstrating all the ornaments of music, and the nobly imaginative scene between Orlando and Charon on the edge of Lethe, which indeed brings us within reach of Sarastro's kingdom.

After *Armida* Haydn wrote no more operas for Esterház, though he was as busy as ever with opera productions right up to 1790 (we know, indeed, that in that year he was planning to produce *Figaro*, for the Esterházy archives possess the performing material). Whether it was sheer pressure of work that held him back, or the revelation of Mozart's incomparable and eclipsing art, we do not know. But from his famous letter to Prague we know that, perhaps for the first time, he felt that his operas had only a local and transitory validity.

Haydn's London engagements, among them a contract for an *opera seria*, brought him back to opera for the last time, with his Orpheus opera, *L'anima del filosofo*. The text, by Carlo Badini, is so hopelessly undramatic that even if the opera had not been killed by intrigue it would have been hard put to it to survive as a viable work for the stage. Yet it contains scenes of remarkable maturity and imaginative power, and Badini's text (designed as it was for the forces available in a full-scale opera-house) gives Haydn one opportunity hitherto denied to him: that of making dramatic use of the chorus. And this opportunity Haydn seizes again and again with both hands: in the ominous C minor opening chorus, the deceptive gaiety of the women's chorus at the wedding, the warm and tender funeral dirge, and in the choruses of the spirits of the underworld. These, and the scene of Orfeo's death, tempt us indeed to wonder what might have been if Haydn had been enabled to bring his mature art, his lifetime's operatic experience and his new choral technique to the service of a first-class libretto: whether his direct, unsubtle strength and nobility, so much more akin to Gluck than to Mozart, might not have given us a great work of classic tragedy if properly directed and stimulated. But it was not to be. The great upsurge of choral music that marks Haydn's final period flowed into other channels, and opera remained to the end his unrequited love.

APPENDICES

APPENDIX A

(Figures in brackets denote the age reached by the person mentioned during the year in question.)

Year	Age	Life	Contemporary Musicians
1732		Franz Joseph Haydn born March 31/April 1, at Rohrau, Lower Austria, son of Matthias Haydn, wheelwright.	Arne aged 22; Bach 47; Bach (C. P. E.) 18; Bonno 22; Campra 72; Couperin 64; Durante 48; Fux 72; Galuppi 26; Geminiani 52; Gluck 18; Graun 31; Handel 47; Hasse 33; Jommelli 18; Leclair 35; Leo 38; Lotti 65; Martini 26; Pergolesi 22; Piccinni 4; Porpora 46; Rameau 49; Scarlatti (D.) 47; Tartini 40.
1733	1		Couperin (65) dies, Sept. 12.
1734	2		Gossec born, Jan. 17.
1735	3		Bach (J. C.) born, Sept. 5; Eccles (*c.* 72) dies, Jan. 12.
1736	4		Albrechtsberger born, Feb. 3; Gluck (22) comes to Vienna; Pergolesi (26) dies, March 17.
1737	5	Birth of brother, Johann Michael, Sept. 14.	Mysliveček born, March 9.
1738	6	Taken to Hainburg by J. M. Franck, who teaches him music.	
1739	7	Begins to sing and to play the harpsichord and violin.	Dittersdorf born, Nov. 2; Keiser (65) dies, Sept. 12.
1740	8	Enters the cathedral school of St. Stephen's in Vienna under Reutter (32).	Lotti (73) dies, Jan. 5.
1741	9	Gegenbauer and Finsterbusch teach him at the	Barthélemon born, July 27; Desmarets (79) dies, Sept. 7;

205

Haydn

Year	Age	Life	Contemporary Musicians
		cathedral school rather than Reutter (33).	Fux (81) dies, Feb. 13; Gluck's (27) first opera, *Artaserse,* produced in Milan; Grétry born, Feb. 8; Paisiello born, May 9.
1742	10	Acquires great knowledge of current church music.	Bach (C. P. E.) (28) publishes 6 clavier sonatas; Handel's (57) *Messiah* produced at Dublin.
1743	11	Tries his hand at composition, but is not encouraged by Reutter (35).	Boccherini born, Feb. 19.
1744	12		Campra (84) dies, June 29; Leo (50) dies, Oct. 31.
1745	13	His brother Michael (8) joins the St. Stephen's choir. Visit to Maria Theresa at Schönbrunn by the cathedral choir.	
1746	14		
1747	15	Voice begins to break.	
1748	16	His brother Michael (11) takes his place as principal soprano.	Gluck's (34) opera, *Semiramide riconosciuta,* produced in Vienna.
1749	17	Dismissed from St. Stephen's Cathedral choir. He plays in the streets.	Cimarosa born, Dec. 17; Vogler born, June 15.
1750	18	Pilgrimage to Mariazell. *Missa brevis* in F composed. (?) Earliest string Quartets.	Bach (65) dies, July 28; Salieri born, Aug. 19.
1751	19	Plays in and writes for street bands. Kurz commissions a comic opera.	
1752	20	*Der krumme Teufel* produced, spring.	Clementi born, Jan. 24.
1753	21	Begins to study seriously.	Viotti born, May 23.
1754	22	Death of his mother at Rohrau, Feb. 23. He teaches Marianne Martinez (10), meets Metastasio (56)	Bonno's (44) opera, *L'Isola disabitata* (see Haydn, 1779), produced in Vienna; Kozeluch born, Dec. 9.

Year	Age	Life	Contemporary Musicians
		and becomes the valet-pupil of Porpora (68). Visit to Mannersdorf, where he meets Gluck (41).	
~1755	23	Fürnberg invites him to Weinzierl, where he composes for the quartet party.	Durante (71) dies, Aug. 13; Winter born, May 2.
~1756	24	Return to Vienna with better prospects.	Mozart born, Jan. 27; Umlauf born.
1757	25	Makes a modest income by teaching.	Pleyel born, June 1; Domenico Scarlatti (72) dies, July 22; Giuseppe Scarlatti's (34) opera, *L'Isola disabitata* (*see* Haydn, 1779), produced in Vienna.
1758	26	Composes and teaches in Vienna.	
1759	27	Joins the household of Morzin at Lukaveč. First Symphony composed.	Graun (58) dies, Aug. 8; Handel (74) dies, April 14.
1760	28	Makes friends with Dittersdorf (20). Marries Anna Maria Keller (32), Nov. 26.	Cherubini born, Sept. 14; Lesueur born, Feb. 15.
1761	29	Enters the service of Esterházy at Eisenstadt, May.	Dussek born, Feb. 9; Schenk born, Nov. 30.
1762	30	Death of Paul Anton Esterházy and succession of his brother Nicholas, March 18.	Gluck's (48) opera, *Orfeo ed Euridice*, produced in Vienna; Michael Haydn (25) enters the service of the Archbishop of Salzburg; Jommelli's (48) opera, *L'Isola disabitata* (*see* Haydn, 1779), produced at Stuttgart.
1763	31	Opera, *Acide e Galatea*, produced at Eisenstadt on the marriage of Esterházy's son, Jan. 11; death of H.'s father at Rohrau, Sept. 12.	Gyrowetz born, Feb. 19; Méhul born, June 22.

Haydn

Year	Age	Life	Contemporary Musicians
1764	32	*Six Symphonies ou Quatuors dialogués* (i.e. five quartets from Op. 2 and a Cassation) published in Paris. Cantata and Te Deum for return of Esterházy from Frankfort.	Leclair (67) dies, Oct. 22; Rameau (81) dies, Sept. 22.
1765	33	Some instrumental works published at Amsterdam.	
1766	34	Death of Werner and advancement of H. to the post of musical director. Removal from Eisenstadt to Esterház. 'Great Organ Mass.'	Porpora (80) dies, Feb.; Weigl born, March 28 (H. is godfather).
1707	35	Symphony No. 35. Piano Sonatas Nos. 18, 19, ? 46	Gluck's (53) opera, *Alceste*, produced in Vienna; Telemann (86) dies, June 25.
1768	36	Opera, *Lo speziale,* produced at Esterház. Fire at Eisenstadt, in which much of H.'s music is destroyed. Symphony Nos. 49, ? 39.	
1769	37		
1770	38	Visit of the Esterházy musicians to Vienna, March. H. ill with fever.	Beethoven born, Dec. 16; Tartini (78) dies, Feb. 26.
1771	39	Op. 17 Quartets. Piano Sonata No. 20.	Paer born, June 1.
1772	40	Visit to Count Anton Grassalkovicz at Pressburg. Symphonies Nos. 45 ('Farewell'), 46, 47. 'St. Nicholas' Mass. Op. 20 Quartets.	Reutter (64) dies, March 12.
1773	41	Maria Theresa visits Esterház. Opera, *L'Infedeltà delusa,* and Symphony No. 48 performed before her. Piano Sonatas Nos. 21–6.	

Year	Age	Life	Contemporary Musicians
1774	42	Symphonies Nos. 54, 55 ('The Schoolmaster'), 56, 57.	Gassmann (51) dies, Jan. 22; Jommelli (60) dies, Aug. 25; Pleyel (17) becomes H.'s pupil; Spontini born, Nov. 14.
1775	43	Oratorio, *Il ritorno di Tobia*, performed by the Ton-künstlersocietät in Vienna. H., being asked for written promise of compositions in lieu of extra subscription as a country member, withdraws his application for member-ship.	Boieldieu born, Dec. 16.
1776	44	Opera, *La vera costanza*, composed for the Court Theatre in Vienna, which rejects it. Second fire at Eisenstadt, which again destroys many of H.'s MSS. Piano Sonatas Nos. 27–32.	
1777	45	Visit of the Esterház musi-cians to Maria Theresa at Schönbrunn.	Wagenseil (62) dies, March 1.
1778	46		Arne (68) dies, March 5; Hummel born, Nov. 14.
1779	47	Arrival of Luigia Polzelli at Esterház. Opera, *L'isola disabitata*. Theatre in the castle grounds destroyed by fire.	Boyce (69) dies, Feb. 7.
1780	48	New theatre at Esterház in-augurated with the opera, *La fedeltà premiata*, Oct. 15. Polzelli and her husband dis-missed, but reinstated. Piano Sonatas Nos. 35–9 pub-lished by Artaria.	

Year	Age	Life	Contemporary Musicians
1781	49	Meeting with Clementi (29) in Vienna, where the Esterház musicians entertain the Grand Duke Paul of Russia, who is on a visit to the Emperor Joseph II. Friendship with Mozart (25). *Stabat Mater* performed in Paris. First set of songs published by Artaria. Op. 33 ('Russian') Quartets.	Mysliveček (44) dies, Feb. 4.
1782	50	Opera, *Orlando Paladino*, and Mariazell Mass, a mass composed for the shrine of Mariazell.	Auber born, Jan. 29; Bach (J. C.) (47) dies, Jan 1; Field born, July 26; Mozart (26) writes the first of the six string quartets dedicated to H.
1783	51		Hasse (84) dies, Dec. 16.
1784	52	Opera, *Armida*. Second set of songs published. Haydn and Mozart take part in chamber music with Dittersdorf (46) and Wanhal (46) at the lodgings of Stephen Storace. Meeting with Paisiello (43) and Sarti (55) on their way from and to Russia.	Martini (78) dies, Oct. 3; Spohr born, April 5.
1785	53	Setting of *The Seven Words* commissioned by Cadiz Cathedral. At Mozart's lodging H. hears last three quartets dedicated to him and meets Leopold Mozart (66)	Galuppi (79) dies, Jan. 3; Mozart (29) dedicates 6 string quartets to H.
1786	54	Six symphonies for the Concert de la Loge Olympique in Paris completed.	Sacchini (52) dies, Oct 7; Weber born, Dec. 18.
1787	55	Six Quartets (Op. 50) dedicated to Frederick William II of Prussia. Invitation from Ferdinand IV of Naples refused.	Gluck (73) dies, Nov. 15.

Year	Age	Life	Contemporary Musicians
1788	56	Symphonies Nos. 90, 91.	Bach (C. P. E.) (74) dies, Dec. 15; Bonno (78) dies, April 15.
1789	57	Bland visits H. at Esterház and vainly invites him to London. Symphony No. 92 (later named 'Oxford). Publication of Quartets Opp. 54 and 55.	
1790	58	Death of Nicholas Esterhàzy, Sept. 28, and H.'s retirement with a pension. He goes to Vienna. Salomon invites him to London. At Bonn, Dec. 25, where a mass of his is performed, he invites the musicians, including Beethoven (20), to dinner. Op. 64 Quartets.	
1791	59	First visit to London, Jan. 1. First Salomon concert, Mar. 11. Visit to Oxford, July. Mus. Doc. degree, July 8. Pleyel (34) comes to London in opposition to H. Symphonies Nos. 95, 96.	Barthélemon (50), Callcott (25), Gyrowetz (28) and Shield (43) meet H.; Czerny born, Feb. 20; Hérold born, Jan. 28; Meyerbeer born, Sept. 5; Mozart (35) dies. Dec. 5.
1792	60	In London. H. falls in love with Mrs. Schroeter. Return to Vienna, June. Second visit to Bonn. Beethoven (22) becomes his pupil, Dec. Symphonies Nos. 93, 94, 97, 98. *Sinfonia concertante.*	Dussek (31) meets H. in London. At Bonn Beethoven (22) submits a cantata to him. Rossini born, Feb. 29.
1793	61	Beethoven (23) soon abandons him and goes to Schenk (32) for lessons. Quartets Opp. 71, 74. Symphony No. 99.	
1794	62	Second visit to London, Feb.	Dussek (33) and Viotti (41)

Year	*Age*	*Life*	*Contemporary Musicians*
		4. Visit to Rauzzini (47) at Bath. Symphonies Nos. 100, 101. Piano Sonatas Nos. 50–2.	appear with him at the Salomon concerts.
1795	63	Symphonies Nos. 102–104 for a new series of 'Opera Concerts' under Viotti. Return to Vienna, Aug.	Clementi (43) is on friendly terms with H. Marschner born, Aug. 16.
1796	64	'Heiligmesse.' 'Kettledrum' Mass.	Beethoven (26) publishes 3 piano sonatas (Op. 2), dedicated to H.; Umlauf (40) dies, June 8. Weber (10) becomes a chorister under Michael Haydn (59) at Salzburg.
1797	65	Austrian Hymn composed, Jan. Oratorio, *Die Schöpfung* ('The Creation'). String Quartet Op. 76 No. 3 ('Emperor'). H. is elected honorary member of the Tonkünstlersocietät.	Donizetti born, Nov. 25; Schubert born, Jan. 31.
1798	66	First performance of *The Creation*, April 29. 'Nelson' Mass.	
1799	67	First public performance of *The Creation*, March 19. 'Theresa' Mass. Op. 76 Quartets published and Op. 77 Quartets composed.	Dittersdorf (60) dies, Oct. 24; Halévy born, May 27.
1800	68	Death of H.'s wife, March 20. During a vist to Esterházy at Eisenstadt, H. meets Nelson. Oratorio, *Die Jahreszeiten* ('The Seasons'). *The Creation* performed by Steibelt (35) in Paris.	Piccinni (72) dies, May 7.
1801	69	First performance of *The Seasons*, April 24, and first public performance, May 29.	Bellini born, Nov. 1; Cimarosa (52) dies, Jan. 11; Lanner born, April 11.

Year	Age	Life	Contemporary Musicians
1802	70		Sarti (73) dies, July 28.
1803	71	Receives a diploma (Zwölf-fache Bürgermedaille) from the citizens of Vienna.	Berlioz born, Dec. 9; Glinka born, May 20/June 2; Weber (17) visits H.
1804	72	Is nominated honorary citizen of Vienna.	Strauss (J. i) born, March 14.
1805	73	Concert in honour of his birthday held April 8.	Boccherini (62) dies, May 28; Cherubini (45) visits H.
1806	74	Death of his brother Michael (69) at Salzburg, Aug. 10.	Albrechtsberger (70) dedicates a set of canons to H.
1807	75		
1808	76	Although very infirm, H. attends a performance of *The Creation,* March 27.	Barthélemon (67) dies, July 23.
1809	77	Haydn dies in Vienna, May 31.	Albrechtsberger (73) dies, March 7; Mendelssohn born, Feb. 3.

Auber aged 27; Balfe 1; Beethoven 39; Bellini 8; Berlioz 6; Bishop 23; Boieldieu 34; Callcott 43; Cherubini 49; Clementi 57; Donizetti 12; Dussek 48; Field 27; Glinka 6; Gossec 75; Grétry 68; Gyrowetz 46; Halévy 10; Hérold 18; Hummel 31; Kozeluch 55; Lanner 18; Lesueur 49; Marschner 14; Méhul 46; Mercadante 14; Meyerbeer 18; Paer 38; Paisiello 68; Rossini 17; Salieri 59; Schenk 48; Schubert 12; Spohr 25; Spontini 35; Strauss (J. i) 5; Vogler 60; Wanhal 70; Weber 23; Weigl 43; Winter 54; Zelter 51; Zingarelli 57.

APPENDIX B

GROUP I. SYMPHONIES AND OVERTURES

Symphonies

No.	Key	Title (*if any*)	Date
1.	D major		1759
2.	C major		*c.* 1760
3.	G major		*c.* 1760
4.	D major		*c.* 1760
5.	A major		*c.* 1760
6.	D major	Le Matin	*c.* 1761
7.	C major	Le Midi	1761
8.	G major	Le Soir et La Tempête	*c.* 1761
9.	C major		? 1762
10.	E flat major		*c.* 1760–3
11.	E flat major		*c.* 1760
12.	E major		1763
13.	D major		1763
14.	A major		*c.* 1763
15.	D major		*c.* 1763
16.	B flat major		*c.* 1760–3
17.	F major		*c.* 1760–3
18.	G major		*c.* 1760–4
19.	D major		*c.* 1760–3
20.	C major		*c.* 1760–4
21.	A major		1764
22.	E flat major	The Philosopher	1764
23.	G major		1764
24.	D major		1764
25.	C major		*c.* 1760–4
26.	D minor	Lamentatione	*c.* 1767–8
27.	G major		*c.* 1760–5
28.	A major		1765
29.	E major		1765

Appendix B—Catalogue of Works

No.	Key	Title (if any)	Date
30.	C major	Alleluia	1765
31.	D major	Horn Signal	1765
32.	C major		c. 1760–5
33.	C major		c. 1763–5
34.	D minor		c. 1765
35.	B flat major		1767
36.	E flat major		c. 1765–8
37.	C major		c. 1760–5
38.	C major		c. 1767–8
39.	G minor		c. 1768
40.	F major		1763
41.	C major		c. 1770
42.	D major		1771
43.	E flat major	Mercury	c. 1772
44.	E minor	Mourning Symphony	c. 1772
45.	F sharp minor	Farewell	1772
46.	B major		1772
47.	G major		1772
48.	C major	Maria Theresa	? 1772
49.	F minor	La Passione	1768
50.	C major		1773
51.	B flat major		c. 1772–4
52.	C minor		c. 1772–4
53.	D major	L'Impériale	c. 1775
54.	G major		1774
55.	E flat major	The Schoolmaster	1774
56.	C major		1774
57.	D major		1774
58.	F major		c. 1767–8
59.	A major	Fire Symphony	c. 1767–8
60.	C major	Il Distratto	1774[1]
61.	D major		1776
62.	D major		c. 1780

[1] This definite date is provided by references to the music in the *Pressburger Zeitung* of 6th July and 23rd November 1774, newly discovered by H. C. R. Landon (Supplement to *The Symphonies of Joseph Haydn*, 1961, p. 38).

No.	Key	Title (*if any*)	Date
63.	C major	La Roxolane	*c.* 1777–80 [1]
64.	A major		*c.* 1775
65.	A major		*c.* 1772–4
66.	B flat major		*c.* 1778–9
67.	F major		*c.* 1778–9
68.	B flat major		*c.* 1778–9
69.	C major	Laudon	*c.* 1778–9
70.	D major		1779
71.	B flat major		*c.* 1780
72.	D major		*c.* 1761–5
73.	D major	La Chasse	1780 and 1781 [2]
74.	E flat major		*c.* 1780
75.	D major		*c.* 1780
76.	E flat major		*c.* 1782
77.	B flat major		*c.* 1782
78.	C minor		*c.* 1782
79.	F major		*c.* 1784
80.	D minor		*c.* 1784
81.	G major		*c.* 1784
82.	C major	L'Ours	1786
83.	G minor	La Poule	1785
84.	E flat major		1786
85.	B flat major	La Reine (de France)	1785–6
86.	D major		1786
87.	A major		1785
88.	G major		*c.* 1787
89.	F major		1787

[1] H. C. R. Landon (*The Symphonies of Joseph Haydn*, pp. 359 ff.) discusses the various versions of this Symphony, of which the first movement is also the Overture to *Il mondo della luna* (1777). He maintains that the opera overture came first and that other movements were subsequently added to make a symphony.

[2] The Finale was composed in 1780 as the overture to *La fedeltà premiata*; the autograph score is with that of the opera in the Esterházy archives (Landon, Supplement to *The Symphonies of Joseph Haydn*, pp. 51–2). The autograph of the third and part of the second movement was formerly in the Prussian State Library, Berlin; its present whereabouts is unknown.

No.	Key	Title (*if any*)	Date
90.	C major		1788
91.	E flat major		1788
92.	G major	Oxford	1789
93.	D major		1791-2
94.	G major	Surprise	1791
95.	C minor		1791
96.	D major	The Miracle	1791
97.	C major		1792
98.	B flat major		1792
99.	E flat major		1793
100.	G major	Military	1794
101.	D minor and major	The Clock	1794
102.	B flat major		1794
103.	E flat major	Drum-roll	1795
104.	D minor and major	London	1795

No.		Date
105.	Sinfonia Concertante for violin, cello, oboe, bassoon, in B flat major.	1792
106.	D major (lost; listed on p. 2 of Haydn's Draft Catalogue)	not known
107.	B flat major. (Original, authentic version of String Quartet, Op. 1 No. 5)	*c.* 1757-60
108.	B flat major (listed in Haydn's Thematic Catalogue among the symphonies as No. 7; called 'Partita' in some MSS.)	*before* 1765

Overtures

N.B. In this Group, Van Hoboken has retained the numbering of the thematic list in the Breitkopf & Härtel Collected Edition, which is arranged by key and not in chronological order.

No.	Key	Work	Date
1.	C major	*L'infedeltà delusa*	1773 [1]
2.	C minor and major	*Il ritorno di Tobia*	1774-5

[1] The key and scoring of this overture make it appear likely that it belongs to this opera, and the watermarks on the fragments of the autograph date it around 1773, the date of the opera. (See foreword to vocal

No.	Key	*Work*	*Date*
3.	C minor and major	*L'anima del filosofo* (?)	1791[1]
4.	D major		*before* 1785
5.	D major	*Acide e Galatea*	1762
6.	D major	*L'incontro improvviso* (?)	1775[2]
7.	D major		1777[3]
8.	D minor	*Philemon und Baucis*	1773
10.	G major	*Lo Speziale*	*c.* 1766–9
13.	G minor	*L'isola disabitata*	1779
14.	B flat major	*Armida*	1784
15.	B flat major	*La vera costanza*	? 1776
16.	B flat major	*Orlando Paladino*	1782

No. 11 is the orchestral introduction to the opening chorus of *La fedeltà premiata*, No. 12 is the Prelude to Act III of *Il mondo della luna*. No. 9, an overture to *King Lear*, is not by Haydn but by W. G. Stegmann.

The following should be added to the above list:

C major	*Il mondo della luna* (i.e. first movement of Symphony No. 63)	1777
D major	*La fedeltà premiata* (i.e., last movement of Symphony No. 73)	1780

---

score of *L'infedeltà delusa*, ed. H. C. R. Landon, 1961.) On similar grounds Landon assigns Overture No. 6 to *L'incontro improvviso* (*The Symphonies of Joseph Haydn*, p. 19).

[1] The autograph of this overture (incomplete and undated) is in the Preussische Staatsbibliothek with that of the opera *L'anima del filosofo* with which it is also thematically connected. Haydn himself, however, entered it in his Draft Catalogue as 'For an English Opera 1994' [*sic*], and it was probably composed in the first place for J. P. Salomon's opera *Windsor Castle*, produced at Covent Garden on 6th April 1795 (H. C. R. Landon, *The Symphonies of Joseph Haydn*, pp. 19., 541–2, 566; Supplement to *The Symphonies of Joseph Haydn*, pp. 43–4).

[2] See footnote 1, p. 217.

[3] Originally an opera overture, it is frequently found in early MSS. and published editions of Symphony No. 53 as an alternative finale. See Haydn Society Complete Edition, Series I vol. 5, where it is fully discussed and printed as the second of the three alternative finales. See also Landon, *The Symphonies of Joseph Haydn*, pp. 365–6.

GROUP II. DIVERTIMENTI (*without Keyboard*) IN FOUR PARTS AND OVER

N.B. Nos. 1–20 in this group are those listed in Haydn's Thematic Catalogue under the heading *Divertimenti auf verschiedene Instrumenten*, in the order there given.

No.	Key	Scoring	Date
1.	G major	1 fl., 1 ob., 2 vlns., bass (vc.)	c. 1755–60
2.	G major	2 vlns., 2 vlas., bass (vc.)	c. 1753
3.	G major	2 ob. 2 bassoons, 2 horns	c. 1760[1]
4.	F major	2 cl., 1 bassoon, 2 horns	Lost
5.	F major	2 cl., 1 bassoon, 2 horns	c. 1760–2
6.	E flat major	String Quartet (Op. 1 No. 1 in some early editions)	before 1765
7.	C major (*Feld Parthie*)	2 ob., 2 bassoons, 2 horns	c. 1760–2
8.	D major	2 fl., 2 horns, 2 vlns., vc.-bass	c. 1761–4
9.	G major	2 lb. (or fl.), 2 horns, 2 vlns., 2 vlas., vc.-bass	c. 1760
10.	D major		Lost
11.	C major	1 fl., 1 ob., 2 vlns., vc., bass.	c. 1755–60
12.	E flat (*Feld Parthie*)	2 cors anglais, 2 horns, 2 bassoons	c. 1760
13.	D major		Lost
14.	C major (*Feld Parthie*)	2 cl., 2 horns	c. 1760
15.	F major (*Feld Parthie*)	2 ob., 2 bassoons, 2 horns	1760
16.	F major (*Feld Parthie*)	2 cors anglais, 2 horns, 2 bassoons, 2 vlns.	1760
17.	C major	2 cl., 2 horns, 2 vlns., 2 vlas., vc.-bass	c. 1761
18.	D major		Lost
19.	G major		Lost
20.	F major	2 ob., 2 horns., 2 vlns., 2 vlas., vc.-bass	c. 1760–5

---

[1] Rediscovered by H. C. Robbins Landon in the Music Archives of Schloss Frýdlant (now National Museum, Prague), and edited by him in Diletto Musicale series (Doblinger), No. 84.

No.	Key	Scoring	Date
21.	E flat major	String Quartet and 2 horns; original, authentic version of string quartets Op. 2 Nos. 3 and 5	
22.	D major		*c.* 1755–60
23.	F major	2 ob., 2 bassoons, 2 horns	*c.* 1760–5
24.	E flat major	1 fl., 2 cors anglais, 1 bassoon, 2 horns, 2 vlns., vla., vc., double bass.	*before* 1775 [1]
25.	C major		
26.	F major	Set of 8 *Notturni* commissioned by King Ferdinand IV of Naples, for 2 *lire organizzate* (or flute and oboe), 2 clarinets (or violins), 2 horns, 2 violas and bass.	Set completed 1790
26.	G major		
28.	F major		
29.	C major		
30.	G major		
31.	C major		
32.	C major		
33.	F major		
34.	C major	Flute, 2 oboes, 2 horns, 2 violins and bass. Listed as *Scherzandi* in Breitkopf's Catalogue for 1765.	Probably *c.* 1760
35.	D major		
36.	G major		
37.	E major		
38.	A major		

Nos. 39–47 are works of which the authenticity is doubtful. No. 39 is the 'Echo' Sextet, Nos. 41–6 are the six *Feldpartiten* of which one contains the *Chorale St. Antoni*, No. 47 is the 'Toy Symphony.' See above, p. 171 n.

To the above Mr. H. C. Robbins Landon has added the following works, published under his editorship by Doblinger in the series *Diletto Musicale* (numbers in this series given in brackets):

Description	Scoring	Series No.	Date
Divertimento, D major	2 ob., 2 bassoons, 2 horns. (Hoboken II. D18)	(D.M.33)	*c.* 1760
Divertimento, G major	2 ob., 2 bassoons, 2 horns	(D.M.85)	*c.* 1760
Divertimento, D major	2 ob., 2 bassoons, 2 horns	(D.M.86)	*c.* 1760

[1] The autograph has only recently come to light; see Van Hoboken's notes on this work.

Description	Scoring	Series No.	Date
Cassation, G major	2 ob., 2 horns, 2 vlns., 2 vlas., vc., bass. (Hoboken II. G1)	(D.M.47)	
Cassation, D major	4 horns, vln., vla., bass	(D.M.66)	*c.* 1761–5

The *Six Divertissements à 8 Parties Concertantes* are listed in Group X.

GROUP III. STRING QUARTETS

The opus numbers are given here in addition to Van Hoboken's numbering.

No.	Op. No.	Key	Remarks	Date
1.	1, 1	B flat major		1755
2.	1, 2	E flat major		
3.	1, 3	D major		
4.	1, 4	G major		
5.	1, 5	B flat major	Originally a symphony, I. 107	
6.	1, 6	C major		
7.	2, 1	A major		
8.	2, 2	E major		
9.	2, 3	E flat major	Originally a divertimento with 2 horns, II. 21	
10.	2, 4	F major		
11.	2, 5	D major	Originally a divertimento with 2 horns, II. 22	
12.	2, 6	B flat major		
13.	3, 1	E major		? 1767
14.	3, 2	C major		
15.	3, 3	G major		
16.	3, 4	B flat major		
17.	3, 5	F major		
18.	3, 6	A major		
19.	9, 1	C major		
20.	9, 2	E flat major		
21.	9, 3	G major		
22.	9, 4	D minor		*pub.* 1769
23.	9, 5	B flat major		
24.	9, 6	A major		

Haydn

No.	Op. No.	Key	Remarks	Date
25.	17, 1	E major		
26.	17, 2	F major		
27.	17, 3	E flat major		
28.	17, 4	C minor		1771
29.	17, 5	G major		
30.	17, 6	D major		
31.	20, 1	E flat major		
32.	20, 2	C major		
33.	20, 3	G minor		
34.	20, 4	D major		1772
35.	20, 5	F minor		
36.	20, 6	A major		
37.	33, 1	B minor		
38.	33, 2	E flat major		
39.	33, 3	C major		
40.	33, 4	B flat major		pub. 1782
41.	33, 5	G major		
42.	33, 6	D major		
43.	42	D minor		1785
44.	50, 1	B flat major		
45.	50, 2	C major		
46.	50, 3	E flat major	Ded. to King Frederick	
47.	50, 4	F sharp minor	William II of Prussia	pub. 1787
48.	50, 5	F major		
49.	50, 6	D major		
50–6.	51, 1–7		*The Seven Words* arr. for Quartet. See below, Group XX	1787
57.	54, 2	C major		
58.	54, 1	G major		
59.	54, 3	E major		
60.	55, 1	A major		pub. 1789
61.	55, 2	F minor and major		
62.	55, 3	B flat major		
63.	64, 5	D major		
64.	64, 6	E flat major		
65.	64, 1	C major		
66.	64, 4	G major		1790
67.	64, 3	B flat major		
68.	64, 2	B minor		

Appendix B—Catalogue of Works

No.	Op. No.	Key	Remarks	Date
69.	71, 1	B flat major		
70.	71, 2	D major		
71.	71, 3	E flat major	Dedicated to Count Anton	
72.	74, 1	C major	Apponyi	1793
73.	74, 2	F major		
74.	74, 3	G minor		
75.	76, 1	G major		
76.	76, 2	D minor		
77.	76, 3	D major	Dedicated to Count Joseph	
78.	76, 4	B flat major	Erdödy	1797
79.	76, 5	D major		
80.	76, 6	E flat major		
81.	77, 1	G major	Dedicated to Prince Lob-	
82.	77, 2	F major	kowitz	1799
83.	103	B flat major—D minor (unfinished)		1803

GROUP IV. DIVERTIMENTI FOR THREE INSTRUMENTS

No.	Key	Scoring	Date
1.	C major	2 fl. and vc.	1794
2.	G major	2 fl. and vc.	1794
3.	G major	2 fl. and vc.	1794
4.	G major	2 fl. and vc.	1794
	(one movement)		
5.	E flat major	Horn, vln. and vc.	1767
6.	D major		
7.	G major		
8.	G major	2 vlns (or fl. and vln.) and vc. Partly *pub.* 1784
9.	C major	arranged from other works	
10.	G major		
11.	A major		

GROUP V. STRING TRIOS

Entered in Haydn's Thematic Catalogue as 'Sonatas for two Violins and Violoncello,' they are in fact Trio Sonatas for two violins and string bass with continuo.   They are early works dating probably from 1750 to 1760.[1]

No	Key	No	Key
1.	E major	12.	E major
2.	F major	13.	B flat major
3.	B minor	14.	B minor
4.	E flat	15.	D major
5.	B major	16.	C major
6.	E flat major	17.	E flat major
7.	A major	18.	B flat major
8.	B flat major	19.	E major
9.	E flat major	20.	G major
10.	F major	21.	D major
11.	E flat major		

GROUP VI.   STRING DUOS

Those of which the authenticity is established are all for violin and viola, and are listed as such in Haydn's Thematic Catalogue.

No.	Key	No	Key
1.	F major	4.	D major
2.	A major	5.	E flat major
3.	B flat major	6.	C major

GROUP VII.   CONCERTOS

(a) Violin

No.	Key	Remarks	Date
1.	C major		before 1765
2.	D major		before 1765
3.	A major		before 1770
4.	G major		before 1769

[1] The *Sechs Sonaten für 2 Violinen und Klavier* (*Violoncello ad lib*) *Opus 8*, edited by A. Gülzow and Wilhelm Weismann (Peters), is a reprint of *Six Sonates à deux Violons & Basse* published by J. J. Hummel, Amsterdam, 1770.   It contains Nos. 4, 20, 3 and 17 of the above list, together with Nos. G2 and A1, the authenticity of which is not established.

(b) Violoncello [1]

No.	Key		Date
1.	C major		
2.	D major		1783

(c) Double Bass

1.	D major		Lost

(d) Horn

No.	Key		Date
1.	D major		Lost
2.	E flat major	(for 2 horns)	Lost
3.	D major		1762
4.	D major	(authenticity not established)	before 1781

(e) Trumpet

1.	E flat major		1796

(f) Flute

1.	D major		Lost
2.	D major	Probably spurious (by Leopold Hoffmann)	

(g) Oboe

1.	C major	Probably spurious

(h) Two Lire Organizzate

No.	Key	Date
1.	C major	1786
2.	G major	1786
3.	G major	1786
4.	F major	1786
5.	F major	1786

The Keyboard Concertos and the F major Concerto for violin and cembalo are listed below in Group XVIII.

The *Sinfonia Concertante* for violin, cello, oboe and bassoon is entered as Symphony No. 105.

---

[1] The lost C major Concerto has recently been found in Prague (information received from Mr. H. C. Robbins Landon). The remaining concertos listed by Van Hoboken (Nos. VII. 4, 5 and G1) are not definitely authentic (see his introduction to this group).

GROUP VIII. MARCHES

No.	Key	Remarks	Date
1.	E flat major	Composed for Sir Henry Harpur, Bart., and presented by him to the Volunteer Cavalry of Derbyshire	1795
2.	C major		
3.	E flat major	Wind-band version composed for Prince of Wales, orchestral version for Royal Society of Musicians [1]	1792
4.	E flat major	Hungarian National March	1802
5.	C major	From *Il mondo della luna*	
6.	E flat major		*before* 1793
7.	E flat major		fragment only

Added by H. C. Robbins Landon:

	G major	Marche Regimento de Marshall	*c.* 1772 [2]

GROUP IX. DANCES

No.	Description	Date
1.	1. 12 Minuets. Undated autograph, Monastery of Seitenstetten	*before* 1760
2.	6 Minuets, listed in Catalogue of Hohenzollern Archives, Sigmaringen (authenticity not established)	*before* 1766
3.	16 Minuets (12 in undated autograph, Esterházy archives, 4 lost; autograph for keyboard, but listed in Breitkopf Catalogue 1767 as for orch.)	*before* 1767
4.	12 Minuets pub. by J. J. Hummel (authenticity not established)	*pub.* 1766
5.	6 Minuets	1776
6.	12 Minuets (last four identical with No. 5, 1–4); authenticity of remaining eight not established)	? 1776
7.	14 *Menuetti ballabili*	*pub.* Artaria 1784
8.	12 Minuets *pour le clavecin ou piano forte*	*pub.* Artaria 1785
9.	6 Deutsche Tänze (*Allemandes*)	*pub.* Artaria 1787
10.	12 Deutsche Tänze (authenticity not established)	? *pub.* 1793

---

[1] Karl Haas, 'Haydn's English Military Marches' (*The Score*, Jan. 1950).

[2] Published as No. 1 of his edition of Haydn's Marches (Verlag Doblinger, *Diletto Musicale* No. 34).

No.	Description	Date
11.	12 Minuets for the Redoutensaal	1792
12.	12 Deutsche Tänze for the Redoutensaal	1792

The remaining numbers (13–30) listed by Van Hoboken are, according to the sources cited by him, of non-proven or doubtful authenticity, with the exception of the following:

23. Minuet in G. Undated autograph in Esterházy archives
24. Minuet in C. Complete undated autograph sketch in Marburg, Westdeutsche Bibliothek (formerly Prussian State Library, Berlin)

GROUP X. DIVERTIMENTI WITH BARYTON

No.	Key	Scoring	Date
1.	D major	Originally scored for baryton, 2 vlns.,	1775
2.	D major	vla., vc., d.-bass, 2 horns, Nos. 1–5	prob. 1775
3.	A minor and major	were published, with No. 12, by Artaria in 1781, replacing the baryton by a flute, as *Six Divertissements*	1775
4.	G major	ton by a flute, as *Six Divertissements*	prob. 1775
5.	G major	*à 8 Parties Concertantes*, Op. 31.	1775
6.	A major	Baryton, 2 vlns., vla., vc., d.-bass, 2 horns	c. 1775
7.	D major	Baryton, vla., bass, 2 horns	Lost
8.	G major	Baryton, vla., vc., (2 horns ?)	Lost
9.	D major	2 barytons, 2 horns	Lost
10.	D major	Baryton, vla., bass, 2 horns	1767–8
11.	D major	Baryton, vc. (bass ?)	before 1770
12.	G major	See note on Nos. 1–5 above. Original scoring not known	before 1781

GROUP XI. BARYTON TRIOS (FOR BARYTON, VIOLA AND VIOLONCELLO)

Date: Nos. 1–96, 1765–71; Nos. 97–126, 1771–5.[1]

1.	A major	4.	A major	7.	A major	10.	A major
2.	A major	5.	A major	8.	A major	11.	D major
3.	A major	6.	A major	9.	A major	12.	A major

[1] See Van Hoboken's introduction to this group, and the volumes published by the Joseph Haydn Institute (Series XIV).

13.	A major	42.	D major	71.	A major	100.	F major
14.	D major	43.	D major	72.	D major	101.	C major
15.	A major	44.	D major	73.	G major	102.	G major
16.	A major	45.	D major	74.	D major	103.	A major
17.	D major	46.	A major	75.	A major	104.	D major
18.	A major	47.	G major	76.	C major	105.	G major
19.	A major	48.	D major	77.	G major	106.	D major
20.	D major	49.	G major	78.	D major	107.	D major
21.	A major	50.	D major	79.	D major	108.	A major
22.	A major	51.	A major	80.	G major	109.	C major
23.	D major	52.	D major	81.	D major	110.	C major
24.	D major	53.	G major	82.	C major	111.	G major
25.	A major	54.	A major	83.	F major	112.	D major
26.	G major	55.	G major	84.	G major	113.	D major
27.	D major	56.	D major	85.	D major	114.	D major
28.	D major	57.	A major	86.	A major	115.	D major
29.	A major	58.	D major	87.	A minor	116.	G major
30.	G major	55.	G major	88.	A major	117.	F major
31.	D major	60.	A major	89.	G major	118.	D major
32.	G major	61.	D major	90.	C major	119.	G major
33.	A major	62.	G major	91.	D major	120.	D major
34.	D major	63.	D major	92.	G major	121.	A major
35.	A major	64.	D major	93.	C major	122.	A major
36.	D major	65.	G major	94.	A major	123.	G major
37.	G major	66.	A major	95.	D major	124.	G major
38.	A major	67.	G major	96.	B minor	125.	G major
39.	D major	68.	A major	97.	D major	126.	C major
40.	D major	69.	D major	98.	D major		
41.	D major	70.	G major	99.	G major		

GROUP XII. BARYTON DUOS

The works in this group are listed on the basis of entries in Haydn's two Thematic Catalogues. The majority (Nos. 2, 3, 6–18, 20–5) are now lost. Those that have been preserved are listed below.

No.	Key	Scoring	Date
1.	A major	Baryton and vc. (with bass ?)	*before* 1770
4.	G major	2 barytons	*before* 1770
5.	D major	2 barytons (with bass ?)	*before* 1770
19.	A and D major	12 short movements. 2 barytons and bass	*before* 1765

Appendix B—Catalogue of Works

GROUP XIII. BARYTON CONCERTOS

1 and 2.	D major	⎫
3.	D major 2 barytons	⎬ Lost

GROUP XIV. DIVERTIMENTI WITH KEYBOARD

No.	Key	Scoring	Date
1.	E flat major	Cembalo, vln., bass, 2 horns	*before* 1766
2.	F major	Cembalo, baryton, 2 vlns.	*before* 1769
3.	C major	Cembalo, 2 vlns., vc.	*c.* 1767
4.	C major	Cembalo, 2 vlns., vc.	1764
5.	D major	Cembalo, 2 vlns., vc.	*before* 1766
6.	G major	Cembalo, 2 vlns., vc.	*before* 1766 [1]
7.	C major	Cembalo, 2 vlns., vc.	*before* 1766
8.	C major	Cembalo, 2 vlns., vc.	*before* 1766
9.	F major	Cembalo, 2 vlns., vc.	*before* 1766
10.	C major	Cembalo, 2 vlns., ?	? [2]
11.	C major	Cembalo, 2 vlns, vc.	1760
12.	C major	Cembalo, 2 vlns., vc.	*before* 1766
13.	G major	Cembalo, 2 vlns., vc.	?

GROUP XV. PIANO TRIOS

Of the works in this group, Nos. 1–31 are the piano trios (mostly mature works) listed as such by Larsen (*Drei Haydn Kataloge*) and published in the Peters Edition. No. 32 is the Sonata in G for violin and piano (see Group XVA). Nos. 33–41 are works of early date, classified by Larsen as Divertimenti with Keyboard.

No.	Peters	Key	Date
1.	19	G minor	*before* 1769
2.	26	F major	*before* 1769
3.	12	C major [3] ⎫	
4.	27	F major ⎬	*before* 1784
5.	28	G major ⎭	

---

[1] i.e. three movements of piano Sonata, XVI. 6; Haydn himself noted it at different times as 'per il Cembalo Solo' and 'con due Violini e Basso.'

[2] Only the cembalo part is extant. See Larsen, *Die Haydn-Überlieferung*, p. 303.

[3] Nos. 3 and 4 are possibly by Michael Haydn. See Van Hoboken, also Larsen, *Die Haydn-Überlieferung*, pp. 141 ff.

No.	Peters	Key	Date
6.	25	F major	1784
7.	10	D major	c. 1785
8.	24	B flat major	c. 1785
9.	15	A major	1875
10.	20	E flat major	c. 1785
11.	16	E flat major	before 1789
12.	7	E minor	before 1789
13.	14	C minor and major	before 1789
14.	11	A flat major	1789–90
15.	31	G major ⎫	
16.	30	D major ⎬ flute trios	1789–90
17.	29	F major ⎭	
18.	13	A major	before 1794
19.	17	G minor	before 1794
20.	9	B flat major	before 1794
21.	21	C major	1794–5
22.	23	E flat major	1794–5
23.	22	D minor and major	1794–5
24.	6	D major ⎫	
25.	1	G major ⎪	
26.	2	F sharp minor ⎪	
27.	3	C major ⎬	1794–5
28.	4	E major ⎪	
29.	5	E flat major ⎭	
30.	8	E flat major	1795
31.	18	E flat minor and major	1795
32.		G major. Violin sonata. See below, XVA.	1793–4
33.		D major	
34.		E major	
35.		A major	prob. before 1760
36.		E flat major	
37.		F major	before 1766
38.		B flat major	
39.		F major (consists mainly of movements from early piano sonatas)	
40.		F major	prob. before 1760
41.		G major	before 1767

Appendix B—Catalogue of Works

GROUP XVA. A DUO SONATAS

In this subsection Van Hoboken lists, without numbers, the works by Haydn published at various times as sonatas for violin and piano. Trio No. XV. 32 in G major = Sonata No. 1 for violin and piano (Peters Edition), which was first published as a trio in London in 1794, although this edition was quickly followed by editions for piano and violin. The remaining works are either (a) piano sonatas published during Haydn's lifetime with a violin 'accompaniment' (noted as such under Group XVI, Piano Sonatas), or (b), arrangements of works for other combinations (e.g. Peters Ed. Nos. 7 and 8, which are arrangements by A. E. Müller of the string Quartets, Op. 77.

GROUP XVI. PIANO SONATAS

The numbers in the Augener and Peters Editions are also given for reference.

No.	Augener	Peters	Key	Date
1.	—	—	C major	before 1760
2.	—	22	B flat major	prob. before 1760
3.	—	—	C major	prob. before 1760
4.	—	—	D major	prob. before 1760
5.	25	23	A major	before 1763
6.	26	37	G major ⎫	
7.	27	—	C major ⎬	before 1766
8.	28	—	G major ⎪	
9.	29	—	F major ⎭	
10.	—	43	C major ⎫	
11.	—	11	G major ⎬	before 1767
12.	30	29	A major ⎪	
13.	17	18	E major ⎭	
14.	11	15	D major	
*15.[1]	—	—	C major	
16.[1]	—	—	E flat major	c. 1767
17.[1]	—	—	B flat major	

* Violin Sonata in Peters Edition.

---

[1] No. 15 is a keyboard version of three movements of Divertimento II. 11. The authenticity of Nos. 16 and 17 is not established.

No.	Augener	Peters	Key	Date
18.	31	19	B flat major	
19.	22	9	D major	1767
20.	32	25	C minor	1771
21.	33	16	C major	
22.	10	40	E major	1773
23.	13	21	F major	
*24.	—	31	D major	
*25.	—	31	E flat major	1773
*26.	—	33	A major	
27.	9	12	G major	
28.	34	13	E flat major	1774–6
29.	8	14	F major	(No. 29 part aut. 1774)
30.	35	36	A major	
31.	24	30	E major	
32.	36	39	B minor	
33.	14	20	D major ⎫	
34.	2	2	E minor ⎬	pub. 1783–4
35.	5	5	C major ⎭	
36.	6	6	C sharp minor	pub. 1780
37.	7	7	D major	
38.	21	35	E flat major	
39.	12	17	G major	
40.	16	10	G major ⎫	
41.	19	27	B flat major ⎬	1784
42.	20	28	D major ⎭	
*43.	—	41	A flat major	pub. 1783
44.	4	4	G minor	prob. 1766
45.	37	26	E flat major	1766
46.	38	8	A flat major	c. 1770
47.	39	34	F major	pub. 1788
48.	15	24	C major	1789
49.	3	3	E flat major	1789–90
50.	23	42	C major	1794–5
51.	18	38	D major	prob. 1794
52.	1	1	E flat major	1794

The 8 sonatas listed in Haydn's Draft Catalogue and now lost are entered by Van Hoboken as Nos. 2a–h.

* Violin Sonatas in Peters Edition.

Appendix B—Catalogue of Works

Group XVII. Piano Pieces

Of the works in this group Nos. 1–6 are authenticated by entries in Haydn's Thematic Catalogue. Nos. 7–12, though authenticated in other ways, are impossible to date with certainty.

No.	Description	Date
1.	Capriccio, G major	1765
2.	Arietta con Variazioni, A major	*before* 1771
3.	Arietta con Variazioni, E flat major	*before* 1774
4.	Fantasia, C major	1789
5.	Variations, C major	1790
6.	Variations, F minor	1793
7.	Variations, D major	*before* 1766
8.	Variations, D major	
9.	Adagio, F major	
10.	Allegretto, G major	*prob.* 1793
11.	Andante, C major	
12.	Andante con Variazioni, B flat major	

Group XVIIa. Piano Duets

No.	Description	Date
1.	Variations, F major (*Il maestro e lo scolare*)	*before* 1778
2.	Allegro and Minuet and Trio, F major	

Group XVIII. Keyboard Concertos

No.	Key	Date
1.	C major ('Concerto per l'Organo')	1756
2.	D major	*before* 1767
3.	F major	*before* 1771
4.	G major	*c.* 1770
5.	C major	*before* 1763
6.	F major, for violin and cembalo	*before* 1766
7.	F major	*before* 1766
8.	C major	*prob. before* 1760
9.	G major	*before* 1767
10.	C major	*before* 1771
11.	D major	*before* 1782

Haydn

GROUP XIX. PIECES FOR MUSICAL CLOCK

This group lists the 32 short pieces written by Haydn for different musical clocks and published by E. F. Schmid as *Joseph Haydn: Werke für das Laufwerk* (Nagels Musik Archiv No. 1, 1932, revised edition 1954). The numbers in brackets refer to this edition. Thirteen of the pieces are variants of movements from other works.

Clock of 1772

1. (13) F major
2. (14) F major
3. (15) F major
4. (16) C major
5. (17) F major
6. (18) F major

Clocks of 1772 and 1792

7. (8) C major
8. (6) C major
9. (11) C major
10. (2) C major

Clocks of 1772 and 1793

11. (19) C major
12. (20) C major
13. (21) C major
14. (22) C major
15. (23) C major
16. (24) C major

Clock of 1792

17. (1) C major
18. (3) C major
19. (4) C major
20. (5) C major
21. (7) G major
22. (9) C major
23. (10) C major

Clock of 1793

24. (12) C major
25. (25) D major
26. (26) E major
27. (27) G major
28. (28) C major
29. (29) C major
30. (30) G major

On none of the three clocks

31. (31) C major
32. (32) F major

GROUP XX. THE SEVEN WORDS OF OUR SAVIOUR ON THE CROSS

		Date
1		
(a)	Original orchestral version	1785
(b)	Version for string quartet made by Haydn	pub. 1787
(c)	Piano reduction, approved by Haydn	pub. 1787
2		
(d)	Vocal version	1799

GROUP XXI. ORATORIOS

Title	Date
Il ritorno di Tobia	1774–5
Die Schöpfung (*The Creation*)	1796–8
Die Jahreszeiten (*The Seasons*)	1798–1801

GROUP XXII. MASSES

No.		Date
1.	Missa brevis, F major	*c.* 1749–50
2.	Missa in honorem beatissimae Virginis Mariae, E flat major (Great Organ Mass)	? 1766
3.	Missa Sanctae Caeciliae, C major	*c.* 1769–73
4.	Missa Sancti Nicolai, G major	1772
5.	Missa brevis Sancti Joannis de Deo, B flat major (Little Organ Mass)	*c.* 1775
6.	Missa Cellensis, C major (Mariazell Mass)	1782
7.	Missa in tempore belli, C major (*Paukenmesse*, i.e. 'Kettledrum' Mass)	1796
8.	Missa Sancti Bernardi de Offida, B flat major (*Heiligmesse*)	1796
9.	Missa in Angustiis, D minor ('Nelson' Mass)[1]	1798
10.	Mass in B flat major (*Theresienmesse*)	1799
11.	Mass in B flat major (*Schöpfungsmesse*, i.e. 'Creation' Mass)	1801
12.	Mass in B flat major (*Harmoniemesse*, i.e. 'Wind-band' Mass)	1802
13.	Mass 'Sunt bona mixta malis,' D minor	Lost
14.	Mass 'Rorate coeli desuper'	*c.* 1749–50[2]

GROUP XXIII. OTHER CHURCH WORKS

Te Deum	Date
C major	*before* 1764
C major	*c.* 1799–1800

---

[1] Also, for no apparent reason, known as the 'Imperial' or 'Coronation' Mass.

[2] This Mass, long believed to be lost, was rediscovered in 1957 by H. C. Robbins Landon in the music archives of Göttweig Abbey. It was published under his editorship by the Haydn-Mozart Press, London.

Haydn

	Date
Stabat Mater	
G minor	1767–8
Ave Regina	
A major [1]	
F major [1]	
Salve Regina	
E major	1756
G minor	1771
E flat major [1]	*c.* 1760–70
G major [1]	*c.* 1761–70
Litania de B.V.M.	
C major	*c.* 1780

Offertories and Motets

  Accurrite hunc mortales ⎫ from Esterházy Cantata
  Plausus honores date   ⎭

  O Jesu te invocamus   ⎫ from *Applausus*
  Concertantes jugiter per calamitatem ⎭

  Insanae et vanae curae ⎫
  Audi clamorem   ⎬ from *Il ritorno di Tobia*
  Alleluia   ⎭

  Ad aras convolate [1]
  Animae Deo gratae
  Ens aeternum attende votis ('Walte gnädig, O ewige Liebe')
  Non nobis Domine
  Sankta Thekla
  Super flumina (Motetto de tempore)

Arias and duets

  Christus coeli atria ⎫
  Resonant tympanae   ⎬ from *Applausus*
  Dictamina mea   ⎭

  Cantilena pro Adventu, 'Ein' Magd, ein' Dienerin,' A major
  Aria pro Adventu, 'Mutter Gottes, mir erlaube'
  Aria pro Adventu, 'Maria die Reine' (arranged from *Philemon und Baucis*)
  Aria de Venerabili, *Lauda Sion Salvatorem*

---

[1] Authenticity not established.

Six settings of metrical psalms contributed to 'Improved Psalmody . . . The Psalms of David from a Poetical Version originally written by the late Reverend James Merrick, A.M. . . . with new Music collected from the most Eminent Composers by the Reverend William Dechair Tattersall.' Vol. I, London 1794. Haydn's settings comprise selected verses of Psalms 26, 31, 41, 50, 62 and 69.

GROUP XXIV. CHORUSES, CANTATAS AND ARIAS WITH ORCHESTRA

(a) *Choral*

	Date
Cantata for Prince Nicholas Esterházy, *Destatevi o miei fidi*, G major	1763
Cantata for Prince Nicholas Esterházy, *Sembra que in questo giorno* (possibly a sequel to foregoing), G major	1763
Cantata, *Qual dubbio*, A major	1764
Applausus for the birthday of an Abbot	1768
Die Erwählung eines Kapellmeisters, cantata buffa	? 1770
The Storm, for soli, chorus and orchestra	1792
Mare Clausum (unfinished)	1794
What Art Expresses, for solo, chorus and piano (text by Dr. Harington of Bath)	1794
Vivan gl' illustri sposi Al tuo arrivo felice Dei clementi	Lost [1]

(b) *Concerted Solo Works* [2]

Terzetto, Pietà di me, benigni Dei (2 sopranos and tenor)	*prob.* 1795
Terzetto, Levatevi presto (male voices) for pasticcio *La Circe*	1789
Duet, Dunque o Di quando sperai (alto and tenor)	*before* 1790

---

[1] Regarding the assumption by some writers that these three works were based on movements of baryton trios, see Larsen, *Die Haydn-Überlieferung*, pp. 237, 290, and Van Hoboken's remarks on Baryton Trio No. 116.

[2] The terzetto *Pietà di me, benigni Dei* was composed for Mrs. Billington (H. C. R. Landon, *The Symphonies of Joseph Haydn*, p. 861). The duet *Quel cor umano e tenero* (not listed) is simply the duet of Eurilla and Pasquale, 'Quel tuo visetto amabile,' from *Armida*, with a fresh text. (H. C. R. Landon, Supplement to *The Symphonies of Joseph Haydn*, pp. 42-3.)

Haydn

(c) Solo Cantatas and Concert Arias	Date
Ah, come il cuore mi palpita	c. 1782
Deutschlands Klage über den Tod Friedrichs des Grossen.	
(Lost; fragment only preserved)	1786
Cantata, *Miseri noi, misera patria*	c. 1790
Scena, *Berenice, che fai?*	1795
Concert Aria, *Solo e pensoso*	1798

(d) Arias

1. For his own operas

Title	Opera	Date
Tergi i vezzosi rai (text re- composed for bass)	*Acide e Galatea* (1762)	1773
Or vicino a ti il mio core	*L'incontro improvviso* (1775)	c. 1780
L'amore di natura	*La fedeltà premiata* (1780)	before 1782
Deh, soccorre un'infelice	*La fedeltà premiata*	
Dove son che miro intorno	*La fedeltà premiata*	
Placidi ruscelletti (two versions)	*La fedeltà premiata*	
Tornate per mia bella	*La fedeltà premiata*	

2. For operas by other composers

Title	Opera	Date
Quando la rosa	Anfossi, *Metilde ritrovata*	1779
Dice benissimo	Salieri, *La scuola de' gelosi*	1780
Dica pure che vuol dire	Anfossi, *Il geloso in cimento*	before 1785
Signor voi sapete	Anfossi, *Il matrimonio per inganno*	1785
Sono Alcina	Gazzaniga, *L'isola d'Alcina*	1786
Ah, tu non senti, amico	Traetta, *Ifigenia in Tauride*	1786
Un cor si tenero in petto forte	Bianchi, *Il disertore*	1787
Vada adagio Signorina	Guglielmi, *La Quakera spiritosa*	1787
Chi vive amante	Bianchi, *Alessandro nell'Indie* (text by Metastasio)	1787
Se tu me sprezzi, ingrata	Sarti, *I finti erede*	1788
Infelice, sventurata	Cimarosa, *I due supposti Conti*	1789
Son due ore che giro	*La Circe* (pasticcio)	1789
Son pietosa, son bonina	*La Circe* (pasticcio)	1789

238

Title	Opera	Date
Da che penso a maritarmi	Gassmann, *L'amore artigiano*	1790
Il meglio mio carattere	Cimarosa, *L'impresario in angustie*	1790
La moglie quando e buona	Cimarosa, *Giannina e Bernardone*	1790
Costretta piangere	probably Cimarosa, *Il credulo*	
D'una sposa meschinella	possibly Paisiello, *La frascatana*	? 1777

N.B. This list is based on the list of Haydn's *Einlage-arien* given in *Haydn als Opernkapellmeister*, by Dénes Bartha and László Somfai. It includes, however, only those of which the complete text and music have been preserved, and does not include Haydn's revisions of arias by other composers.

GROUP XXV. PARTSONGS
(Joseph Haydn Institute, Series XXX)

1. Der Augenblick
2. Die Harmonie in der Ehe
3. Alles hat seiner Zeit
4. Die Beredsamkeit
5. Der Greis
6. An den Vetter
7. Daphnens einziger Fehler
8. Die Warnung
9. Betrachtung des Todes
10. Wider den Übermuth
11. An die Frauen
12. Danklied zu Gott
13. Abendlied zu Gott

GROUP XXVI. SOLO SONGS AND CANTATAS WITH KEYBOARD

1. SONGS (Joseph Haydn Institute, Series XXIX, Vol. 1)

I. *24 German Songs*

(a) XII Lieder für das Klavier—Erster Teil (1781)

1. Das strickende Mädchen
2. Cupido
3. Der erste Kuss

Appendix B—Catalogue of Works

35. Piercing Eyes
36. Content
36a. Der verdienstvolle Sylvius (Ich bin der Verliebteste)
    Original German version of No. 36.

III. *Miscellaneous Songs*

37. Beim Schmerz, der dieses Herz durchwühlet
38. Der schlaue und dienstfertige Pudel
39. Trachten will ich nicht auf Erden
40. Abschiedslied
41. The Spirit's Song
42. O Tuneful Voice
43. Gott, erhalte Franz den Kaiser
44. Als einst mit Weibes Schönheit
45. Ein kleines Haus (Un tetto umil)
46. Vergiss mein nicht (Antwort auf die Frage eines Mädchens)

Appendix (*Songs of doubtful authenticity*)

1. The Lady's Looking Glass (Trust not too much to that enchanting face)
2. Bald wehen uns des Frühlings Lüfte

2. CANTATAS AND DUETS

Duets	Date
Saper vorrei si m'amı	1796
Guarda qui, che lo vedrai	1796
Cantatas	
Arianna a Naxos	1789
Lines from 'The Battle of the Nile'	1800

GROUP XXVII. CANONS

(Joseph Haydn Institute Complete Edition, Series XXXI)

I. Die heiligen Zehn Gebote (The Ten Commandments) 1791–5
II. Secular Canons   1790–1800

No.	Title	First Line
1.	Hilar an Narziss	O stelle dich, Narziss, doch morgen bei mir ein!
2.	Auf einem adeligen Dummkopf	Das nenn' ich einen Edelmann.

No.	*Title*	*First line*
3.	Der Schuster bleib bei seinem Leist	Ein jeder bleib bei seinem Stand
4.	Herr von Gänsewitz zu seinem Kammerdiener	Befehlt doch draussen still zu schweigen
5.	An den Marull	Gross willst du und auch artig sein?
6.	Die Mutter an ihr Kind in der Wiege	Höre, Mädchen, meine Bitte!
7.	Der Menschenfreund	O wollte doch der Mensch
8.	Gottes Macht und Vorsehung	Ist Gott mein Schutz
9.	An Dorilis	Wie grausam, Dorilis
10.	Vixi	Ille potens sui laetusque deget
11.	Der Kobold	Du, merke dir die Lehre
12.	Der Fuchs und der Marder	Wer Schwache leiten will
13.	Abschied	Kenne Gott, die Welt und dich
14.	Die Hoffstellungen	Es stecket Ja in linken
15.	Aus Nichts wird Nichts/Nichts gewonnen, Nichts verloren	Nackt ward ich zu Welt geboren
16.	Cacatum non est pictum	Beherzigt doch das Dictum
17.	Tre cose	Aspettare e non venire
18.	Vergebliches Glück	Es is umsonst
19.	Grabschrift	Hier liegt Hans Lau
20.	Das Reitpferd	Wie manche schliefen hier mit Ehren
21.	Tod und Schlaf	Tod ist ein langer Schlaf
22.	An einen Geizingen	Ich dich beneiden?
23.	Das böse Weib	Ein einzig böses Weib
24.	Der Verlust	Alles ging für mich verloren
25.	Der Freigeist	Fliehe, fliehe, wenn dein Wohl heilig ist
26.	Die Liebe der Feinde	Nie will ich dem zu schaden suchen
27.	Der Furchtsame	Kaum seh' ich den Donner die Himmel umziehen
28.	Die Gewissheit	Ob ich morgen leben werde
29.	Phöbus und sein Sohn	Zwischen Gott und unsern Sinnen
30.	Die Tulipane	So war der Mensch zu allen Zeiten

No.	Title	First Line
31.	Das grösste Gut	Ein weises Herz und guter Mut
32.	Der Hirsch	Jeder prüfe seine Stärke!
33.	Überschrift eines Weinhauses	Wein, Bad und Liebe
34.	Der Esel und die Dohle	Ein Narr trifft allemal
35.	Schalksnarren	Ein Herr, der Narren hält
36.	Zweierlei Feinde	Dein kleinster Feind ist der
37.	Der Bäcker und die Maus	Wer leichtlich zürnt
38.	Die Flinte und der Hase	Was hilft Gesetz
39.	Der Nachbar	Sehr nützlich is uns oft ein Feind
40.	Liebe zur Kunst	Wer Lust zu lernen hat
41.	Frag und Antwort zweier Fuhrleute	Geh, sag mir nur
42.	Der Fuchs und der Adler	Je höher Stand, je mehr Gefahr
43.	Wunsch	Langweiliger Besuch macht Zeit und Zimmer enger
44.	Gott in Herzen	Gott in Herzen
45.	Turk was a Faithful Dog	Turk was a faithful dog
46.	Thy Voice, O Harmony	Thy voice, O Harmony

GROUP XXVIII. OPERAS

	Date
Acide e Galatea, festa teatrale (Migliavacca)	1762
La Canterina, intermezzo	1765
Lo speziale, dramma giocoso (Goldoni)	1768
Le pescatrici, dramma giocoso (Goldoni)	1769
L'infedeltà delusa, burletta (Coltellini)	1773
L'incontro improvviso, dramma giocoso (Friberth, after Dancourt's *La Rencontre imprévue*)	1775
La vera costanza, dramma giocoso (Puttini and Travaglia)	1776
Il mondo della luna, dramma giocoso (Goldoni)	1777
L'isola disabitata, azione teatrale (Metastasio)	1779
La fedeltà premiata, dramma giocoso	1780
Orlando Paladino, dramma eroi-comico (Nunziato Porta)	1782
Armida, dramma eroica (Durandi)	1784
L'anima del filosofo, opera seria (Badini). Extracts later published under the title *Orfeo ed Euridice—Dramma per musica*	1791

Haydn

Lost

Der krumme Teufel ⎫ Singspiel (Felix Kurz-Bernardon)	1751
Der neue krumme Teufel ⎭	1758
La Marchesa Nepola (? di Napoli) (fragments preserved) [1]	1762

Group XXIX. Marionette Operas

Die bestrafte Rachgier oder das abgebrannte Haus [2]
Philemon und Baucis (Singspiel)   1773

Lost

Der Götterat, oder Jupiters Reise auf der Erde (Prelude to *Philemon und Baucis*)	1773
Hexenschabbas	1773
Didone abbandonata	1777
Genovefens 4ter Teil	1777

Group XXX. Incidental Music

Der Zerstreute (trans. of *Le Distrait*, by Jean-Francois Regnard), i.e. Symphony No. 60 [3]	1774
Alfred oder der Patriotische König (Bicknell, trans. J. W. Cowmeadow). Duet, aria and Chorus of Danes	1796

Group XXXI. Arrangements of Scottish and Welsh Airs

402 arrangements in the following collections:

William Napier
1792-4. 'A Selection of Original Scots Songs . . .'   Vols. II (1792)

---

[1] Five complete and two incomplete arias are preserved in the National Library, Budapest, in an autograph headed 'arie per la Comedia Marchese.' The title of the work is entered in Haydn's Draft Catalogue as 'Comedia La Marchesa Nepola'; the three following entries, 'Comedia La Vedova,' 'Comedia Il Dottore' and 'Comedia Il Scanarello,' have long been regarded as titles of other lost operas; but Bartha and Somfai suggest that they may be dramatis personae in *La Marchesa Nepola*, of which one of the arias is for 'Scanarello.' (*Haydn als Opernkapellmeister*, Chap. VII.)

[2] See footnote 2, p. 195.

[3] See H. C. R. Landon, *The Symphonies of Joseph Haydn*, pp. 349–53, and Supplement to *The Symphonies of Joseph Haydn*, p. 38.

and III (1794) contain 100 and 50 airs respectively, all arranged by Haydn.

Joseph Haydn Institute Complete Edition, Series XXXII, Vol. I, contains the 100 songs of Napier, Vol. II.

George Thomson

1800–5. 'A Select Collection of Original Scottish Airs . . .' The various editions of, and supplements to, this collection contain 144 settings by Haydn.

'A Select Collection of Original Welsh Airs . . .' Contains 42 settings by Haydn.

'A Select Collection of Irish Airs . . .' Contains 1 setting by Haydn (the rest by Beethoven).

William Whyte

1800–5. 'A Collection of Scottish Airs harmonized for Voice and Pianoforte . . .' Vols. I and II, 65 settings, all by Haydn.

An additional 43 unpublished arrangements are mentioned by Karl Geiringer in his article 'Haydn and the Folksong of the British Isles' (*Musical Quarterly*, April 1949); of these, 37 are in the British Museum (Add. MS. 28613, 35272–5). His total, however, includes the *Six Admired Scotch Airs, arranged as Rondos* . . . which were published by Preston in 1805, and which are instrumental settings of airs which Haydn had already arranged for Thomson's collections.

APPENDIX C

Abaco, Evaristo Felice Dall' (1675–1742), violinist and composer at Bavarian court.

Abingdon, Willoughby Bertie, fourth Earl of (1740–99), Whig politician and writer, patron of music and amateur composer.

Alberti, Domenico (*c.* 1710–40), Italian composer, singer and harpsichord player. The keyboard device known as the 'Alberti bass' is so called from his frequent use of it.

Albrechtsberger, Johann Georg (1736–1809), theorist, composer and teacher, settled in Vienna.

Bach, Johann (John) Christian (1735–82), youngest son of Johann Sebastian Bach, composer and clavier player, settled in London.

Baldesturla, Costanza, Italian soprano, employed at Esterház, 1779–85. Went to Leipzig and married J. G. Schicht (1753–1810), who became cantor at the Thomasschule.

Barthélemon, François Hippolyte (1741–1808), French composer and violinist, settled in London.

Billington, Elizabeth, born *Weichsel* (*c.* 1768–1818), English soprano singer of German extraction, born in London. Married James Billington, a double-bass player.

Boccherini, Luigi (1743–1805), Italian composer and violoncellist, settled in Madrid after 1769 and for a time in Berlin.

Burney, Charles (1726–1814), English musical historian, organist and composer, author of *A General History of Music.* Father of Fanny Burney.

Caldara, Antonio (1670–1736), Venetian composer, settled in Vienna as Vice-Kapellmeister to J. J. Fux (*q.v.*).

Cannabich, Christian (1731–98), composer of the Mannheim school, also violinist and conductor there, and later at Munich.

Carpani, Giuseppe Antonio (1752–1825), Italian poet and writer on music, settled in Vienna, friend and biographer of Haydn.

Clement, Franz (1780–1842), Viennese violinist; first appeared in Vienna in 1789 and in London in 1790. Leader at the Theater an der Wien in Vienna, 1802–11.

Clementi, Muzio (1752–1832), Italian pianist, composer, publisher and piano manufacturer. Lived in England but made many continental tours.

Cramer, Wilhelm (1745–99), German violinist, settled in London in 1772. Leader of the king's band and many important concert organizations, including the 'Professional Concerts.' Father of J. B. Cramer (1771–1858), pianist and composer.

Davide, Giacomo (1750–1830), Italian tenor singer. First appeared in London in 1791.

Dies, Albert Christoph (1755–1822), landscape painter, friend and biographer of Haydn.

Dittersdorf, Karl Ditters von (1739–99), composer and violinist, friend of Haydn. Prolific composer in various branches of music.

Dragonetti, Domenico (1763–1846), Italian double-bass virtuoso. Appeared in London in 1794, and settled there.

Dussek, Jan Ladislav (1761–1812), Bohemian pianist and composer; lived in London 1790–1800. Married Sophia Corri (1775–1847), soprano singer.

Elssler, Johann (1767–1843), Haydn's servant and copyist. Father of the dancer Fanny Elssler (1810–84).

Fischer, Ludwig (1745–1825), German bass singer of European repute. Appeared in London in 1794.

Forster, William (1739–1808), violin maker, music seller and publisher in London.

Franz, Karl (1738–1802), horn and baryton player in Esterházy orchestra 1763–76. Later travelled as baryton virtuoso, and settled at Munich.

Friberth, Karl (1736–1816), Austrian tenor singer, composer and librettist. Worked for the Esterházys, 1759–76, and later in Vienna.

Fux, Johann Joseph (1660–1741), Austrian composer and theorist, appointed court *Kapellmeister* in Vienna in 1715. Author of the treatise on counterpoint, *Gradus ad Parnassum*.

Gallini, Giovanni Andrea Battista (Sir John) (1728–1805), Italian dancing master and theatrical manager, settled in London.

Gassmann, Florian Leopold (1723–74), Bohemian composer settled in Vienna, appointed musical director to the court in 1772. Father of soprano singer, Therese Gassmann.

Giardini, Felice de (1716–96), Italian violinist settled in London.

Appendix C—Personalia

Giornovichi, Giovanni (1740-1804), Italian violinist and composer, much travelled. Lived in London, 1791-6.

Griesinger, Georg August (died 1828), German tutor and diplomat, friend and biographer of Haydn.

Gyrowetz, Adalbert (1763-1850), Bohemian composer, prolific writer of orchestral, operatic and chamber music.

Harington, Henry (1727-1816), physician and composer settled at Bath. May have composed familiar setting of *Drink to me only*.

Hasse, Johann Adolph (1699-1783), German composer of Italian operas and oratorios. Husband of the Italian singer Faustina Bordoni (1700-81).

Haydn, Johann Evangelist (1743-1805), tenor singer of mediocre abilities, brother of Joseph Haydn.

Haydn, Johann Michael (1737-1806), composer and organist, brother of Joseph Haydn. Appointed musical director to the Bishop of Gross-wardein in 1757 and in 1762 became conductor to the Archbishop of Salzburg, where he was afterwards organist. Married the singer Maria Magdalena Lipp in 1768.

Janiewicz, Felix (1762-1848), Polish violinist, studied in Vienna and appeared in Paris and London.

Jansen, Therese (c. 1770-1843), German-born pianist, settled in England, pupil of Clementi (q.v.). Married Gaetano Bartolozzi, son of engraver Francesco Bartolozzi, in 1795. Mother of the actress Lucia Elizabeth Vestris.

Kelly, Michael (1762-1826), Irish tenor singer and composer, friend of Haydn and Mozart in Vienna.

Kraft, Anton (1752-1820), Bohemian violoncellist, baryton player and composer, employed at Esterház from 1778 to 1790.

Lidl, Andreas (c. 1740-before 1789), Austrian baryton (*viola di bordone*) virtuoso, first at Esterház, later throughout Europe.

Mannheim School, a group of composers so named for having their centre in the court of Mannheim. *See* Cannabich, Stamitz. Other members of the school were Filtz, Holzbauer, Richter and Toeschi.

Mara, Gertrud Elisabeth, born *Schmeling* (1749-1833), German soprano singer in Dresden, Vienna and London.

Martinez, Marianne (1744–1812), Austrian composer and clavier player of Spanish descent, daughter of the master of ceremonies to the papal nuncio in Vienna, pupil of Metastasio, Porpora and Haydn.

Mattheson, Johann (1681–1764), German theorist, composer and organist. Author of treatise *Der vollkommene Capellmeister.*

Monn, Georg Matthias (1717–50), Austrian composer, organist at the Karlskirche in Vienna and instrumental composer of the transitional Viennese school.

Neukomm, Sigismund von (1778–1858), Austrian composer and conductor, pupil of Haydn. Became director of the German Theatre at St. Petersburg, 1806. Later lived in England and France.

Pacchierotti, Gasparo (1744–1821), Italian male soprano singer. First appeared in London in 1778.

Palotta, Matteo (1680–1758), Italian priest and composer, appointed as court composer in Vienna.

Parke, William Thomas (1762–1841), oboe player in London. Author of *Musical Memoirs.* Uncle of Maria Hester Parke (1775–1822), soprano singer, pianist and composer.

Pleyel, Ignaz Joseph (1757–1831), Austrian composer and clavier player, pupil of Haydn. Later settled in Paris as piano manufacturer, and published a complete edition of Haydn's quartets in 1802.

Porpora, Niccolò Antonio (1686–1766), Italian composer, theorist and singing teacher. Master of Haydn.

Pugnani, Gaetano (1731–98), Italian violinist and composer. Toured Europe, visiting Paris and London, and finally settled at Turin.

Rauzzini, Venanzio (1746–1810), Italian singer, teacher and composer, settled at Bath from 1787 onwards.

Reichardt, Johann Friedrich (1752–1814), German composer and writer on music, one of the early composers of German songs.

Reutter, Johann Adam Karl Georg von (1708–72), composer in Vienna, *Kapellmeister* of the Cathedral of St. Stephen from 1738. Haydn's master.

Rosetti (or *Roessler*), *Antonio* (*c.* 1745–92), Bohemian violinist and composer, member of Esterházy orchestra, 1776–81. Later orchestral director to Prince Oettingen-Wallerstein and Duke of Mecklenburg-Schwerin.

Salieri, Antonio (1750–1825), Italian composer who settled in Vienna in 1766, studied under Gassmann (q.v.) and succeeded Bonno as court *Kapellmeister* in 1788.

Appendix C—Personalia

Salomon, Johann Peter (1745–1815), German violinist, settled in London from 1781. Appeared as soloist with the Professional Concerts, and later organized his own series of subscription concerts.

Sammartini, Giovanni Battista (c. 1701–75). Italian composer, mainly of instrumental music, in Milan. Master of Gluck.

Schenk, Johann (1753–1836), Austrian composer and theorist.

Schikaneder, Emanuel (1748–1812), German actor, singer, playwright and theatrical manager settled in Vienna. Part librettist of Mozart's *The Magic Flute.*

Schroeter, Johann Samuel (1750–88), German pianist and composer, brother of the singer Corona Schroeter (1751–1802). Appeared in England in 1772 and succeeded J. C. Bach (q.v.) as music master to Queen Charlotte in 1782.

Schulz, Johann Abraham Peter (1747–1800), German composer, conductor and writer on music. Composed numerous songs.

Shield, William (1748–1829), violinist and composer in London. Composer to Covent Garden Theatre, 1778–91 and 1792–7.

Smart, George Thomas (1776–1867), conductor, organist and composer in London.

Stamitz, Johann Wenzel Anton (1717–57), Bohemian composer, musical director to the court of Mannheim and founder of the Mannheim school of composers. Father of Karl Stamitz (1746–1801), another symphonist of the same group.

Storace, Stephen (1763–96), English composer of Italian descent, brother of Ann (Nancy) Storace (1766–1817) and pupil of Mozart.

Swieten, Gottfried van, Baron (1734–1803), Austrian diplomat, court librarian and musical amateur in Vienna.

Thomson, George (1757–1851), Scottish official and musical collector, who published collections of national airs arranged by Haydn, Beethoven, Kozeluch and others.

Tomasini, Luigi (1741–1808), Italian violinist, leader of the orchestra at Eisenstadt and Esterház under Haydn.

Tost, Johann, wealthy merchant and amateur violinist in Vienna, to whom Haydn dedicated his string quartets Opp. 54, 55 and 64. (*See* footnote on p. 59 for discussion of his possible identity and past history.)

Tuma, Franz (1704–74), Bohemian composer, pupil of Fux. Musical director to Dowager Empress Elisabeth in Vienna, 1741–50.

Vanhall. See Wanhal.

Viotti, Giovanni Battista (1753–1824), Italian violinist and composer for his instrument. Appeared in Paris in 1782 and settled in London in 1792.

Wagenseil, Georg Christoph (1715–77), Austrian composer, pupil of Fux (q.v.), music master to Maria Theresa and her daughters, composer of operas and instrumental music and the leading figure of the Viennese transitional symphonic school.

Waldstein, Ferdinand Ernst Gabriel, Count (1762–1823), musical amateur, patron of Beethoven.

Wanhal (or Vanhall), Johann Baptist (1739–1813), Bohemian composer, pupil of Dittersdorf, settled in Vienna.

Weidinger, Anton, court trumpeter in Vienna. Inventor of valve trumpet, which he produced in 1801.

Weigl, Joseph (1740–1820), Austrian violoncellist in the Esterházy orchestra; from 1769 member of the Imperal Opera Orchestra in Vienna.

Weigl, Joseph (1766–1846), Austrian composer, son of the preceding, godson of Haydn and pupil of Albrechtsberger and Salieri (q.v.).

Werner, Gregor Joseph (1695?–1766), composer, musical director to the Esterházy family, predecessor of Haydn and his superior for five years.

Zelter, Carl Friedrich (1758–1832), composer, conductor and teacher in Berlin, friend of Goethe, teacher of Mendelssohn.

APPENDIX D

BIBLIOGRAPHY

Abert, Hermann, 'Joseph Haydns Klavierwerke.' Z.M.W., II and III. (1920–1.)

Adler, Guido, 'Handbuch der Musikgeschichte,' 2nd edition. (Leipzig, 1920.)

——, 'Haydn and the Viennese Classical School.' (M.Q. 1932.)

——, Preface to D.T.Ö., XV, xix, 2, 'Wiener Instrumentalmusik vor und um 1750.'

Amoroso, Ferruccio, 'Haydn.' (Turin, 1933.)

Arnold, J. F., 'Joseph Haydn.' (Erfurt, 1810.)

Artaria, F., and *Botstiber, H.,* 'Joseph Haydn und das Verlagshaus Artaria.' (Vienna, 1909.)

Baresel, Alfred, 'Joseph Haydn: Leben und Werk.' (Leipzig, 1938.)

Bartha, Dénes, and *Somfai, László,* 'Haydn als Opernkapellmeister. Die Haydn-Dokumente der Esterházy-Opernsammlung.' (Budapest and Mainz, 1960.)

Besseler, Heinrich, 'Einflusse der Contratanzmusik auf Joseph Haydn.' Bericht uber die internationale Konferenz zum Andenken Joseph Haydns, Budapest, 1959.) (Budapest, 1961.)

Blume, Friedrich, 'Joseph Haydns künstlerische Persönlichkeit in seinen Streichquartetten.' (J.M.P., XXXVIII, 1932.)

Botstiber, H., 'Zur Entstehung der schottischen Lieder von Josef Haydn. Mit 16 ungedruckten Briefen des Meisters.' ('Der Merker,' Jahrg. 1, Heft 19, 10 July 1910.)

Brand, Carl Maria, 'Die Messen von Joseph Haydn.' (Würzburg, 1941.)

Brenet, Michel, 'Haydn,' translated by C. Leonard Leese. (Oxford, 1926.)

Carpani, Giuseppe, 'Le Haydine, ovvero Lettere sulla vita e sulle opere del celebre maestro Giuseppe Haydn.' (Milan, 1812.)

Conrat, H., 'Joseph Haydn und das kroatische Volkslied.' ('Die Musik,' XIV, 1904–5.)

Cuming, Geoffrey, 'Haydn: where to begin.' (M. & L., 1949.)

Deutsch, Otto Erich, 'Haydn in Cambridge.' ('Cambridge Review,' 1941.) 'Haydn und Nelson.' ('Die Musik,' XXIV, 6, Mar. 1932.)

——, 'Haydn's Hymn and Burney's Translation.' (M. Rev., IV, 1943.)

——, 'Haydn's Kanons.' (Z.M.W., XV, Dec. 1932.)

Appendix D—Bibliography

Dies, A. C., 'Biographische Nachrichten über Joseph Haydn.' (Vienna, 1810.)

Dunhill, Thomas F., 'Franz Joseph Haydn,' in 'The Heritage of Music,' Vol. I. (Oxford, 1927 and 1948.)

Dworschak, F., 'Joseph Haydn und Karl Joseph von Fürnberg.' ('Unsere Heimat,' Vienna, Nos. 6, 7, 1932.)

Engl, J. E., 'Haydns handschriftliches Tagebuch des 2. Aufenthaltes in London.' (Leipzig, 1909.)

Fox, D. G. A., 'Haydn: an Introduction.' (Oxford, 1930.)

Framéry, N., 'Notice sur Joseph Haydn.' (Paris, 1810.)

Friedländer, Max, 'Van Swieten und das Textbuch zu Haydns Jahreszeiten.' (J.M.P., 1909.)

Fröhlich, Joseph, 'Joseph Haydn,' new edition by Adolf Sandberger. (Ratisbon, 1936.)

Geiringer, Karl, Article in Thompson's 'International Cyclopedia of Music.' (New York, 1939.)

——, 'Haydn: a Creative Life in Music.' (London, 1947.)

——, 'Haydn and the Folk Song of the British Isles.' (M.Q. XXXV, April 1949.)

——, 'Haydn as an Opera Composer.' (Proc. Mus. Ass., LXVI, 1940).

——, 'Haydn's Sketches for "The Creation."' (M.Q., 1932.)

——, 'Joseph Haydn.' (Potsdam, 1932.)

——, 'Joseph Haydn. Der schöpferische Werdegang eines Meisters der Klassik.' (Mainz, 1959.)

——, 'Sidelights on Haydn's activities in the field of Sacred Music.' (Bericht über die internationale Konferenz zum Andenken Joseph Haydns, Budapest, 1959.) (Budapest, 1961.)

——, 'The Operas of Haydn.' (Musical America, 1940.)

Gerber, E. K., Article in 'Neues Lexikon der Tonkunst.' (1790–2 and 1812.)

Griesinger, G. A., 'Biographische Notizen über Joseph Haydn.' (Leipzig, 1810.)

Grosser, J. G., 'Biographische Notizen über Joseph Haydn.' (Hirschberg, 1826.)

Haas, Karl, 'Haydn's English Military Marches.' ('The Score,' Jan. 1950.)

Hadden, J. Cuthbert, 'George Thomson, the friend of Burns.' (London, 1898.)

——, 'Haydn,' revised edition. (London, 1932.)

Hadow, W. H., 'A Croatian Composer,' reproduced in 'Collected Essays.' (Oxford, 1928.)

Haydn

Harich, János, 'Das Repertoire des Opernkapellmeisters Joseph Haydn in Esterháza (1780–90).' (Haydn Year Book, Vol. I, 1962.)

Hase, Hermann von, 'Joseph Haydn und Breitkopf & Härtel.' (Leipzig, 1909.)

Hinderberger, A., 'Die Motivik in Haydns Streichquartetten.' (Turbenthal, 1935.)

Hopkinson, Cecil, and *Oldman, C. B.,* 'Haydn's Settings of Scottish Songs in the Collections of Napier and Whyte.' (Bibliog. Soc. Transactions, Edinburgh, Vol. III, Part 2, Sessions 1949–50, 1950–1.)

——, 'Thomson's Collections of National Song, with Special Reference to the Contributions of Haydn and Beethoven.' (Bibliog. Soc. Transactions, Edinburgh, 1938–9.)

Horanyi, M., 'Das Esterházysche Feenreich.' ('Beitrag zur ungarlandischen Theatergeschichte des 18. Jahrhunderts.') (Budapest, 1959.)

Karajan, T. von, 'Joseph Haydn in London, 1791 und 1792.' (Vienna, 1861.) (Contains his letters to Marianne von Genzinger.)

Katz, Adele T., 'Challenge to Musical Tradition.' (New York, 1945.)

Klafsky, Anton M., 'Michael Haydn als Kirchenkomponist.' ('Studien zue Musikwissenschaft,' 1915.)

Kobald, C., 'Joseph Haydn: Bild seines Lebens und seiner Zeit.' (Vienna, 1932.)

Koch, Lajos, 'Joseph Haydn,' 1732–1932. (Bibliography.) (Budapest, 1932.)

Krebbiel, H. E., 'Music and Manners in the Classical Period.' (New York, 1896.) (Contains translated extracts from the notebook of the first London visit.)

Kubač, F. S., 'Josip Haydn i Hrvatske narodne popievke.' (Zagreb, 1880.)

Lachmann, Robert, 'Die Haydn Autographen der Staatsbibliothek zu Berlin.' (Z.M.W., XIV, March 1932.)

Landon, H. C. Robbins, 'The Symphonies of Joseph Haydn.' (London, 1955.)

——, Supplement to 'The Symphonies of Joseph Haydn.' (London, 1961.)

—— (ed.), 'The Complete Correspondence and London Notebooks of Joseph Haydn.' (London, 1959.)

—— and *Larsen, Jens Peter,* article 'Haydn' in 'Die Musik in Geschichte und Gegenwart,' Vol. V. (Kassel and Basel, 1956.)

——, 'Haydn's Marionette Operas and the Repertoire of the Marionette Theatre at Esterhaz Castle.' (Haydn Year Book, Vol. I, 1962.)

Larsen, Jens Peter, 'Die Haydn-Überlieferung.' (Copenhagen, 1939.)

——, 'Drei Haydn Kataloge in Faksimile, mit Einleitung und ergänzenden Themenverzeichnissen.' (Copenhagen, 1941.)

Larsen, Jens Peter, 'Joseph Haydn's künstlerische Entwicklung.' (Fischer-Festschrift, Innsbruck, 1956.)

Le Breton, J., 'Notice historique sur la vie et les ouvrages de Joseph Haydn.' (Paris, 1822.)

Major, E., 'Ungarische Tanzmelodien in Haydns Bearbeitung.' (Z.M.W., II, 1920.)

Michel, Henri, 'La Sonate pour clavier avant Beethoven.' (Paris, 1908.)

Müller, R. F., 'Heiratsbriefe, Testament und Hinterlassenschaft der Gattin Haydns.' ('Die Musik,' XX, 2.)

Nohl, Ludwig, 'Haydn,' new edition by Alfred Schnerich. (Leipzig, 1931.)

——, 'Musikerbriefe.' (Leipzig, 1867.)

Nowak, Leopold, 'Joseph Haydn.' (Vienna, 1951.)

Pohl, Carl Ferdinand, 'Joseph Haydn,' 2 vols. (Berlin, 1875–82). Vol. III by Hugo Botstiber. (Leipzig, 1927.)

——, 'Mozart und Haydn in London,' II, 'Haydn in London.' (Vienna, 1867.)

Radcliffe, Philip, 'The Piano Sonatas of Joseph Haydn.' (M. Rev., VII, 1946, p. 139.)

Reich, Willi, 'Joseph Haydn: Leben, Briefe, Schaffen.' (Lucerne, 1946.)

Reissman, A., 'Joseph Haydn: sein Leben und seine Werke.' (Berlin, 1812.)

Rywosch, B., 'Beiträge zur Entwicklung in Joseph Haydns Symphonik.' (Turbental, 1934.)

Saint-Foix, Georges de, 'Haydn and Clementi.' (M.Q., 1932.)

Sandberger, Adolf, 'Zur Entwicklungsgeschichte von Haydns "Sieben Worten,"' in 'Gesammelte Aufsätze.' (Munich, 1921.)

——, 'Zur Geschichte des Haydnschen Streichquartetts,' *ibid.*

Sandys, William, and *Forster, S. A.,* 'The History of the Violin.' (London, 1864.)

Schmid, E. F., 'Josef Haydn und Carl Philipp Emmanuel Bach.' (Z.M.W., XIV, March 1932.)

——, 'Joseph Haydn: ein Buch von Vorfahren und Heimat des Meisters.' (Cassel, 1934.)

——, 'Joseph Haydn und die Flötenuhr.' (Z.M.W., 1932.)

Schmidt, Leopold, 'Joseph Haydn.' (Berlin, 1898 and 1907.)

Schnerich, A., 'Joseph Haydn und seine Sendung,' 2nd edition. (Vienna, 1926.)

——, 'Messe und Requiem seit Haydn und Mozart.' (Vienna, 1909.)

——, 'Messen-Typus von Haydn bis Schubert.' (Vienna, 1893.)

Schnyder von Wartensee, X., 'Aesthetische Betrachtungen über die "Jahreszeiten" von Joseph Haydn.' (Frankfort-on-Main, 1861.)

Scott, Marion M., 'Haydn: Fresh Facts and Old Fancies.' (Proc. Mus. Ass., 1941–2.)

——, 'Haydn and Folk Song.' (M. & L., April 1950.)

——, 'Haydn Stayed Here!' (M. & L., January 1951.)

——, 'Haydn in England.' (M.Q., 1932.)

——, 'Haydn: Relics and Reminiscences in England.' (M. & L., XIII, 1932, p. 126.)

——, 'Haydn's "83"' (String Quartets). (M. & L., XI, 1930, p. 207.)

——, 'Haydn's Opp. 2 and 3.' (Proc. Mus. Ass., LXI, 1934.)

——, 'The Opera Concerts of 1795.' (M. Rev., January 1951.)

——, Preface to Haydn's first String Quartet. (Oxford, 1931.)

——, 'Some English Affinities and Associations in Haydn's songs.' (M. & L., XXV, 1944, p. 1.)

Smith, Carleton Sprague, 'Haydn's Chamber Music and the Flute.' (M.Q., 1933.)

Sondheimer, Robert, 'Haydn. A Historical and Psychological Study.' (London, 1951.)

Stendhal, 'Vie de Haydn, Mozart et Métastase,' new edition by D. Müller. (Paris, 1914.)

Strunk, Oliver, 'Haydn' in 'From Bach to Stravinsky,' edited by David Ewen. (New York, 1933.)

——, 'Haydn's Divertimenti for Baryton, Viola and Bass.' (M.Q., 1932.)

——, 'Notes on a Haydn Autograph.' (M.Q., 1934.)

Stuber, Robert, 'Die Klavierbegleitung im Liede von Haydn, Mozart und Beethoven. Eine Stilstudie.' (Biel, 1958.)

Szabolcsi, Bence, 'Haydn und die ungarische Musik.' (Bericht über die internationale Konferenz zum Andenken Joseph Haydns, Budapest, 1959.) (Budapest, 1961.)

Tenschert, Roland, 'Frauen um Haydn.' (Vienna, 1947.)

——, 'Joseph Haydn.' (Berlin, 1932.)

——, 'Joseph Haydn: sein Leben in Bildern.' (Leipzig, 1936.)

Therstappen, H. J., 'Joseph Haydns sinfonisches Vermächtnis (Die Londoner Sinfonien).' (Wolfenbüttel, 1941.)

Appendix D—Bibliography

Tovey, D. F., Article in Cobbett's 'Cyclopaedic Survey of Chamber Music.' (London, 1929.)

Townsend, Pauline, 'Joseph Haydn.' (London, 1894.)

Vecsey, Jenö (ed.), 'Haydn Compositions in the Music Collection of the National Szechenyi Library, Budapest.' (Budapest, 1960.)

Wendschuh, L., 'Über Joseph Haydns Opern.' (Halle, 1896.)

Wirth, Helmut, 'Joseph Haydn als Dramatiker.' (Wolfenbüttel, 1940.)

Wurzbach, C., 'Joseph Haydn und sein Bruder Michael.' (Vienna, 1862.)

Wyzewa, Teodor de, 'À propos du centenaire de Haydn.' ('Revue des Deux Mondes,' Paris, 1909.)

ABBREVIATIONS

D.T.Ö.—Denkmäler der Tonkunst in Österreich.

J.M.P.—Jahrbuch der Musikbibliothek Peters.

M. & L.—Music & Letters.

M.Q.—Musical Quarterly.

M. Rev.—Music Review.

Proc. Mus. Ass.—Proceeding of the (Royal) Musical Association.

Z.M.W.—Zeitschrift der Musikwissenschaft.

INDEX

INDEX

Index

Esterházy, Princess Maria Elisabeth, 61, 86

Esterházy, Princess Maria Hermenegildis, 96, 106, 142, 148

Esterházy, Prince Nicholas (I), 7, 36, 37, 39, 40, 41, 42, 44, 46, 51, 55, 58, 61–2, 63, 96, 126, 128, 147, 194, 195, 196

Esterházy, Prince Nicholas (II), 87, 93, 95–6, 106, 128, 149

Esterházy, Dowager Princess Octavia, 23, 32, 37

Esterházy, Prince Paul, 32

Esterházy, Prince Paul Anton, 31, 32, 36, 37, 42, 174

Fantasia for piano, C major, 146

Farinelli, 15

Fedeltà premiata, La, opera, 58, 59

Ferdinand IV, King of Naples, 62, 63, 171

Finsterbusch, 12

Fischer, Ludwig, 77, 89, 247

Fitzherbert, Mrs., 93

Fonteski, 50

Forster, William, publisher, 51, 63, 147, 247

Fox, Charles James, 66

Framéry, Nicolas E., 15

Francis I, emperor, 11

Francis II, emperor, 55, 62, 85, 98, 103

Franck, Johann Matthias, 5–9

Franck, Rosina, 5, 6

Franz, Karl, 42, 247

Frederick William II, King of Prussia, 77, 161

Friberth, Karl, 43, 247

Fries, Count, 105

Fuchs, Johann, 104

Fürnberg, Baron, 27, 28, 151

Fux, Johann Joseph, 11, 12, 13, 247

Gallini, Sir John, 63, 68, 69, 72, 73, 80, 247

Gassmann, Florian, 48, 96, 247

Gassmann, Therese, 96, 101, 247

Gebet zu Gott, song, 122

Gegenbauer, Adam, 12

Geiringer, Karl, v, 2, 21, 27, 36, 42, 45, 54, 72, 74, 93, 123, 138, 150, 153

Gellert, 48

Genzinger, Franz von, 61

Genzinger, Josepha von, 61

Genzinger, Marianne von, 60–2, 65, 71, 75, 76, 78, 81, 87, 143, 145

Genzinger, Dr. Peter Leopold von, 60, 107

George III, 66, 67, 92–3, 94

George, Prince of Wales, later George IV, 66, 69, 70, 72, 77, 92–3

Gerardi, Christine, 100, 103

Giardini, Felice de, 83, 247

Giornovichi, Giovanni, 69, 248

Gluck, Christoph Willibald von, 25, 111, 139, 198, 201

Goethe, 36

Goldoni, 196, 197

Goldsmid, Jane, 98

Gott erhalte Franz den Kaiser. See *Austrian Hymn*

Grassalkovics, Count, 41, 62

Grassi, Anton, 105, 107

Index

No. 8, E flat major, 147, 149
No. 9, B flat major, 147, 148
No. 10, D major, 147
No. 11, A flat major, 147
No. 13, A major, 147, 148
No. 14, C minor-major, 147
No. 15, A major, 147
No. 16, E flat major, 147
No. 17, G minor, 147, 148
No. 18, E flat minor, 147, 148-9
No. 19, G minor, 147
No. 20, E flat major, 147
No. 21, C major, 147, 148
No. 22, D minor-major, 147, 148
No. 23, E flat major, 147, 148
No. 24, B flat major, 147
No. 25, F major, 147
No. 29, F major, 147
No. 30, D major, 147
No. 31, G major, 147
Trost unglücklicher Liebe, song, 122
Tuma, Franz, 12, 250

Vanhall. *See* Wanhal
Variations for piano in F minor, 146
Vera costanza, La, opera, 48, 195, 199
Verai, 196
Verlassene, Die, song, 122
Viotti, Giovanni Battista, 89, 92, 93, 250

Vivaldi, Antonio, 111
Volkmann, H., 172

Wagenseil, Georg Christoph, 110, 140, 251
Wagner, Richard, 138
Waldstein, Count, 149, 251
Wanderer, The, song, 122
Wanhal, Johann Baptist, 56, 251
Weber, Fritz, Edmund and Carl Maria von, 56
Weidinger, Anton, 98, 172, 251
Weigl, Joseph, 42, 45, 251
Weigl, Joseph (son), 43, 251
Weissenwolf, Countess, 86
Welsh songs, arrangements of, 102, 123
Werner, Gregor Joseph, 31, 32, 33, 37, 39, 104, 251
Whyte, publisher, 102, 123
Wolcot, John ('Peter Pindar'), 80, 133
Wrastil, Father, 18
Wyzewa, Teodor de, 45, 114

York, Duke of, 77, 88, 92
York, Duchess of, 77, 84, 94
Young, Arthur, 69
Yriarte, Tomás de, 50

Zelter, Carl Friedrich, 105, 251